Luminos is the Open Access monograph publishing program from UC Press. Luminos provides a framework for preserving and reinvigorating monograph publishing for the future and increases the reach and visibility of important scholarly work. Titles published in the UC Press Luminos model are published with the same high standards for selection, peer review, production, and marketing as those in our traditional program. www.luminosoa.org

Male Survivors of Wartime Sexual Violence

Male Survivors of Wartime Sexual Violence

Perspectives from Northern Uganda

Philipp Schulz

UNIVERSITY OF CALIFORNIA PRESS

University of California Press
Oakland, California

© 2021 by Philipp Schulz

Suggested citation: Schulz, P. *Male Survivors of Wartime Sexual Violence: Perspectives from Northern Uganda*. Oakland: University of California Press, 2020. DOI: https://doi.org/10.1525/luminos.95

Library of Congress Cataloging-in-Publication Data
Names: Schulz, Philipp, author.
Title: Male survivors of wartime sexual violence : perspectives from
    northern Uganda / Philipp Schulz.
Description: Oakland, California : University of California Press, [2021] |
    Includes bibliographical references and index.
Identifiers: LCCN 2020015360 (print) | LCCN 2020015361 (ebook) |
    ISBN 9780520303744 (paperback) | ISBN 9780520972865 (ebook)
Subjects: LCSH: Male rape victims—Uganda—Case studies. | Rape as a
    weapon of war.
Classification: LCC HV6569.U33 S38 2021 (print) | LCC HV6569.U33
    (ebook) | DDC 362.8830811/096761—dc23
LC record available at https://lccn.loc.gov/2020015360
LC ebook record available at https://lccn.loc.gov/2020015361

Manufactured in the United States

30   29   28   27   26   25   24   23   22   21
10   9   8   7   6   5   4   3   2   1

*For the extraordinary Men of Courage from northern Uganda,
and the extraordinary people supporting them*

*For Sarah and Freya, for always and lovingly supporting
me in more ways than imaginable*

CONTENTS

LIST OF ILLUSTRATIONS

MAPS

FIGURES

ACKNOWLEDGMENTS

The struggles and difficulties—emotionally, organizationally, and intellectually—of writing this book are outbalanced by the many relationships and friendships formed during the process. In particular the field research time in northern Uganda, despite the nature of the topic and the at times heartbreaking stories, was a time of revelations of various sorts, joy, and friendships. I therefore want to thank in particular the male survivors, and the associations they form, who participated in this study. While this book is also *about* you, it is primarily *by* you and *for* you. I would not write these words on these pages if you had not shared your stories, experiences, and perspectives with me. You are indeed extraordinary *Men of Courage*.

I also want to acknowledge the many amazing individuals in Uganda who made this work happen: Fred Ngomokwe, Steven Oola, Benard Okot Kasozi, Kenneth Oyot Odong, Alice Otto, Jackson Odong, Adam Buliisa, Patrick Otim, Gilbert Nuwagira, Okwir Isaac Odiya, Patrick Odong, Patrick Otim, Lino Ogora, Evelyn Amony, and Stella Lanam. Thank you for your assistance, generosity, and friendship. On the institutional side, my affiliation as a research associate with the Refugee Law Project in Gulu not only facilitated the work but also helped me to understand the context in a way that would otherwise not have been possible. Special appreciation is due to Chris Dolan for continuously inspiring me in so many different ways. I also would like to thank in particular Lars for having had the patience to live with me and for making the time in Gulu the fun time it was, and Stine, Holly, Julian, Alice, and many others in Gulu and beyond for joyful dinners and thoughtful discussions.

The research underpinning this book was initially conducted for a doctoral dissertation, completed and defended at the Transitional Justice Institute (TJI) at Ulster University in December 2017. Particular thanks are due to my doctoral supervisors, Fionnuala Ní Aoláin, Brandon Hamber, and Louise Mallinder, from whom I learned a great deal and who continuously challenged me, which immensely fueled my thinking and writing. For your inspiration and support I am grateful. To Fionnuala in particular, your generosity and kindness continues to inspire and shape what kind of scholar I would like to become—thank you for that. Also thanks to friends and colleagues at TJI, and in particular Seamus Campbell, Daire McGill, and Hedley Abernethy, for making me feel at home in Belfast, but also Rory O'Connell, Cath Collins, Lisa Thompson, Catherine O'Rourke, Thomas Hansen, and many more, for creating a generous and collegial working and research environment.

During the writing of the initial dissertation, I was based as a guest researcher at the Hugo Valentin Centre at Uppsala University in Sweden. Here particular thanks and immense appreciation is due to Roland Kostic and Sverker Finnström for thoughtful conversations and lots of coffee, as well as to Tomislav Dulic. For the subsequent writing of this book, I was based as a postdoctoral researcher at the Institute for Intercultural and International Studies at the University of Bremen. At the University of California Press, I am particularly thankful to my editors, Maura Roessner and Madison Wetzell, for believing in this work from the beginning, for guiding me throughout the process, and for always answering my (many) questions.

In addition, various friends and colleagues have accompanied me along the way and have offered comments on drafts, agreed to discuss ideas, or listened to my concerns and struggles. Particular thanks first and foremost for Heleen Touquet for constantly providing me with inspiration and always offering an ear. Throughout the process of writing this project, you have not only become a close colleague and coauthor, but also a dear friend, for which I am thankful. I also extend many thanks and much appreciation to numerous other colleagues and friends, —too many to list here,— but who include Kate Lonergan, Goran Miljan, Anne-Kathrin Kreft, Lewis Turner, Henri Myrttinen, Roxani Krystalli, Erin Baines, Sebastian Möller, Roy Karadag, and Caterina Bonora. Specific thanks also to Stefan Döring, who produced the illustrative maps for this book.

The fieldwork underpinning this research was generously supported by external grants from the Socio-Legal Studies Association; the British Institute in Eastern Africa; the Broadening Horizons Scholarship Fund at Ulster University; and the French Institute for Research in Africa. My sincerest appreciation for supporting this work and believing in its value. The open access publication of this book was made possible through financial assistance from the University of Bremen and the German Research Foundation—for which I am particularly grateful, as it enables a potentially wider readership.

Parts of the analysis in chapter 4 were previously published as: Schulz, P. 2018. Displacement from Gendered Personhood: Sexual violence and masculinities in northern Uganda. *International Affairs*, 94(5): 1101–1119. Parts of the analysis in chapter 5 were previously published as: Schulz, P. 2019. "To me, justice means to be in a group": Survivors' Group as a Pathway to Justice in Northern Uganda. *Journal of Human Rights Practice*, 11(1): 171–189; and as Touquet, H. and Schulz, P. 2020. Navigating Vulnerabilities and Masculinities: How Gendered Contexts Shape the Agency of Male Sexual Violence Survivors. Security Dialogue: 1–19. Parts of chapter 6 were previously published as: Schulz, P. 2020. Examining Male Wartime Rape Survivors' Perspectives on Justice in Northern Uganda. *Social & Legal Studies*, 29(1): 19–40.

Particular appreciation goes of course also to my parents, and to my sister, for always believing in me and supporting me in so many ways. Most important, and above all, thank you to Sarah, for your love, for bearing with me, and for tremendously assisting me over the years with this work and beyond. Every day you help me to become the person I want to be, and for that I will be eternally grateful. This book is dedicated to you, and to what we have together, as well as to our daughter, Freya, who was born into the final stages of the initial dissertation and who is growing up to be her own independent and most incredible person and whose constant joy and adorable laughter always boost my spirit and show me the *really* important sides of life.

LIST OF ACRONYMS

AWDCA	Acholi War Debt Claimants Associations
BJP	Beyond Juba Project
CAR	Central African Republic
CVR	Comisión para la Verdad y Reconciliation
CSO	Civil Society Organization
DRC	Democratic Republic of the Congo
GBV	Gender-Based Violence
GoU	Government of the Republic of Uganda
HSM	Holy Spirit Movement
HSMF	Holy Spirit Mobile Forces
IACHR	Inter-American Commission on Human Rights
IATJ	Institute for African Transitional Justice
ICC	International Criminal Court
ICD	International Crimes Division (of the High Court Uganda)
ICTR	International Criminal Tribunal for Rwanda
ICTY	International Criminal Tribunal for the former Yugoslavia
IDP	Internally Displaced Person
JLOS	Justice, Law and Order Sector
JRP	Justice and Reconciliation Project
LC	Local Council
LRA	Lord's Resistance Army
MOC	Men of Courage
MOH(RAU)	Men of Hope (Refugee Association Uganda)
MOP	Men of Peace

NGO	Non-Governmental Organization
NRA/M	National Resistance Army / Movement
OTP	Office of the Prosecutor
PAR	Participatory Action Research
PRDP	Peace and Recovery Development Plan
RLP	Refugee Law Project
SGBV	Sexual and Gender-Based Violence
SOGI	Sexual Orientation and Gender Identity
SSI	South-South Institute
TJWG	Transitional Justice Working Group
TRC	Truth and Reconciliation Commission
UHRC	Uganda Human Rights Commission
UNLA	Uganda National Liberation Army
UNOCHA	United Nations Office for the Coordination of Humanitarian Affairs
UNOHCHR	United Nations Office of the High Commissioner for Human Rights
UNSC(R)	United Nations Security Council (Resolution)
UPDA	Uganda People's Democratic Army
UPDF	Uganda People's Defence Force
VSLA	Village Savings and Loan Associations
WAN	Women's Advocacy Network
WNBF	West Nile Bank Front
WPS	Women Peace and Security

MAP 1. Map of Uganda.

Introduction

Male Survivors' Experiences in Context

One night in April 1987, while Okwera was asleep, rebels of the Lord's Resistance Army (LRA) camped against his will in his homestead in rural northern Uganda. The next day, neighbors and other community members who were concerned about the rebels' presence in the area informed the nearby stationed government soldiers about the rebels' whereabouts. The following day, at about four o'clock in the morning, Okwera woke up to the sound of gumboots in his compound. Suspecting either that the LRA rebels had returned or that government soldiers of the National Resistance Army (NRA) under the command of incumbent President Museveni had come to interrogate him about the rebel incident, Okwera alerted his wife. But before they were able to go into hiding, the soldiers had already surrounded the homestead. The NRA cadres forced him to open the door, but Okwera refused. Equipped with the power of their guns, a group of soldiers eventually forced their way in and began to loot, while others stood guard outside or proceeded to neighboring compounds. With a gun pressed against his back, Okwera was dragged outside, behind his kitchen hut, while his wife had to remain inside the hut with several other soldiers. The soldiers accused Okwera of "being a father to the rebels," and after further intimidation, they ordered him to kneel down and bend over. In a testimony recorded and published by the Refugee Law Project (RLP), Okwera recalls: "My hesitation earned me a kick '*kwara*' and a bayonet pointed in my back. Not knowing what to do, I complied. They removed my trousers and each penetrated me in turn. I could tell that those who penetrated me were three in number because each of them would do it in turn and then leave."

Along with countless other civilian men across the entire Acholi subregion during the early phase of the war, Okwera was sexually violated by the NRA government soldiers. As he was sexually violated, his wife—who was about seven months pregnant with twins at that time—was also raped by another group

of soldiers who remained with her in the hut. At that time, during his own violation, Okwera did not know about this and only found out after the soldiers had left.
Three weeks later, his wife suffered a miscarriage and died soon thereafter as a result
of injuries caused by the sexual assault. "It was a very traumatizing moment for
the whole family," Okwera recalled. During a conversation we had in March 2016, he
explained that he felt extremely devastated, lonely and isolated for years after this.

Regarding this own sexual violation, Okwera described it as "the most painful experience ever." But due to shame and fear, he decided to keep it to himself.
He did not tell his children what had happened to him, and he felt that he could
not report the violation officially, since the soldiers who committed the violence
belonged to the same government that remains in power today. "We did not
have any voice," Okwera said. Although these crimes were widespread across the
entire war-torn Acholi subregion—as I will demonstrate throughout this book—
nobody spoke openly about it, and survivors had no actual opportunities or spaces
to share their stories or narrate their testimonies. Okwera himself also did not
share his experience, because he felt it was too dehumanizing and shameful.

About ten years later, in the midst of the conflict during the mid- and late
1990s, the government forced up to 95 percent of the civilian population into
internally displaced persons (IDPs) camps, which according to Chris Dolan
(2009) constituted their own form of "social torture." In the camps, civilian communities were forced to live side by side in overcrowded conditions, which further strained the already ruptured social fabric of life and relationships. Rumors
quickly began to spread about different stories related to the war, including about
who was a victim of male rape or other humiliations. Even though Okwera began
to understand that he was not alone and that others must have endured similar
experiences, he still heard of only one other case, and he did not know any other
survivor personally.

In 1999, after more than twelve years of silence, Okwera nevertheless eventually
gathered his courage to report the violation to the Uganda Human Rights Commission (UHRC). At the time, the commission was the only institution Okwera
knew of that was dealing with human rights abuses during the war. The commission, however, turned him away, arguing that the violations occurred outside the
temporal and definitional scope of their mandate. Okwera felt extremely demoral-
ized and disappointed. Even though he (at least temporarily) accepted the stigmatization that he anticipated to follow his report, he was turned away without any
support. He felt he had been denied the opportunity to share this testimony, to be
listened to, and to seek justice and redress. Elsewhere I have described this experience as "ethical loneliness" (Schulz 2018b), understood as "a condition undergone by persons who have been unjustly treated and dehumanized by human
beings and political structures, who emerge from that injustice only to find that
the surrounding world will not listen to or cannot properly hear their testimony"
(Stauffer 2015: 1).

During the postencampment period and in the final stages of the LRA's presence in northern Uganda, from about 2006, rumors and stories continued to spread within the camps and the communities about different violations and humiliations committed during the conflict. Okwera's children became more inquisitive and wanted to know what happened to him during the war and how their mother died. "I became deeply troubled and had nightmares about that experience," Okwera recalls. Still feeling shame and fearing stigmatization, however, he did not yet tell them about his violent ordeal. Hoping to find ways to cope, he joined a church group and regularly attended local counseling sessions as well as community events organized by different humanitarian and civil society actors. During one of these events in 2008, Okwera met staff from the Refugee Law Project (RLP). Okwera appreciated that, unlike other humanitarian agencies or service providers at that time, "they listened carefully" to what he had to say. After much consideration, various visits, and a sense of mutual trust that had begun to develop, Okwera decided to share his full testimony with them. The fact that they *listened carefully,* and did not further silence or ignore him, was a paramount reason Okwera broke his silence.

Despite early hesitation and even some resentments, after a long and continuous process of building trust and relationships, further catalyzed by the gradual passing of time, fellow survivors eventually shared their experiences as well, talking about *tek-gungu*—how male rape is locally referred to—and encouraging other male victims of sexual violations to tell their stories and support one another. Coordinated by Okwera, a support group was formed: the Men of Courage. The group is composed exclusively of and led by survivors, and primarily engages in peer counseling, income-generating economic activities, and advocacy. For Okwera, as well as for many other male survivors, being in this group enables them to exercise agency and even facilitates a sense of justice on the micro-level (chapter 5). Today Okwera has narrated his testimony on his own terms, and his account has been published by the Refugee Law Project (RLP) and is featured in two widely viewed RLP-produced video documentaries. He has articulated male survivors' needs and demands in various forums locally, nationally, and internationally—for instance, during meetings and workshops in northern Uganda, regional conferences such as the annual Institute for African Transitional Justice (IATJ), and the global South-South Institute (SSI) on sexual violence against men and boys in Uganda (in 2013 and 2019) and Cambodia (in 2015). As of this book's writing, he continues to coordinate the Men of Courage support group, raise awareness, and advocate for justice on behalf of male survivors.

THE CENTRAL ARGUMENT

This book is about the diverse stories, experiences, and viewpoints of not only Okwera but numerous male sexual violence survivors in northern Uganda more broadly. By centralizing their lived realities, this book seeks to broaden and deepen our understanding of the gender dynamics of armed conflicts in general, and of conflict-related sexual violence in particular. In many ways, Okwera's narrative—and in particular his contemporary role as an advocate—is exceptional and not necessarily representative for the majority of male survivors of sexual violence in northern Uganda, or across the globe. Nevertheless, his experience and viewpoints as well as his inspiring transformation are certainly illustrative for many of the arguments I pursue throughout this book. Okwera, just as most other male sexual violence survivors in this context, experienced different and intersecting layers of gendered harms caused by the violations committed against him. As I demonstrate throughout this book, wartime sexual violence against men was widespread in northern Uganda, perpetrated by soldiers of the government army against civilian men in the early stages of the country's civil war, during the late 1980s and early 1990s. Yet for years, and most often even decades, survivors like Okwera were silenced—by society, their communities around them, or by bodies and organizations initially designed to assist them. Due to the shame and stigma surrounding their experiences, many survivors did not reveal their experiences to anyone, and many continue to uphold this protective silence in the current postwar context. As a result, crimes of tek-gungu remain notoriously under-explored in the contemporary Acholi context, so that a persistent vacuum of assistance, support and justice for male sexual violence prevails, reflective of the overall inattentiveness to sexual violence against men globally.

At the same time, however, survivors also grapple and engage with their harmful experiences in myriad ways, thereby resisting and subverting the stereotypical image of the ever-vulnerable and inevitable passive survivor of sexual violence. As I will explore in this book, survivors form and engage in support groups, break the silence surrounding their experiences on different levels and in different spheres, and advocate for justice. Within the absence of official measures, male survivors in Acholiland therefore exercise agency on their own terms, primarily through their participation in survivors' groups, but they also articulate demands for state-driven assistance and support, especially in form of acknowledgment of their otherwise silenced experiences. The central argument that I posit in this book thus holds that sexual violence against men can significantly impact male survivors' masculine identities, but that survivors in the contemporary postconflict context seek to respond to, engage with, and remedy these gendered harms in various endogenous and exogenous ways.

Recognizing this heterogeneity and complexity of survivors' experiences, this book paints a detailed and holistic picture of wartime sexual violence against men in northern Uganda by placing male survivors' diverse lived realities under the microscope and by centralizing their perspectives. The book thereby follows feminist scholar Donna Haraway's (1988) methodological approach of "situated knowledge(s)," whereby "diverse views from below, clearly rooted in life experiences" (Cockburn 2010: 141) can help us to construct embedded accounts of the world in all its complexities and lived realities. In light of this, the central premise of this book is the construction of a holistic narrative of survivors' experiences in terms of gendered harms, but it is also attentive to various postviolation elements with regard to agency and justice. While in the last decade various empirical, conceptual, and political inroads have been made into recognizing men and boys as victims of sexual violence, much remains unknown about the dynamics surrounding these crimes, and about male survivors' lived realities in particular.

This book therefore addresses a twofold gap in existing research on wartime sexual violence, and on gender and armed conflict more generally, as well as on the conflict in northern Uganda: On the one hand, although conflict-related sexual violence against men is committed more frequently than assumed, these crimes continue to be underexplored and silenced, and much remains unknown about the dynamics surrounding this type of violence. Survivors' experiences in particular remain strikingly absent from the increasing scholarly and political engagement with this issue. On the other hand, while much has been written about the war in northern Uganda, and in particular about the horrendous atrocities committed by the LRA, human rights violations by the Ugandan army, including male-directed sexual violence, have thus far received only insufficient attention. By documenting, discussing, and analyzing crimes of sexual violence against civilian men in northern Uganda—through the eyes, voices, and experiences of male survivors directly—this book therefore engages with both of these areas of study, and thereby answers persistent questions regarding male survivors' lived realities in conflict zones.

The book draws upon and speaks to intersecting bodies of scholarship broadly situated within International Relations (IR), including most importantly feminist IR scholarship as well as research on political violence and armed conflict. In methodological and epistemological terms, the book is also guided by ethnographic approaches to and ideals of research, as elaborated upon below, and therefore perhaps also speaks to scholars from across disciplines, beyond the boundaries of IR.

WARTIME SEXUAL VIOLENCE AGAINST MEN

Much like the IR literature more broadly, the study of armed conflict was traditionally silent on gender.[1] As noted by Laura Sjoberg, "the great majority of studies seeking constitutive understandings of or causal explanations for war do not consider gender . . . as potential cases or elements" (2013: 4). Despite this neglect of gender as an analytical tool in IR and conflict studies in general, however, recent decades nevertheless witnessed an increasing utilization of gender perspectives and in particular of diverse feminist theories to elucidate the gendered dimensions of armed conflicts. Predominantly guided by feminist curiosities to comprehend, unravel, and uproot patriarchal structures and gendered inequalities within theaters of war, as Enloe (2004) puts it, a diverse set of studies increasingly seeks to examine conflict, violence, and peace building through a gender lens. As emphasized by Cockburn (2001), these interventions are much needed, as "being alert to the power relations of gender enables us to see features of armed conflict and political violence that are otherwise overlooked" (13). The underlying premise of my position taken in this book is that wars and armed conflicts cannot be fully understood without centralizing gender. Following Jill Steans, applying a gender lens to the study of armed conflict thereby means "to focus on gender as a particular kind of power relation, or to trace out the ways in which gender is central to understanding international processes" (1998: 5).

Crucially, this growing body of scholarship has convincingly documented how war is constituted by and at the same time constitutes gender. Diverse feminist approaches to theorizing war have laid open the multiple and embedded ways in which war is a gendered concept and follows a gendered logic. Among the arguably more influential insights of feminist war theorizing is the standpoint that patriarchal gender relations are among the root causes of and set "favorable conditions" for the onset of armed conflicts, positioning patriarchy (and its intersections with national and economic power) as causal in militarization and war. Feminist IR scholar Kimberly Hutchings similarly identifies a connection between gender relations, and in particular certain hegemonic and militarized conceptions of masculinities, and war. "Masculinity is linked to war because the formal, relational properties of masculinity provide a framework through which war can be rendered both intelligible and acceptable as a social practice and institution," Hutchings writes (2008: 389). According to these diverse feminist insights, therefore, "gendering is a key cause of war as a well as a key impact" (Sjoberg 2013: 6). Much of this engagement with gender in the context of conflict and security arguably comes through a focus on sexual and gender-based violence (SGBV), widely considered a phenomenon exacerbated by war and conflict and forming the overarching focus of this book.[2]

At the same time, throughout most of the literature on violence and conflict, however, employing a "gender perspective" is frequently equated with feminist perspectives and is thereby (erroneously) perceived as exclusively highlighting the roles, needs, rights, and vulnerabilities of women and girls. Owing to the pervasive marginalization of women and female experiences, during conflict and beyond, such a focus is urgently needed and warranted. In scholarship and practice, however, there often seems to be a tendency to equate *gender* with *women*. Chris Dolan (2015) consequently proclaims, "If gender is a potentially powerful analytical, practical and political engine"—which it undoubtedly is—"it is one which is currently firing on only half its cylinders" (486). As a result, and despite the increasing utilization of gender lenses, specific masculinities perspectives—and careful consideration of men and their experiences *as gendered*—as well as queer lenses oftentimes remain missing from gender analyses of armed conflicts.

Since crimes of SGBV against men are immediately underpinned by masculinities, it is inevitable that we use a masculinity lens—namely, that we foreground the roles, structuring, and positioning of masculine identities and highlight the experiences of men and boys, or of masculine bodies and actors, as gendered. Quite generally, masculinities are socially constructed gender norms, referring to the multiple ways of "doing male." Over the past decades, a growing body of interdisciplinary literature has begun to pay critical attention to masculinities and their relations to and positioning in the global gender order, including their roles in political and social structuring.[3] Although still underresearched, the study of masculinities in recent years has also increasingly extended toward analyses of armed conflicts. Consequently, and despite a prevailing lack of *systematic* and *holistic* attention to masculinities during conflicts and transition, a "fairly substantial amount of literature has been generated over the years regarding the forms of masculinity that emerge in times of armed conflict and war" (Ní Aoláin, Haynes, and Cahn 2011: 104).

However, investigating armed conflicts through a masculinities lens and paying attention to men's gendered experiences and roles during war must not be misappropriated toward diverting attention from women's experiences and feminist approaches. Examinations of masculinities can therefore not be decoupled from analyses of patriarchal gender hierarchies more broadly. Rather, studies of men's roles and experiences in (post)conflict contexts must maintain a holistic gendered focus. Caution is also required so that centralizing a masculinities perspectives does not reinforce gender binaries, which "have been remarkably consistent across time, place and culture in human social and political relations" (Sjoberg 2016: 4). Therefore, despite this study's focus male survivors' experiences as underpinned by masculinities, careful consideration of gender as a fluid spectrum and of the elasticity of gender identities is required. The inclusive recognition of gender nonconforming, intersex and/or trans, or queer identities is consequently necessary to fully comprehend studies of war.

At the same time, while the roles of masculinities during armed conflict are slowly but increasingly recognized, this "research has tended to be focused on certain groups and to employ a relatively narrow scope" only (Myrttinen et al. 2016: 1). Indeed, most dominant research on men and masculinities in the context of war focuses on the "violences of men" (Hearn 1998) and the linkages between (militarized) masculinities and the various forms of aggression and violence associated with them. All too often these examinations have (re)produced an unreconstructed view of men as universal aggressors and women as universal victims during armed conflicts. In her groundbreaking work on the gender politics of militarism, Cynthia Enloe (2004) critically exposed these essentialist binary categorizations of "all the men are in the militias and all the women are victims."

Empirically, however, this is a gross "over-simplification that both reinforces ideas about violence being natural to men and fails to explain for women's roles in conflict" (Cleaver 2002: 17). Problematically, and as pointed out by a growing body of critical scholarship, the literature's persisting focus on hyper- and militarized masculinities omits attention from the gendered experiences of nonviolent, non-soldiering, and civilian men.[4] As MacKenzie and Foster (2017) note, "Although there is a rich and growing literature on masculinities and war, there remains little understanding of how non-combatant civilian men and civilian masculinities are impacted by war, conflict, occupation and militarization" (210).

As a consequence, men as victims and male vulnerabilities in theaters of war are only insufficiently addressed and frequently overlooked, largely due to stereotypical gender assumptions about women's and men's roles in society. This misrecognition and denial of masculine vulnerabilities is wrongheaded and irritating. Vulnerabilities are fundamentally human, constituting an "underlying, ever present and abiding undercurrent of our natural state," as poet David Whyte (2018: 233) puts it. In line with Hannah Arendt, Martha Fineman (2008) further argues that "vulnerability is universal and constant, inherent in the human condition, . . . arising from our embodiment, which carries with it the ever-present possibility of harm, injury and misfortune" (Fineman 2008: 9). Somewhat ironically, however, and even though vulnerability is ultimately beyond human control, dominant hetero-patriarchal assumptions of gender nevertheless presume masculinities to be irreconcilable with victimhood, instead expecting men to invulnerable. Owing to these socially constructed premises, the intersections between masculinities and vulnerabilities, despite emerging scholarship, remain heavily undertheorized and underresearched, and it seems that "we do not really have any idea of the full extent of male vulnerability" (Dolan 2011: 135) in conflict scenarios. In particular the seemingly mundane and everyday gendered harms and vulnerabilities experienced by men in conflict-affected contexts, during displacement, or under militant occupation remain particularly neglected. To obtain a realistic and holistic understanding of the workings and functioning of gender in conflict-affected contexts, however, "the scope of studying masculinities in these situations needs to be broadened to go beyond merely examining the violences of men" (Myrttinen et al. 2016: 1) to include male vulnerabilities.

One scholarly and politically relevant entry point for analyzing masculine vulnerabilities in conflict settings are crimes of wartime sexual violence against men and boys. Although still largely ignored in dominant global conceptions of conflict-related gender-based violence, violence against men has increasingly received attention from academics and humanitarian actors in the past decade.[5] However, despite some newly gained attention and important theoretical, empirical, and political inroads, much remains unknown about the dynamics of male-directed sexual violence. In this introduction, and even more so in the following chapter, I identify numerous lacunae in the growing literature on male-directed sexual abuse in conflict settings, which I then seek to engage with throughout the book. By and large, much of the growing yet limited body of scholarship is largely descriptive or conceptually dominated and lacks both theory and, even more so, empirical foundations, with only few noteworthy exceptions.

Empirically grounded in-depth case study analyses and documentation of the dynamics surrounding wartime sexual violence within (or across, for that matter) specific cases remain particularly underdeveloped. For instance, while the LRA's horrendous atrocities in northern Uganda have been subjected to extensive scholarly debate and have received widespread media coverage, the pervasive human rights violations committed by the Ugandan government armed forces have received significantly less attention. Within this context, crimes of male rape committed by the government's National Resistance Army (NRA) in the early phase of the war, during the late 1980s and early 1990s, are particularly poorly documented. While scholars have brought detailed attention to gender-based violence against women and girls, who remain disproportionately affected, only occasional references to male-directed sexual violence in Acholiland exist, which in turn lack empirical data and analytical depth. By painting a detailed and empirically grounded picture of conflict-related sexual violence against men in Acholiland—situated within the overall historical and political context and intersecting episodes of violence and war—the analysis in this book thereby offers a more nuanced and comprehensive understanding of the war in northern Uganda, as well as of the dynamics of wartime sexual violence more broadly.

By examining questions of context, gendered harms, agency, and justice, in this book I intend to complicate dominant conceptions of the gender dynamics of armed conflict in general and to deepen our understanding of wartime sexual violence and of male survivors' experiences in particular. This book serves as an empirically grounded response to the growing body of scholarship on wartime sexual violence that still largely ignores male survivors and has not yet carefully enough engaged with survivors' lived realities.

DISPLACEMENT FROM GENDERED PERSONHOOD

To analyze male survivors' experiences in holistic ways, I employ the conceptual framework of "displacement from gendered personhood."[6] While this framework will be analytically employed most centrally in chapter 4, which analyzes the impact of sexual violence on male survivors' masculinities, the temporal and spatial dimensions of this framework are indeed indicative of the wider argument I make about male survivors' overall experiences across time and space—and thus warrant sufficient explanation here.

Most of the existing scholarship on the topic suggest that sexual violence against men compromises or thwarts male survivors' gender identities as men.

What in existing scholarship is almost exclusively referred to as "emasculation" through "feminization" and/or "homosexualization" is frequently portrayed at once as a motivation for sexual violence to occur and as its primary consequence. In existing scholarship, there appears to be a consensus that "sexual violence against men involves forms of emasculation in which perpetrators seek to feminize their victims by rendering them weak, violated and passive, in contradistinction to stereotypical masculine ideals" (Auchter 2018: 1440). The vast majority of studies on sexual violence against men indeed argue that "emasculating" victims is among the most common drivers, if not the single most prevalent driver, of male-directed sexual violence and simultaneously its primary consequence and harm. These global assumptions reflect the ways in which sexual violence against men is locally made sense of in Acholiland. Among the conflict-affected community, and situated within hetero-patriarchal gender relations, men who were raped are perceived as "less of a man" and "stripped of their manhood."

Yet despite initial conceptual insights, how exactly sexual violence impacts upon male survivors' lives, and in particular how the compromising of masculinities unfolds, and what it entails, are questions that remain insufficiently understood. Most discussions about wartime sexual violence against men are conceptually dominated, abstract-descriptive and consistently lack empirical data on survivors' experiences. Conditioned by the methodological and ethical challenges of collecting data on this topic, insights into the longitudinal effects of gender-based violence against men from a survivor perspective remain mostly absent from the existing literature. At the same time, existing scholarship has not yet sufficiently enough engaged critically with the analytical categories and associated terminologies of "emasculation," "feminization," and "homosexualization," which are characterized by different normative and analytical challenges.

Throughout the expanding and interdisciplinary literature on gender, war and (in)security, including feminist theorizing, "feminization" is broadly conceptualized as devalorization and devaluation, illuminating the gendered power inequalities constituted by the asymmetric privileging of masculine over feminine qualities inherent in global gender orders. For Peterson (2010), the ultimate effect of rendering someone (or something) female—that is, of "feminizing"—is a reduction in legitimacy, status, and value, associated with rejection and weakness. In studies on wartime male sexual assault, "feminization" is thus used as a synonym for degradation and humiliation. In this reading, "emasculation" by way of "feminization" and/or "homosexualization" is underpinned by the premise that femininities, as well as the female (and/or homosexuality), are seen as inherently undesirable and problematic. Such dynamics and assumptions in many ways rely upon (implicit and explicit) misogyny, gender essentialism, and homophobia. This marginalization and infantilization of the female and femininities, which lies at the core of the "feminization" terminology, has been critiqued by decades of feminist IR scholarship.

In light of this, I am concerned that employing this language without critically examining and questioning it can imply the risk of accepting and normalizing these patriarchal assumptions behind unequal gender expectations, orders, and relations, in which women and homosexuals are automatically subordinate to all (heterosexual) men. Ultimately, the dichotomous assumptions of inviolable and invulnerable masculinities vis-à-vis infantilized females and femininities that underpin the language of "feminization," specifically when employed for male sexual assault, risk reinforcing dominant ideas about masculinities and heterosexualities. While I recognize that simply avoiding the use of this language cannot change these assumptions and gender inequalities, my motivation in refraining from employing this terminology nevertheless in part constitutes a normatively driven endeavor of not wanting to reproduce these presumptions.

In addition to these normative challenges, the concept of "emasculation" is furthermore characterized by analytical shortcomings. As predominantly applied throughout the interdisciplinary literature on sexual violence against men, "emasculation" is predominantly understood as the *ultimate* loss of manhood, and survivors are seen as being *completely* and *indefinitely* stripped of their masculine identities. In his groundbreaking and widely cited article on the topic, Sivakumaran (2007), for instance, posits that sexual violence *robs* victims of their masculine status—thereby implicitly suggesting ultimate, nonreversible effects. Empirically, however, there often is a misfit between the idea of "emasculation," which appears static and unambiguous, and survivors' lived realities, which often are dynamic, fluid, and variable—as demonstrated throughout this book.

Mindful of these normative and analytical shortcomings, I instead adopt the idea and wording of "displacement from gendered personhood." In a recent examination of the lived realities of refugee survivors of male sexual violence from the Democratic Republic of the Congo (DRC) living in Uganda, Edström, Dolan, and colleagues (2016) refer to the effects of male-directed sexual violence as "displacement from self and personhood." Drawing on this, here I seek to unpack and further develop this framework, and specifically its gendered components and applicability.

Importantly, the displacement terminology suggests that—like physical displacement, for instance in a refugee camp—"displacement from gendered personhood" can potentially be mitigated, of course not without leaving its physical and psychological marks. Linked to survivors' harms, employing the language of displacement in this context thus illustrates that survivors' harmful experiences are potentially temporary and can possibly be alleviated, preventing us from employing terminology that freezes dynamic experiences into time and space. As poignantly argued by Gray, Stern, and Dolan, the "unmaking" of survivors' personhood and subjectivities as a result of sexual violence frequently "occurs in tandem with a 'remaking' of the self and the world in which the self inhabits" (2019: 7). To illustrate, and as unpacked in chapter 4, male survivors in northern Uganda often felt they were "less of a man" as a result of the sexual violations they had experienced. In the local Acholi context, constructions of personhood play a fundamentally important role in identity formation and societal structuring in northern Uganda (p'Bitek 1986), and are inherently linked to and constructed through gender (Porter 2016). Similarly, the concept of "displacement from gendered personhood" accommodates different intertwined harms composed of physical, psychological, social, and physiological effects that reflect survivors' long-term lived realities, thereby emphasizing that the impact of violence on gender identities frequently is a layered process perpetuated over time and composed of layered vulnerabilities, rather than a singular event exclusively linked to particular acts of rape (chapter 4).

At the same time, however, for numerous survivors these perceptions regarding their impacted masculine identities were able to change again over time, shaped by different factors, such as membership in survivors' groups or access to physical rehabilitative support. The analysis underpinning this book therefore evidences that these gendered harms do shape male survivors' lived realities in different ways, but do not always and indefinitely define them as ever-vulnerable, helpless, and "emasculated" victims. Instead, survivors' viewpoints and their experiences show that these harms and vulnerabilities, as associated with normative gender constructs, are contextually dependent and often are potentially malleable through sociopolitical and economic assistance. This can include ways in which survivors themselves exercise varying forms of political agency as well as different forms of justice in response to their sexual harms, as I explore throughout this book.

"THE LONG STICK CANNOT KILL A SNAKE"

In northern Uganda's subregion of Acholiland, much sociocultural knowledge and wisdom is communicated through proverbs. What Chinua Achebe in *Things Fall Apart* (1958) writes in a beautifully poetic way about the Ibo (in the novel) in Nigeria—that "proverbs are the palm-oil with which words are eaten"—similarly applies to the Acholi in northern Uganda. The careful reader will notice that throughout the book I illustrate certain contextual and culturally specific interpretations or arguments through Acholi proverbs or idioms, many of which were recorded in the writings of the late Acholi poet-artist-academic Okot p'Bitek. I use one particular Acholi proverb as a guiding framework for this book and its argumentation: *Odoo mabor pe neko twol*—"A long stick cannot kill a snake." In borrowing and applying this particular proverb, I am inspired by Holly Porter's (2016) application of it in her own work.

The proverb's explanation or interpretation, as put forward by both Okot p'Bitek and Holly Porter, goes as follows: If one tries to kill a snake by hitting it with a long stick, and is thereby far away from the snake, one's efforts will most likely not be rewarded with success. If one tries to hit the snake with a long stick and from afar with only weak blows, the snake will inevitably curl around the end of the stick, latching on. As the stick is raised to deliver another blow, there is a danger that the snake releases and falls on the person holding the stick. At the same time, the relatively low force of the blow with a long stick ultimately cannot kill the snake either. Being far away from the snake with a long stick therefore does not work, and in fact can even prove counterproductive. Instead, one will have to get closer to the snake, with a shorter stick, and deliver strong, decisive hits in order to kill it. The moral of the proverb, according to both p'Bitek and Porter, is "If you are too far away from a problem, you cannot contribute to the solution" (Porter 2013: 107). One needs to get close to the problem in order to deal with it, resolve it, and contribute to a potential solution.

Based on this interpretation, I first employ this Acholi proverb in methodological and epistemological terms: In this study, I get close to the stories, experiences, and lived realities of male survivors of sexual violence in northern Uganda and listen to their perspectives and priorities, including those about the current postconflict context or about justice. I therefore follow what can be called an epistemology from below, guided by the experiences and viewpoints of survivors themselves. This attentiveness to survivors' perspectives, which is unique in comparison to existing research on the topic, is also crucial in order to get close to and contribute to a solution—thus metaphorically using a short stick—instead of listening only to, for instance, external service providers, and therefore being too far away from the problem, which would figuratively resemble using a long stick.

Second, conceptually, I get close to the "problem" by carefully analyzing and understanding the sexual and gendered harms experienced by male survivors of sexual violence before considering appropriate responses, remedies, or processes. I thus get close to the "problem," or the harm resulting from the violations, in order to then be able to think about possible appropriate "solutions," such as survivors' agentic capacities or quests for justice. As argued by Porter (2013), any appropriate response to wrongdoing and crimes, and any consideration of how to engage with the ensuing harm, "must begin with an understanding of the act itself, and how it is perceived in terms of its damage and harm" (69). This will be done in chapter 4, which unpacks the harms experienced by Acholi male survivors, specifically examining how sexual violence impacts their gender identities.

Third, in analytical terms, throughout this book I demonstrate that in responding to sexual violence against men in northern Uganda, different processes—such as avenues for agency or justice measures—must be contextual, culturally appropriate, and in direct response to local needs and concerns in order to potentially contribute to the solution. Rather than "distanced" responses to violence and crime, solutions that are close to the problem, embedded in the local context, and driven by conflict-affected communities themselves (for instance, survivors' support groups) are necessary. This approach follows how Porter (2013) utilizes the proverb in her work and necessitates as well as embodies a survivor-centric approach, as put forward toward the end of this book.

REFLECTIONS ON METHODOLOGIES AND ETHICS

Although I have conducted research in northern Uganda since 2011, the empirical material underpinning this book derives primarily from a total of nine months of field-based research conducted in Acholiland in northern Uganda. Following a preparatory visit in May 2015, I collected the bulk of the data between January and July 2016, followed by two shorter spells of research in June and September 2018. During this period, I was affiliated as a research associate with the Refugee Law Project (RLP) at the School of Law at Makerere University, which I reflect upon in more detail below. Overall, the data derive from different triangulated qualitative data-collection techniques, including four participatory workshop discussions with a total of 46 male survivors of sexual violence who are members of survivor support groups; 79 in-depth key-informant interviews; two focus-group discussions with male elders; and ethnographic participant "reflection." The data collection was also made possible through the diligent and thorough assistance of my research collaborator and translator, Kenneth Oyet Odong.

The focus on northern Uganda as one in-depth case study, based on embedded qualitative field research, facilitates a holistic and grounded examination of the dynamics of sexual violence against men within a particular context. This approach specifically allows me to foreground the experiences and viewpoints of male survivors directly. Conducting a single case study analysis on northern Uganda thus allows for what Geertz (1983) labels in ethnographic terms as "thick descriptions."[7]

A variety of methodological and ethical criteria as well as feasibility and practicality aspects influenced the focus on northern Uganda as a case study. In methodological terms, northern Uganda is among a growing list of conflicts in which sexual violence against men occurred, and for which at least initial documentation exists. Crimes of sexual violence against men, however, remain absent and marginalized from dominant analyses of the conflict and are insufficiently explained, understood, and explored. In addition to this widespread occurrence of sexual violence against men in northern Uganda, the region also constitutes an interesting and exemplary case of a relatively diverse postconflict landscape, which includes numerous implemented and proposed transitional justice and peace-building mechanisms. This diversity of ongoing and attempted postconflict initiatives thus enables me to engage with broader and related questions of survivors' views on justice and the ways in which they exercise agency. In addition to these underlying methodological considerations, practicality and feasibility considerations likewise informed the case selection. The research was facilitated by my basic knowledge of the local language, Acholi—which enabled me to have social conversations but was not good enough to conduct thorough interviews or research-related exchanges—coupled with contacts across northern Uganda that I have developed through research and advocacy work since 2011.

It was also during my prior engagement in northern Uganda in late 2011 that I first heard about the occurrence and dynamics of sexual violence against men in this context. Together with a colleague from the Justice and Reconciliation Project (JRP), we interviewed representatives of various survivors' associations. During one of those interviews in Kitgum district, after diligently having answered our questions, the leader of a massacre survivors' group continued to describe to us the manifold ways in which his community had been affected by episodes of violence and brutality throughout the war, not only by the LRA but also by government soldiers. What appeared to be most memorable and noteworthy to him was a particularly gruesome act of sexual torture of a male community member by the NRA in the early 1990s, which he graphically recounted to us. I had read as many books and articles about the conflict as I possibly could, and had conducted several interviews across Acholiland for the previous four months, and so I naively thought that I roughly knew about the various forms of violence perpetrated during the conflict. Up to that point, however, I had not yet heard anything about sexual crimes perpetrated against men in this context. Later in the car, on our way back to Kitgum town, I asked my colleague whether this instance of male-directed sexual abuse was an isolated case. "It was widespread and happened a lot, but people do not talk about it at all," my colleague explained to me. "This is why you and even most people from here have never heard about it," I was told.

Since then, I have been intellectually and personally interested in the dynamics of these crimes and in male survivors' experiences. Why did these crimes occur? Why are they seldom discussed locally and internationally? What characterizes the lived realities of male survivors? How do survivors experience the silencing of their harms for more than twenty years, and how do they want these crimes to be redressed? Out of those deliberations and over time grew not only my academic but also my personal interest and curiosity, which underpins this inquiry.

Reflections on Positionality

As a young, white, European academic, I am obviously an outsider, even a stranger to Acholiland and thus to most of my respondents. A *munu,* as the Acholi would say. In many ways, I could not be any more different from the elderly Acholi survivor I engaged with for this study. At times our gender identities were the only obvious and visible common personal characteristics; and yet we did have much more in common that initially appeared. In retrospect, I think that in particular my sexual and gender identity as a heterosexual man constituted a crucial enabling factor for me to conduct the research. I specifically believe that as a heterosexual man, I have been able to relate in a variety of ways not only to my male colleagues at RLP (and thus with some of my key informants), but also to the male survivors who participated in the study. I believe that especially our conversations about the physiological impact of the sexual violations on male survivors' sexualities were made possible in part because of my own positionality in that regard. At the same time, however, I am of course fully aware of the power asymmetries that characterized my relationships with research participants in heavily gendered and racialized ways (see Schulz 2020b). As a young, white researcher (now with a PhD, at the time of researching the bulk of the material in the process of acquiring that title) I without a doubt enjoy a tremendous amount of socioeconomic, cultural, and political privileges vis-à-vis the vast majority of my respondents and collaborators, which in turn shape the power dynamics that structured our engagement and relationships.

My external appearance resembles those of the countless expatriate aid workers, students, Christian missionaries, travelers, and tourists who populate Gulu, particularly during the summer months. However, to the best of my abilities, I have attempted to distance myself from assumptions and expectations related to this status and to transcend the obvious differences and boundaries between me and my interlocutors. I tried to learn the local language Acholi as best as I could, although my inability to have a fluent professional conversation or to conduct an interview must be acknowledged as a methodological limitation. I also tried to participate in my informants' lives as much as I could. I attended funerals, weddings, graduation parties, and traditional ceremonies. I spent countless afternoons or evenings in local bars or at the kiosk around the corner from my house, participating in everyday activities and tasks and learning as much about culture, sociality, and gender identities and relations as I could. When traveling to the field, when and wherever possible, I also made a purposeful and methodologically informed choice of traveling by motorbike—locally called a *boda-boda*—rather than by car to visibly distance myself from other expatriate aid-workers who frequently travel in air-conditioned SUVs. I thus concur with Ryan (2017: 377), who, reflecting on her own field research in Sierra Leone, attests that "turning up on the same mode of transport frequently used to travel to markets, or to health centres, or to visit relatives made me more relatable to the communities I visited."

During one of our numerous stays in "the field," a group of villagers gave me a new Acholi name: *Omara*—the "loved one," or the "one who loves." The name, they explained, reflected what they saw as my appreciation, perhaps even love, for Acholi culture and Acholi ways of life. I am aware that this is not necessarily unique, and yet it meant (and continues to mean) a great deal to me. Indeed, these were among the experiences where conducting this empirically rich research just felt, as Sverker Finnström (2008) has put it, "like the exact right thing to do."

It probably goes without saying that conducting the research and engaging with the survivors was not easy emotionally and psychologically. Many a time, as I sat with the survivors and listened to their stories, tears were shed—tears of sorrow, of compassion, but at times also tears of relief. Many sleepless nights I lay awake recounting the horrors of the stories and thinking about the past, the present, and the future that is linked to these narratives. These emotional and psychological impacts that accompany research on sensitive topics must be commonplace, but their effects on researchers too often go underacknowledged and remain undiscussed. My intention here is absolutely not to (re)center my own experiences at the expense of decentring my research participants' realities and stories. Rather, I want to be honest and transparent about how engaging with these at times heartbreaking narratives has shaped me in some ways and therefore also the research process and its output, in the form of this book.

As I left the field in the summer of 2016 and returned first to Northern Ireland and then to Sweden, where I was based for the initial analysis and drafting of the dissertation, these stories (obviously) traveled with me, on paper in my notebook and on my laptop, but also in my mind and heart. In many ways I found it much more difficult to reread and reengage with these narratives in this context of greater spatial and geographical (but also emotional) separation from Acholiland and my research participants. To some extent this was probably due to the absence of the support network that I had built and nurtured in northern Uganda, primarily composed of my colleagues at RLP, as described below, but also of friends and colleagues with whom I could talk about the challenges I faced. In other ways, as I was back home I was often accompanied by feelings of concern, if not guilt, of simultaneously having done (or rather asked) too much and of not having done enough to support and be there for the survivors who so generously and compassionately shared their stories and worries. Maintaining regular, often daily, contact with my colleagues at RLP via social media was one way of trying to extend that presence. Follow-up visits in 2018, during which I had a chance to engage with some of the survivors and share copies of my dissertation, also constituted small steps in countering these concerns.

Nevertheless, the last thing I want is for any of the survivors who participated in this study to feel that they and their stories have been exploited and have been taken advantage of. Trying to do justice to that and to their stories, and trying to respectfully, truthfully, and sensitively convey them in the pages of this book, have thus far been one of the hardest but also most rewarding tasks I have taken on. At this stage, it must suffice to say that these stories resonated with me not only on an intellectual or political level but also more deeply on a personal level. They brought out many uncomfortable truths but also helped me to make sense of certain questions, issues, and lived realities myself.

Joining an Established Process: My Institutional Affiliation with RLP

For the field research period, I was affiliated as a research associate with the Refugee Law Project (RLP), an outreach project at the School of Law at Makerere University in Uganda. Between January and July 2016, I was based in the organization's Gulu office and closely worked with its staff there. Cooperating and being affiliated with RLP allowed me to become part of an established and sustainable process of engaging with male sexual violence survivors in a participatory approach and enabled me to closely partner with local experts on the topic. For the past ten years, RLP has engaged with male survivors of sexual violence in an inclusive, empowering, and ethically sensitive way. Specifically, RLP is working with three institutionalized and organized victims' groups composed of male survivors of sexual violence. One of these groups specifically unites Acholi male survivors and is based in northern Uganda: The Men of Courage umbrella association is composed of three subgroups located in three separate locations across Acholiland.

The collaboration with RLP was particularly important not only in gaining physical access to male survivors but also in developing mutual trust, between me and my research collaborators at RLP as well as between me and the research participants who are members of the survivors' groups. Due to their prolonged and sustained engagement with male survivors, RLP has been able to establish a level of mutual trust between the organizations and its staff as well as the groups of survivors. A recent study about the cooperation between RLP and the Men of Hope Refugee Association Uganda (MOHRU) of male survivors—one of Men of Courage's partner associations based in Kampala—refers to this continuous process and cooperation as "engaged excellence," "meaning that the work is dependent upon it linking to and involving those who are at the heart of the change they wish to see" (Dolan, Edström, et al. 2016: 37).

By becoming an integral component of this process, some of the trust the survivors have in the institution (and by association its staff) was transferred to me as an affiliated researcher. During my engagement and meetings with the survivors, many emphasized that they felt reassured and comfortable to participate in the discussions precisely because they were conducted in cooperation with RLP and accompanied by staff with whom they had engaged with over a prolonged period of time. To further build trust, my RLP collaborators and I also regularly engaged with members of the group on an informal basis prior to each of the more formal data collection exercises, to ensure that the participating survivors had an opportunity to at least meet and engage with me before agreeing to share their viewpoints and experiences. The cooperation and affiliation with RLP also allowed me to conduct the discussions with male survivors in the presence of experts in the field. One of my colleagues is a trained psychological counselor who regularly conducts counseling sessions with conflict-affected communities in northern Uganda, including the groups of male sexual violence survivors. By joining the workshops, he was able to provide immediate psychological and psychosocial services to respondents if and when necessary.[8]

At the same time, my cooperation with RLP was not a one-way street characterized only by their support of my research. Rather, our relationship was one of mutual collaboration. Especially in the early months of my affiliation with RLP, I regularly assisted and supported my colleagues' daily work-related activities, traveled to the field for consecutive days to implement RLP's programming, and immersed myself in the organization's work. Taken together, these different levels of involvement with RLP's work were not just unique and fascinating opportunities for me to obtain a deeper understanding and appreciation of the local context; they were also intended as my active part in a collaborative process. They thus constitute elements of my giving back to a process I benefited from immensely, something that is of particular concern to scholarly discussions about ethical research.

Data Collection

Most of the contextual background about the war as well as gender identities and relations in northern Uganda is based on in-depth interviews conducted with key informants. The experiences and viewpoints of male survivors, on the other hand, constituting the empirical core of this book, specifically derive from four workshop discussions with a total of forty-six male survivors who are members of survivors' support groups. In conducting these workshop discussions, I was inspired by normative and methodological principles of a participatory research approach, which seeks to conduct research *with* people, rather than *on* them, in order to "ground knowledge production in the everyday lives of those most affected" (Robins and Wilson 2015: 236). Such an approach to research likewise "rejects the liberal value of neutrality in social research and aims to advance the goal of a particular community" (Robins and Wilson 2015: 228). Indeed, I am increasingly convinced that attempting neutrality or value-free engagement in the context of sensitive research with populations in marginalized, victimized, and vulnerable situations in general often does not only seem impossible but would at times also be highly undesirable or even unethical. The careful reader will therefore notice that remaining entirely neutral or value-free in light of survivors' heartbreaking stories and experiences is not something I managed or something I, in full honesty, truly aspired to. Rather than staying entirely value-free, my normative aim here is to foreground and elucidate the harmful experiences of marginalized and victimized male sexual violence survivors in northern Uganda.

In practical terms, the workshop sampling strategy of engaging only with survivors who are members of organized support groups is underpinned by various ethical considerations. Specifically, the Men of Courage umbrella group has clearly defined political and societal agendas and follows a commitment to advocate for justice on behalf of male survivors. Deriving from this premise, the voluntarily participating members within the group had a predefined interest in workshops on these themes. However, only including male survivors who are members of institutionalized survivors' associations also implies methodological limitations for the representativeness of the argument, and in particular the findings on justice cannot necessarily be extended toward male survivors who are not part of these groups, but require further examination. Furthermore, through their membership in groups and their linkages to RLP (see further below), the participants, to differing degrees, were already exposed to dominant international and national discourses, specifically with regard to dealing with the past. As such, this degree of familiarity and experience with these discourses may well be expected to have shaped their viewpoints on questions of postconflict justice and social reconstruction. While I thus acknowledge the limitations of engaging only with survivors who are members of survivors' groups with close links to an organization, I emphasize the ethical integrity of this approach that situates the study as part of a continuous process of working with male survivors.

The Men of Courage association specifically consists of three subgroups in separate locations in across Acholiland (see chapter 5). To preserve survivors' anonymity and confidentiality, the exact locations of these groups will not be revealed. One participatory workshop was conducted with each of these groups, in addition to a final workshop, which brought together representatives from each of the three groups. For each of these workshops, only voluntarily participating members joined the discussion. Two of the workshops were conducted in the familiar locations where the groups usually held their meetings, which in both cases were members' homesteads. One of these discussions preceded the group's weekly meeting, which ensured that numerous members were already present and that survivors did not have to devote too much extra time to the research project. Another workshop took place in a nearby school compound (during the school holidays). Members of the group chose this location because they deemed it safe for discussing their viewpoints without raising the community's attention or suspicion. The fourth workshop, which brought together representatives of all three organizations, was held in RLP's office in Gulu.

Rather than following a more imposed and rigid group interview or focus-group discussion format, these workshops were less guided and confrontational, and more open and participatory. For the first three workshops, I posed one guiding question:, "What does justice mean to you?" This then initiated a longer discussion. I thus primarily served as a facilitator rather than the research director, while participants had some agency over the workshop process and the direction of the discussion. All four workshops were conducted in Acholi, and two RLP colleagues translated for me.[9] Due to the focus of the workshops, and for ethical reasons, I did not include any questions about their harmful experiences of sexual violence directly. In each of the discussions, however, survivors themselves always situated their perspectives in relation to their respective experiences and harms, and at times openly spoke about their sexual violations. Various survivors expressed that "talking has really helped, and it was important to get this out." We therefore never interrupted these elaborations, letting survivors speak freely and then linking their input back to the initial focus of the discussions.

The fourth workshop, bringing together representatives from each of the groups in Gulu town, was designed slightly differently. At the beginning, I gave a presentation on the Ugandan government's draft transitional justice policy in order to allow for a sufficiently informed discussion about contextual postconflict developments. In preparation for this workshop, together with my colleagues, I compiled a summary of the draft policy. The summary was then translated into Acholi and copies were provided to the participants. Following the presentation on the draft policy, we asked survivors to position their views and perspectives on justice in relation to the draft policy and its proposed justice mechanisms. The discussion then followed a similar open structure comparable to the previous three workshop discussions and was directed by the same guiding question.

The fourth workshop was also followed by a meeting for members and representatives of the groups to collectively work toward the future development of the separate groups and the Men of Courage umbrella association. Based on previous deliberations within the group, a strategy meeting for the future of the group was determined as the right approach and thus formed the focus of the latter part of the workshop. During the meeting, members confirmed their commitment to further formalize the structure of the groups in order to officially register as an association at the local government level. Toward this end, a constitution was needed for the Men of Courage umbrella group. Following the workshop discussion, we thus began to jointly develop a constitution, which I together with representatives of the group and colleagues at RLP continued working on after the workshop. Providing this space for the group thereby constituted an aspect of actively involving research participants in the process and was part of my objective to "return to the community something of real value, in forms determined by participants themselves" (Pittaway, Bartolomei, and Hugman 2010: 234).

Overall, participants regularly stated that the workshops were empowering and emancipatory. "I am glad you are giving us a chance for telling the truth and we shall use the information accordingly," one survivor proclaimed. Another survivor attested that this "research is also justice, because the truth will come out during research." In relation to such viewpoints and expectations specifically but also during the research more generally, I attempted to manage my informants' expectations about the actual expected outcome of the study. To this end, I continually emphasized that the purpose of the research was for an academic study, and that I could not promise that any of this would ensure that "the truth will come out" or that survivors would immediately benefit from this.

Throughout my period in the field, I also constantly listened, observed, and learned, and thus engaged in the ethnographic method of "participant reflection." While most ethnographic research refers to this method as "participant observation," I am instead inspired by Swedish anthropologist Finnström (2003), who describes ethnographers' predominant data collection techniques as participant "reflection" rather than "observation." In his groundbreaking study on the conflict in northern Uganda, Finnström (2008) explains that "we do the best to participate in the works, questions, joys and sorrows of our informants' everyday life. Then we take a few steps back, to be able to *reflect* upon what we have learnt and experienced, again to step forward to participate. This we do daily in the fieldwork encounter" (29, emphasis added).

This process of participating, listening, and learning and then taking a few steps back to *reflect* upon the newly learned insights adequately reflects my own approach of conducting empirical research in northern Uganda, thus leading me to adapt and borrow Finnström's (2003) consideration of participant reflection.

In the field, and during the data collection period, simply engaging with non-work-related activities, or taking on another task, for instance with RLP, helped me to maintain a certain distance for reflection on the stories I heard during the interviews and workshops. In addition to these more structured methods of gathering information, countless more informal and often unexpected conversations with a range of individuals—often initiated by stopping at the side of the road and taking notes (Finnström 2008)—proved to be equally important and relevant, at times even more so.

ORGANIZATION OF THE BOOK

Guided by feminist research methods in the social sciences, throughout this book I use direct quotations as much as possible and when appropriate, to "enable the reader to 'hear' what the researcher heard" (Reinharz and Davidman 1992: 39) and to avoid the all-too-common problem of speaking for others—of depriving them of the opportunity to speak in their own words, on their own terms. Important feminist critique, including by Linda Alcoff, has long argued that "speaking for others is arrogant, vain, unethical and politically illegitimate" (1991: 6), and so I seek to let survivors speak for themselves by (re)citing their views and words. In doing so, I concur with Boesten (2014) that "in order to understand the gendered nature of war, we need to listen to the complex experiences of women [and men] beyond any prewritten assumptions and scripts" (112).

Although I draw on the experiences of male survivors and at times include their testimonies of violence and abuse, as illustrated by the case study narrative that opened this Introduction, I am nevertheless also mindful of not engaging in what others have termed a "pornography of violence" (Daniel 1996). I therefore do not describe in detail the violent sexual acts perpetrated against male survivors as at times narrated to me by research participants themselves, but rather focus on their phenomenological lived realities of gendered harms and the ways in which they come to terms with their experiences in the contemporary post-conflict context.

Furthermore, by homing in on the experiences of male sexual violence survivors, under no circumstances do I mean to divert attention from and resources for female sexual violence survivors, who across time and space remain disproportionately affected by such violence. I also do not mean to hierarchically classify wartime male rape in comparison to sexual violence against women, or other conflict-related harms experienced by women and men alike. As poignantly stated by Audre Lorde, "There is no hierarchy of oppressions" (1983: 9).

"When a mushroom grows, it no longer fears the sun"—A Note on
Names and Anonymity

In the interest of anonymity and confidentiality, and particularly in the interest of survivors, no respondents' personal identities and locations are revealed. An exception to this strict preservation of anonymity is the in-depth case study of Okwera that opened this chapter and that will follow us throughout this book. Okwera's story, including his full name, location, and experience, has previously been published as a written narrative (RLP 2014) and is included in RLP's video documentaries on sexual violence against men and boys. Okwera himself explicitly stated to me, as well as to many of my RLP colleagues, that "when a mushroom has grown, it no longer fears the sun," to confirm that he wanted his identity revealed and his story publicly known. Finnström similarly utilizes the Acholi proverb "The growing millet does not fear the sun" (*bel ka otwi pe lworo ceng*) (2003: 15) in relation to some of his informants insisting on having their full names and identities mentioned throughout his ethnography, "which they claimed gave authenticity to the stories" (ibid.). Anthropologist van der Geest (2003) reflects upon his experience of conducting ethnographic research when he argues that more often than not, informants want to be remembered for what they say and how they contributed to the study. To this end, I follow Okwera's request, as I feel that disrespecting his wish and anonymizing his narrative would in turn be the unethical thing to do.

Chapter Organization

Following this introduction, the following chapter turns to offer a global perspective about the occurrence, dynamics, and scope of conflict-related sexual violence against men across time and space. Chapter 2 systematically reviews the growing literature on wartime sexual violence against men, thereby situating the book in existing scholarship and in relation to what is already known and what remains to be known about the phenomenon under scrutiny here. The examination in chapter 2 then includes an overview of existing evidence regarding the scope, frequency, and prevalence of conflict-related sexual violence against men across and within contemporary armed conflicts. The chapter likewise includes a systematic outline of dominant explanatory frameworks regarding the causes of wartime sexual violence, framed within feminist theorizing and insights about the gendered dynamics of war and violence more broadly.

Turning to the locally specific dynamics in northern Uganda, chapter 3 then situates crimes of sexual violence against men within the context of the more than two-decades-long war between the Ugandan government and the Lord's Resistance Army (LRA) rebel group. While much as been written about the northern Ugandan conflict, government-perpetrated human rights abuses, and in particular crimes of male rape, are only poorly documented and remain almost entirely absent from any scholarly analysis of the conflict. Painting a detailed picture of the dynamics surrounding conflict-related male rape in Acholiland, I evidence that these crimes were geographically widespread and perpetrated across vast areas of the conflict-ridden north, leading the local population to invent a new vocabulary to describe these crimes as *tek-gungu,* which translates as "to bend over" (*gungu*) "hard" or "forcefully" (*tek*), or as "the way that is hard to bend." Perpetrated by government forces of the National Resistance Army (NRA) under the command of incumbent President Museveni and embedded in a protracted web of postcolonial historical developments and intersecting conflict dynamics, these crimes formed an integral component of wider systematic and strategic warfare operations against the civilian population, centered around retaliation, punishment, and terrorization.

Building on this contextualization, chapter 4 then specifically scrutinizes male survivors' lived realities of gendered vulnerabilities and harms. It specifically analyzes the impact of sexual violence on male survivors' masculinities. Despite the increasing realization and/or assumption that sexual violence against men compromises male survivors' masculine identities, how exactly such perceived processes of gender subordination and the compromising of masculinities unfold, and what they entail, are only poorly understood. To understand the impact of war and violence on masculinities, a prior conceptual understanding of locally contingent gender constructions and identities is needed in the first place. This chapter therefore begins with conceptual reflections and an empirically grounded examination of Acholi gender identities and relations. Building on these theoretical and contextual premises, I then analyze how sexual violence impacts male survivors' identities in myriad ways. I show how penetrative anal rape subordinates male survivors along gender hierarchies, and how the effects of such violence render male survivors unable to protect, provide, and procreate, all of which signify survivors' inabilities to live up to socially constructed expectations of masculinities.

In response to the impact of wartime rape, and in the absence of formalized support avenues, numerous male survivors in northern Uganda began forming survivors' support groups. These groups constitute a poignant way in which survivors exercise agency in order to engage with their harmful experiences, which constitutes the focus of chapter 5. To commence this examination, I review dominant framings of wartime sexual violence against men, which largely fall into a tendency to represent male survivors as ever-vulnerable victims without a voice and without any agency. Although agency is usually attributed as a masculine trait, men who were sexually violated and are perceived to have been compromised in their gender identities are likewise seen as having been deprived of their agency. To remedy this, I take inspiration from emerging research within critical feminist IR, which in recent years not only has begun to draw out the manifold ways in which women and girls in situations of armed conflict are passively subjected to violence,

but which also considers women's active roles and positions in war zones, rang
ing from political agents to combatants. My analysis thereby demonstrates that
within the context of support groups, survivors exercise agency in numerous ways,
including by repairing impacted gender identities, rebuilding social relations, and
obtaining recognition of their harmed but largely neglected experiences.

Despite engaging with their harms on their own terms in the context of support
groups, however, male survivors in northern Uganda also articulate diverse exogenous justice-related needs. While recent attention has been gathered to remedy
sexual violence against women, the growing literature on transitional justice has
thus far turned a blind eye to redress for male survivors of gender-based violence.
Chapter 6 therefore explores how male survivors conceptualize justice and what
their respective remedy and redress priorities are. This chapter discusses gendered
political, societal, and cultural barriers male survivors face in accessing the secular
justice sector and standardized transitional justice processes in northern Uganda
but also globally. Drawing on survivors' viewpoints and priorities, the analysis
reveals the importance of broader recognition and of government acknowledgment of male survivors' harms and experiences.

Chapter 7 concludes the book by summarizing its main findings and providing
an overview of key arguments. The chapter specifically lays out a survivor-centric
approach of responding to sexual violence against men and of engaging with male
survivors, both in terms of policy and scholarship, built from the findings and
insights offered in the preceding chapters.

2

Conflict-Related Sexual Violence against Men

A Global Perspective

Across time and space, wartime sexual violence against men is committed more frequently than commonly assumed. The past decade in particular witnessed an increase in scholarly and political attention on male-directed sexual violence during war, contributing toward the steady and continuous inclusion of male victims in dominant conceptualizations of conflict-related sexual violence.[1] In policy terms, the United Nations Security Council Resolution (UNSCR) 2106 from June 2013 and more recently resolution 2467 from May 2019 constituted particularly significant political moves toward recognizing male-directed sexual violence. Despite important progress, however, male survivors of sexual violence arguably remain only a marginal concern, and dominant work on gender-based violence often continues to imply that wartime sexual violence against men constitutes a (rare) exception to the norm.

Even in 2019, at the time of writing this book, men and boys as victims are often not more than a mere afterthought in scholarship and policy-making on the topic. To illustrate: In late May 2019—and in the wake of the Nobel Peace Prize being awarded to Nadia Murad and Dr. Denis Mukwege for their efforts to prevent and respond to wartime sexual violence—various UN agencies, (mostly Western) governments, the International Committee of the Red Cross (ICRC), and civil society organizations came together in Norway for a high-level conference on ending sexual and gender-based violence in humanitarian crises. Both in the official conference material as well as in the media reporting about the event, it was merely noted that "boys and men are affected too," without any further exploration. Even though recent years saw "a major shift towards including male victims in international policy on wartime sexual violence" (Touquet and Gorris 2016: 1), and a marked increase in scholarly publications, much remains unknown about the scope, forms, and dynamics of sexual violence against men.

In light of this global neglect of this type of gender-based violence, in this chapter I critically review the existing body of knowledge on conflict-related sexual violence against men from a global perspective. Pulling together the existing scholarship into one overarching framework, I situate this book within this body of literature. By comprehensively reviewing this relatively new area of study that emerged within the past decade, I build on intersecting bodies of interdisciplinary literature, specifically within the (sub)fields of feminist international relations and masculinities studies, as well as the constantly growing body of research on conflict-related sexual violence. The overview in this chapter thereby evidences that much prevailing scholarship on the topic remains largely descriptive and undertheorized, characterized by a lack of empirical data. Despite a few noteworthy exceptions, male survivors' experiences and perspectives remain strikingly underexplored. This then constitutes the epistemological point of departure for this book, which centralizes male survivors' voices in order to uncover and make sense of their lived realities.

The overview pursued throughout this chapter is structured in accordance with the most prevalent themes reflected in existing research. The chapter commences by revisiting the conceptual links between masculinities and sexual violence against men. I then critically examine existing definitions and conceptualize the understanding of conflict-related sexual violence against men adopted in this book. The next part examines the scope and frequency of male-directed sexual violence during armed conflicts across time and space, evidencing that sexual violence is committed more frequently than commonly acknowledged. I proceed by reviewing numerous explanations regarding the occurrence of sexual violence as prevalent throughout the literature.

MASCULINITIES, CONFLICT, AND SEXUAL VIOLENCE

Since crimes of sexual violence against men are immediately underpinned by masculinities constructions, I open this chapter by reflecting upon the conceptual and theoretical relationships between masculinities and sexual violence. I specifically focus on the conceptual linkages between masculinities and violence as well as masculine vulnerabilities, both of which are fundamentally important for understanding the dynamics of male-directed sexual violence. Even though the study of armed conflict was traditionally silent on gender, recent decades nevertheless witnessed an increasing utilization of gender lenses and particularly diverse feminist theories[2] to elucidate the gendered dimensions of armed conflicts.[3] Predominantly guided by feminist curiosities to comprehend, unravel, and uproot patriarchal structures and gendered inequalities within theaters of war, a diverse set of studies increasingly seeks to examine conflict, violence, and peace-building through a gender lens.[4] Feminist scholarship on gender and armed conflict has provided crucial explanations for causalities between gender relations and war, for the gendered dynamics and consequences of political violence, as well as for the occurrence of gender-based violence, including (sexual) violence against women and girls.

Although significant contextual variation and gendered specificities exist between sexual violence against women and men, much of this feminist theorizing is instrumental for understanding the gender dynamics and dimensions of male-directed sexual violence. As Solangon and Patel (2012) attest, analyses of sexual violence against men can well be explored "through applying causal theories based on female victims of sexual violence" (417). Sivakumaran (2007) likewise observes synergies between many of the conceptual and theoretical building blocks that can be utilized to explain sexual violence perpetrated against both women and men. Somewhat surprisingly, however, I find that much of the existing scholarship on the topic of sexual violence against men, with only a few exceptions, fails to sufficiently draw on and incorporate this body of feminist work and theorizing into their analyses. As noted by feminist legal scholar Nancy Dowd (2010) on a more general level, integrating feminist theorizing with masculinities perspectives can foster a more holistic and robust understanding of the gender dynamics of international politics in general and of sexual and gender-based violence (against women and men) specifically. Dowd argues that "what masculinities has to offer feminist theory, in general, is the enrichment, contextualization and refinement of theory, as well as making men simply visible! What feminism has to offer masculinities theory is a set of tools to address much more strongly inequality, subordination and how to shift from power-over to power-with" (231).

Linking existing feminist theoretical explanations for the gendered dynamics of conflict to the related phenomenon of conflict-related sexual violence against men, as I attempt to do in this book, can therefore help us to develop a more holistic understanding of these forms of violence.

Masculinities and Violence

One obvious and necessary way to build upon extant feminist theorizing is to deconstruct the ways in which wartime sexual violence against men (as well as against women) is immediately underpinned by masculinities. In brief, and as elaborated in the introduction, male-directed sexual violence is predominantly understood to compromise male survivors' masculine identities, while simultaneously awarding a sense of hypermasculinity to the (mostly but not always) male perpetrators.

Recent years in particular have witnessed increasing attention to masculinities in scholarship on gender and armed conflict.[5] The majority of these studies, however, have focused narrowly on hyper- and militarized masculinities—largely at the expense of the diversity of other masculinities constructions, as well as masculine vulnerabilities. This concentration on the intersections between masculinities and the various forms of violence associated with them constituted a primary unit of analysis for many of the earlier critical masculinities studies. If masculinities are integrated into gendered analyses of war and armed conflict, much of the existing literature thus tends to focus on the men who commit violence and the forms of violence perpetrated by men.[6]

Arguably, analyzing the "violences of men" (Hearn 1998) seems sensible and understandable, given that certain notions of masculinities are a driving force behind many of the obvious gender inequalities prevalent throughout society and much of the (gender-based and sexual) violence perpetrated against both women and men. A key point to this analysis is the observation that most male survivors of sexual violence have been violated by men, exposing the empirical reality that when engaging men as victims of violence, we similarly predominantly encounter men as perpetrators.[7]

Michael Kimmel (2010), one of the founding members of the (sub)field of men and masculinities studies, states that violence often constitutes one significant, if not *the* single most important, marker of manhood. Across time and space as well as statistically, it is men who predominantly commit violence, whether during peacetime or armed conflicts. Similarly, men (or masculine actors) predominantly control systems of institutionalized violence, such as prisons, the police, and the military. Influential gender scholars such as Connell (2000), Cockburn (2001), and Hutchings (2008) have found clear (causal) linkages between certain forms of hyper- and militarized masculinities on the one hand and violence and militarism on the other hand. As poignantly argued by Cynthia Cockburn (2010), for instance, certain notions of masculinities and militarization are dependent upon and constitutive of each other, whereby masculinity needs militarization and violence for its fulfilment, and militarization needs (militarized) masculinities. Similarly, Kimberly Hutchings identifies a connection between masculinities and war, grounded in a set of substantial commonalities and shared norms, whereby "the standards that govern the being and conduct of men overlap with the standards that govern the being and conduct of war makers" (2008: 391). Deriving from these apparent correlations between (militarized) masculinities and the perpetration of violence, it perhaps seems not surprising that it is also men who predominantly engage in warfare. At the same time, however, it is also men who across time and space remain disproportionally affected by many (albeit not all) forms of conflict-related violence, and men indeed make up for the vast majority of battle-related deaths during armed conflict.

Instead of equating men and masculinities with violence, it is important to recognize that most men are not violent; yet when violence occurs, it is most often perpetrated by men (see Kimmel 2010; Cockburn 2001). Drawing connections between masculinities and violence is therefore not to suggest that all men are naturally violent. Rather, "interrogating where and how men are situated in relation to the creation, perpetration and institutionalization of violence" (Cahn, Ní Aoláin, and Haynes 2009: 104) reveals that especially within the context of war, certain forms of militarized and hypermasculinities are more closely linked to violence than other often more common and peaceful conceptions of manhood. Frequently, although not universally, these forms of hyper and militarized masculinities may materialize in order to aspire to a hegemonic conception of manhood that stands at the top of the gender hierarchy.[8]

Against the backdrop of this evidence regarding some men's disproportionate perpetration of violence, the enduring question arises of why some masculinities notions are so closely connected to violence. Although we want to avoid oversimplifying or essentializing, it is important to point out that in many societies, violence "may literally make the man" (Ní Aoláin, Haynes, and Cahn 2009: 104) and often constitutes an important element to attaining dominant and hegemonic conceptions of masculinity. Since (hegemonic) masculinity is not automatically a given but rather socially constructed and must be achieved, it requires particular behaviors and actions in specific situations. Frequently in various societal contexts, and at certain points in time (such as war, political or economic instability, disaster emergencies), violence may be seen as either necessary or at least acceptable and tolerated in order to attain hegemonic masculine attributes. Cahn, Ní Aoláin, and Haynes (2009) point out that "in multiple contexts, engaging in violence is a rational choice for men when few other opportunities may be provided to gain economic security . . . , social status and value within their communities, and security . . . for their families and communities" (107). As argued by Cynthia Cockburn, war therefore deepens already existing sexual and gendered divisions, "emphasizing the male as perpetrator of violence, women as victims" (2010: 144).

In light of these insights, feminist scholars in particular have posited the "frustration-aggression" hypothesis for understanding the linkages between some norms of masculinities and violence (see Porter 2013). According to this explanation, especially in situations of armed conflict, turmoil, or economic insecurity, men are confronted with significant barriers to achieving the dominant or traditional markers of manhood, which in turn can cause "feelings of shame, humiliation, frustration, inadequacy and loss of dignity" (Porter 2013: 488). The inability to live up to masculine expectations in more conventional ways may then lead to frustrations, which some men may respond to with violence to attain socially expected standards of manhood. Explaining violence as an expression of, or a reaction to, frustration thereby supports Dolan's (2002) claim that violence is not an inherent or embodied masculine trait, but rather constitutes a response of men feeling unable to fulfill hegemonic but increasingly unattainable models of masculinity. From this perspective violence "represents both an expression of power and dominance and simultaneously an expression of masculinity nostalgia, disempowerment and male vulnerability" (MacKenzie and Foster 2017: 14). Importantly, these reflections do not attempt to justify or excuse violent behaviour, but rather aim to aid our understanding of and explanations for masculine violence.

Such explanations and observations, however, have all too often resulted in false and misleading portrayals of men as universal aggressors in armed conflict and women as universal victims. Interestingly, these essentialist and dichotomous categorizations of "all the men are in the militias, and all the women are victims"—as Cynthia Enloe (2004) has fittingly put it—are criticized from what can be seen as two quite distinct yet partially interlinked lines of argumentation. On the one hand, critical feminist scholarship criticizes much of the prevailing gender discourse for essentializing women as weak and vulnerable victims in need of patriarchal (and often white, Western) protection from the global gender order, challenging the dominant framing of women as passive and vulnerable victims. Previous studies have convincingly argued that these simplistic portrayals automatically render women as ever vulnerable, ignore the diverse experiences and roles women embody within the context of armed conflicts, and overshadow their (political) agency.[9]

Another group of scholars in turn criticizes the mainstream gender discourse for putting forward an unreconstructed view of men that essentializes them as perpetrators only, thereby neglecting men as potential victims and ignoring male vulnerabilities.[10] According to this body of research, common gendered stereotypes risk reducing men as (naturally) violent and exclusively view them in their instrumentalist capacities as perpetrators, or potentially as agents of change in the fight against violence against women, but not as possible victims. This ignores men's diverse experiences of victimhood during armed conflicts, as well as the manifold ways that men are vulnerable to violence and impacted by masculinities constructions themselves—foregrounding the all-encompassing destructive potential of patriarchy in all its manifestations (Enloe 2017).

Even though approaching the problem from partially different angles and with diverging areas of focus, both lines of argumentation express concern regarding the mainstream literature's view on gender relations. Perceiving men solely as perpetrators (and rarely as vulnerable) and women overwhelmingly as victims (and rarely as agents and actors) is therefore a "heavily gendered narrative of war" (Zarkov 2001: 71). This dominant account neglects women's agency while simultaneously ignoring masculine vulnerabilities during wars. Even though dominant conceptions of masculinities are seen as incompatible with victimhood, as deconstructed in the introduction, vulnerabilities are fundamentally human and thus unavoidable. Among the forms of conflict-related male vulnerabilities that in recent years have received increasing attention are crimes of sexual violence against.

CONCEPTUALIZING SEXUAL VIOLENCE
AGAINST MEN

Drawing on these theoretical reflections, let us turn to conceptualizing and defining conflict-related sexual violence against men. To this end, here I scrutinize different definitions of male-directed conflict-related sexual violence as prevalent throughout the literature in order to lay out the foundational understanding of such violence employed in this book. This overview demonstrates that previous conceptions of SGBV during war largely marginalized violence against men while at the same time placing a heavy emphasis on penetrative rape over other forms of sexual violence. These exclusions ultimately necessitate a gender-inclusive and holistic conceptualization of sexual violence, inclusive of male victims and a variety of sexual crimes, as laid out in this section.

While conflict-related sexual violence broadly constitutes a form of gender-based violence (GBV)—an umbrella term for any harmful act that is perpetrated against a person's will based on socially ascribed gender differences—in this book I specifically focus on *sexual violence* as one poignant manifestation of GBV.[11] While much criticism has rightfully been directed toward the hyperattention to and hypervisibility of sexual violence (over other forms of gender-based violence and discrimination), these assertions do not (yet) necessarily apply to sexual violence against men, which remains underexplored.

According to feminist scholar Skjelsbaek (2001), sexual violence can broadly be understood as any form of "violence with a sexual manifestation" (212). Defining what constitutes sexual violence, however, can be difficult and is conditioned by various theoretical, conceptual, and methodological challenges, as well as different contextual, cultural, and social factors. As Leiby (2009) observes, "what is understood as sexual violence varies widely across ethnic, religious and social groups" (81), as well as across scholarly disciplines, and therefore different definitions circulate across the literature. Many of these existing definitions are problematic in different ways and from various perspectives, as they (implicitly or explicitly) exclude sexual violence against men and/or place a heavy emphasis on penetrative rape.

Earlier classifications of sexual violence were often too narrow, reductionist, essentialist, or exclusive, frequently not at all acknowledging men and boys as victims.[12] These exclusions are exemplified through studies that emphasize that sexual violence is committed exclusively against women and girls. To provide just one example, Sharlach (2001: 1) defines rape as "any sexual penetration of a *female* by a male (or with an object) that takes place without *her* consent." Furthermore, most of the earlier UNSC resolutions on conflict and gender under the framework of the Women Peace and Security (WPS) agenda exclusively include women and girls (or at times women and children) as potential victims.[13] These definitions thereby systematically excluded the possibility of men as victims of sexual violence. Only in 2013, with UNSCR 2106, was sexual violence against men acknowledged by the UN's WPS agenda for the first time.

Despite these shortcomings, however, more recent definitions have tended to employ gender-neutral language, thereby also recognizing men and boys alongside women and girls as potential victims of sexual violence. Progress in this regard, and within the policy sphere, can be observed over time: In fact, the most recent resolution of the WPS agenda—UNSCR 2467, passed in April 2019—six times explicitly mentions men and boys as (potential) victims, more than any other resolution before that. Despite these advances, however, the binary framing of women/girls and men/boys leaves out gender-nonconforming identities as recognized victims of sexual violence, necessitating further efforts to queer not only the Women Peace and Security Agenda but international politics and discourses around gender-based violence more broadly (Hagen 2016).

In addition to these gendered biases, various conceptualizations of conflict-related sexual violence similarly place a heavy emphasis on penetrative rape, thereby excluding and ignoring various other forms of sexual (and gender-based) violence, such as sexual torture, forced castration, and sexual threats. According to Rubio-Marin and Sandoval (2011), "limiting the analysis to a rape-centred understanding of sexual violence may obscure other forms of equally grave sexual and reproductive violence" (1065). Only concentrating on rape overlooks the multiple ways in which people are otherwise sexually victimized. Similarly, various definitions of SGBV primarily concentrate on sexual violence while not including other manifestations of gender-based violence, which receive less attention and resources and are considered less significant or relevant. Critical feminist scholars in particular therefore emphasize the need for a broader conceptualization of sexual and gender-based violence, beyond sexualized crimes only, including other manifestations of structural and systematic gendered violence and discrimination along a continuum.[14]

Definitions of conflict-related sexual violence specifically against men often include various physical acts of sexual violence, such as rape, sexual torture, and/or genital beatings, while not paying sufficient attention to what Ní Aoláin (2000) refers to as "connected" harms. Examples of connected forms of sexual violence (also) affecting men may include instances where men are forced (often at gunpoint) to themselves commit sexual violence, often against (female) family or community members. Other forms of connected sexual harms include situations where men are forced to watch (mostly female) members of their families and communities being sexually violated in front of them. The following case provides an example of such indirect or connected forms of sexual violence, quoted from Coulter (2009: 145) and taken from the Sierra Leonean context: "John's mother and his aunt were raped and sexually abused in front of him. John said that this all happened in his presence and that it hurt him immensely, but most of all, he said, he was shamed by the sexual violation of his mother in his presence; perhaps also he was ashamed on a personal level as he could do nothing to protect her."

In these cases, the sexual violations are clearly acted out on female bodies, and women and girls are without a doubt the immediate physical and psychological victims, even though men may also be targeted psychologically and/or emotionally. In the northern Ugandan context, there are various cases of NRA government soldiers or LRA rebels either forcing abductees (in the case of the LRA) or civilians to rape female family members, or forcefully making them watch armed combatants rape their sisters, daughters, or wives.

Feminist scholarship has demonstrated that these harms can be linked to the (perceived) "masculine loss of power demonstrated in the inability to protect 'their' women" (Ní Aoláin 2000: 79). While the dynamics surrounding these connected harms can thus problematically be framed around patriarchal assumptions of vulnerable women in need of male protection, they nevertheless also reflect the lived realities and harms experienced by many men in situations of armed conflict. The exclusion of these harms from dominant conceptions of sexual violence against men thus potentially results in a too narrow understanding of such crimes, underacknowledging complex and intertwined gendered and sexual harms.

At the same time, sexual violence against men is frequently coded, classified, and categorized as torture, often without any recognition of the sexual component and nature of the crime. Only in the mid-1990s, in light of the massive perpetration of sexual violence during the Rwandan genocide and the wars in the former Yugoslavia, did scholarly developments and international jurisprudence move toward more fully establishing a connection between what has previously been treated as two distinct categories. Landmark cases at both the Inter-American Commission for Human Rights and the European Court of Human Rights contributed toward recognizing acts of rape and sexual violence (against women) as constituting torture and inhumane treatment. These developments led to the now commonly held conviction that—as articulated by a female sexual violence survivor cited in a recent article by Gray, Stern, and Dolan—"if torture were a tree, then sexual violence would be one of its branches" (2019: 11).

In scholarship and policy making, however, there often seems to be a gendered distinction between the application of these categories to men's and women's experiences respectively. Whereas forms of violence experienced by women are often coded as sexual violence, acts of violence against men—even if they have clear sexual components—are frequently subsumed under the heading of torture. While sexual violence can and often does meet the threshold level of harm to constitute torture, in concert with others, I caution that to exclusively categorize certain acts as torture without recognizing their sexual component, including the resulting sexual and gendered consequences, can be highly problematic. As noted by Sivakumaran (2010), "The danger of characterizing sexual violence against men and boys only under the rubric of torture is that men and boys will continue to be seen as unsusceptible to sexual violence, reinforcing the view that sexual violence is a problem for women and girls only" (273)—reproducing and reinforcing men as "nonsurvivors" of sexual violence. In addition, exclusively classifying sexual violence against men as torture without acknowledging the violations' sexual components may further prohibit men from accessing necessary harm-responsive, gender- and sex-specific health and psychological services, because sexual violence as such is not documented and recognized.

This problem of misrepresenting sexual violence against men as torture, however, is not only conditioned by the external categorizations of the violence, but can also be linked to survivors' self-representations and perceptions of these acts. Classifications of male-directed sexual crimes as either torture *or* sexual violence may thus prove problematic from a survivors' point of view, given that these respective categories can be perceived differently by individual survivors, depending on the gendered social, political, and cultural context. As I examine more carefully and specifically applied to northern Uganda elsewhere in this book (see chapter 4), sexual violence against men is often perceived (by survivors and communities/societies alike) to negatively impact male survivors' masculine identities in many intertwined ways.

In contrast, crimes of torture may not necessarily have such compromising effects on male survivors' masculinities. Indeed, these crimes may at times instead have an opposite effect. Here it is worth referring to recent research by Harriet Gray and Maria Stern, who rightly point out that *torture* is a very slippery term, politically malleable and employable in multiple ways (2019). The way these two categories—sexual violence and torture—"are filled with meaning in international legal and policy spaces . . . is neither fixed nor stable" (Gray, Stern, and Dolan 2019: 8).

Historiographies of torture reveal that traditionally and contemporarily, torture aims to "destroy a person's self and world" (Scary 1985: 35), and various torture methods and techniques were specifically developed and designed to harm men. Having survived such acts may under certain circumstances be associated with a particular masculine status and might to some extent even reward masculinity, albeit of course at great personal, physical, and psychological costs.[15] Categorizing certain violent crimes and harmful acts as either torture or as sexual violence might thus have different effects on survivors' (perceived) masculine identities.

However, there often is "an overlap between these categories," and the terms "slip and slide across one another" (Gray, Stern, and Dolan 2019: 3), thereby complicating the "simplistic assumption that gender norms will call men to frame their experiences as 'torture,' and women, theirs as 'sexual violence'" (ibid.: 19). In these authors' study of refugee (male and female) survivors of sexual violence in Uganda, they found that "many male participants . . . deliberately spoke about the violences to which they have been subjected as 'sexual'—in contrast to the prevalent assumption that men are more likely to describe their experiences under the label of 'torture'" (ibid.: 13). This mirrors my own observations from northern Uganda, where Acholi male survivors explicitly described their experiences as *rape* and *sexual violence* (see chapter 3).

A Holistic Definition of Conflict-Related Sexual Violence against Men

Departing from these challenges and limitations of existing conceptualizations, I define conflict-related sexual violence more inclusively and broadly. I specifically draw upon the understanding of sexual violence as described in the Rome Statute of the International Criminal Court, which has been praised for its progressive and inclusive character, and specifically for its gender-sensitive approach. By utilizing gender-neutral language, the Rome Statute acknowledges that sexual violence can be committed against women and men as well as gender-nonconforming identities alike. The Rome Statute likewise approaches sexual violence in broad terms, including rape, sexual slavery, enforced prostitution, enforced sterilization, and any other form of sexual violence of comparable gravity. Therefore, not only does the definition put "beyond any doubt that men and boys can be raped" (Sivakumaran 2013: 84), it also includes various acts of sexual violence that are not limited to penetrative rape, thereby broadening our understanding of sexual violence.

Building on this broadened approach, conflict-related sexual violence in this book is defined as acts or threats of violence of a sexual nature perpetrated directly on and against victims, which the victim may be forced to perform or watch being performed on others within the family or community. This conception uses gender-neutral language and thus accounts for male, female, and gender-nonconforming victims alike. Male-directed sexual violence in particular can therefore broadly include penetrative anal and/or oral rape, sexual torture, mutilation and beatings of the genitals, castration or enforced sterilization, sexual humiliation, and sexual slavery and enslavement.[16] Cases of men being forced to perform coercive sexual intercourse (often with female family members) and of females being raped in front of male family members can likewise constitute connected forms of male-directed sexual violence.

SCOPE AND PREVALENCE OF SEXUAL VIOLENCE AGAINST MEN

Deriving from this conceptual understanding of conflict-related sexual violence against men, I now turn to the scope and frequency of such violations. This is important to illustrate my argument that male-directed sexual violence is perpetrated more frequently than commonly assumed. While incorporating this examination of prevalence and existing evidence, however, I also underscore that empirically and politically, frequency and numbers should not matter as to whether or not these crimes are addressed. Even if the numbers were significantly lower than they appear to be, male-directed sexual violence requires the attention, recognition, and responses scholars and policy-makers are increasingly advocating for.

Existing Evidence

In recent years, a growing body of literature has offered various examples of male-directed sexual violence in different settings, such as part of military campaigns, in detention, and during displacement and forced migration, as well as in different geographical contexts. Previous research has documented cases of sexual violence against men in over twenty-five conflicts, and in at least fifty-nine when including boys as victims.[17] The existing literature documents male-directed sexual violence during the conflicts in, among others, El Salvador, the former Yugoslavia, Egypt, Northern Ireland, Sri Lanka, Liberia, Sierra Leone, Burundi, the Central African Republic, the Democratic Republic of the Congo, Peru, Syria, Libya, and northern Uganda.

Mirroring dynamics of sexual violence in general, the numbers, intensities, and occurrence of sexual violence against men are characterized by variation and differ across space and time. Variation theory, as primarily applied by Wood (2006) and others (see Swaine 2015), demonstrates huge variability in the scope of conflict-related sexual violence in different cases, which can also be extended to such violence against males. Systematically assessing the frequency of conflict-related sexual violence in general, including against men, proves immensely difficult for a variety of reasons, as discussed in more detail below. Nevertheless, despite numerous conceptual, methodological, and epistemological challenges, existing research offers preliminary insights into the frequency of male-directed sexual violence across different settings.

To provide just a few contemporary examples: Recent evidence about the civil war in Syria uncovers horrible accounts of systematic human rights abuses, including torture, starvation, and widespread sexual violence against civilians and combatants. Research conducted for the UN Refugee Agency (UNHCR) demonstrates that in Syria and in the context of forced migration in neighbouring countries, various forms of sexual violence against men continue to be deployed systematically and are widespread. For instance, according to the findings underpinning that UNHCR report, "between 19.5 to 27 percent of male survey respondents . . . confirmed having experienced sexual harassment or unwanted sexual contact as boys." Similarly, a 2013 rapid assessment of 520 Syrian male youth and boys (ages twelve–twenty-four) in Lebanon "revealed that 10.8 percent had experienced an incident of sexual harm or harassment in the previous three months" (UNHRC 2017: 4). These findings are further supported by a recent report released in 2019 by Lawyers and Doctors for Human Rights, a Syrian human rights group, which "revealed extensive, pervasive and brutal sexual violence against male Syrian political prisoners across time, government security agencies and their detention centers" (Loveluck 2019).

In Libya, the International Commission of Inquiry on Libya of the United Nations similarly documents widespread and systematic sexual abuse of male and female detainees by security forces under the Gadhaffi regime, as well as during the post-Gadhaffi period. More recently, shocking accounts emerged of systematic sexual violence and torture of male and female refugees in migration camps across the country. For instance, a report by the International Organization for Migration from 2016 found that seven out of ten migrants crossing from North Africa to Europe—most of whom transit through and spend time in Libya—had experienced different forms of exploitation, including kidnapping, forced labor, illegal detention, and sexual violence. Mirroring global refugee dynamics, many of these migrants are men.

Another contemporary example of the widespread occurrence of sexual violence against men and boys points to the situation of the Rohingya from Myanmar in Bangladesh. A 2018 report by the Women's Refugee Council (WRC)—the first of its kind to focus on sexual violence against men in this context—documents how government soldiers burned, mutilated, and hacked off the genitals of men and boys, and how they are forced to witness sexual violence perpetrated against female family and community members (WRC 2018: 2).

Focusing on conflict-related sexual violence against men in Peru, Leiby's (2009a) work further uproots common contextual assumption about the extent of sexual violence against men. According to the official report of the Peruvian Truth and Reconciliation Commission (Comisión para la Verdad y Reconciliation, CVR) out of 583 documented cases of sexual violence, "only 11, or 2 percent, were perpetrated against men" (79). Leiby's work in the commission's archives and with additional primary sources, however, demonstrates that "the percentage of male victims of sexual violence is higher than commonly expected and higher than previously reported [by the CVR]" (82). Instead of the 2 percent of male victims referred to in the commission's final report, her work indicates between 22 and 29 percent of male sexual violence survivors among the violations covered by the CVR. One potential explanation for this divergence is the commission's conceptualization of sexual violence, which despite being technically gender neutral focuses solely on penetrative rape, thereby excluding other forms of sexual violence, which were instead coded as torture. Leiby's analysis instead shows that the most frequently reported forms of sexual abuse against men were cases of sexual humiliation (46 percent), sexual mutilation (20 percent), and sexual torture (15 percent). The case of Peru therefore constitutes a poignant example illustrating some of the difficulties of (mis)categorizing male-directed sexual violence as torture and the consequential challenges of too narrow and too reductionist conceptualizations.

In Liberia, a survey of 1,666 adults affected by the country's civil war found that 32.6 percent of male combatants experienced sexual violence, while 16.5 percent were forced to be sexual servants (Johnson et al. 2008). A similar large-N study by Johnson et al. (2010) in the eastern territories of the Democratic Republic of the Congo found that the rate of reported sexual violence among men was 23.6 percent, while 64.5 percent of male study participants reported being exposed to forms of conflict-related sexual violence. According to the empirical data underpinning that study, there are approximately "1.31 million men as survivors of sexual violence in the eastern region of the DRC" (559). Numerical indicators for the eastern DRC, however, vary substantially, with other studies suggesting between 6 and 10 percent of men as victims of sexual violence (Eriksson Baaz and Stern 2013), to about 20 percent of sexually violated men (Peel et al. 2000). A preliminary study by Chris Dolan and RLP screening 447 male refugees residing in settlements in western Uganda, of which the vast majority originated from the DRC, revealed that "13.4 percent had experienced an incident of sexual violence in the preceding 12 months, rising to 38.5 percent if looking at their whole lives' (Dolan 2014: 2). Such statistical discrepancies and divergences in just one case indicate the general difficulty of quantifying the extent of conflict-related sexual violence against men, but also point to its widespread and common occurrence.

In combination, these studies from a variety of case sites suggest that male-directed sexual violence within the context of war and armed conflict is more widespread than has thus far been acknowledged. In addition to these existing initial insights, other conflict situations across time and space are yet to be analyzed with a focus on sexual violence against men. Clearly, more empirical work is needed, especially on the extent to which boys or male adolescents as well as non-heterosexual men and gender-nonconforming identities are victimized by sexual violence in (post)conflict scenarios.

Challenges of Quantifying Sexual Violence

There are, however, significant challenges with regard to quantifying sexual violence against men, underpinned by stereotypical views of gender that are partially (co)responsible for the underreporting and misrecognition of sexual violence against men. According to Dolan (2014), "As with efforts to document sexual violence against women and girls, precise evidence of prevalence against males is hard to come by in most conflict-affected countries. Internalised feelings of shame, fear of stigmatisation, and legal frameworks and social services that do not recognise men as victims prevent the majority of victims from reporting to the authorities" (2).

Assessing the frequency of sexual violence against men thus proves difficult "because of the extreme stigma attached to sexual abuse of males and the ensuing reluctance to report such rapes" (and other cases of sexual violence) (Eriksson Baaz and Stern 2010: 45). A subsequent effect of this under- or nonreporting is the "invisibility of men and boys as (non-)survivors of sexual violence" (ibid.) and a systematic silencing of such forms of violence.

Caution is required, however, not to oversimplify the potential reasons for the under- and nonreporting of sexual violence against men and to refrain from implicitly blaming victims for the difficulty of establishing more concrete numbers. A study by RLP therefore proposes three potential reasons, in addition to fear and stigma, for why male survivors may be hesitant to report sexual violations committed against them: (1) fear of arrest on suspicion or accusation of being homosexual; (2) fear of social and familial ostracism; (3) lack of access to services. In fact, it is not only the problem of nonreporting that makes it difficult to determine the extent of the violence; it is also the ways sexual violations of men are treated and considered from the outside, and in particular how they are often marginalized, silenced, and neglected.

For instance, men's reluctance to report their sexual victimizations may often be exacerbated by legislation that criminalizes homosexual acts, making survivors fear prosecution. Such is evidently the case in northern Uganda, as documented later in this book, where sexual violence against men is often falsely equated with homosexuality, and where same-sex acts are criminalized and outlawed, punishable by life in prison—further exacerbated by the tabled but then withdrawn Anti-Homosexuality Bill. Furthermore, external service providers and those working with male survivors, such as NGO representatives, medical professionals, and social workers, often do not recognize the physical and psychological signs of male-directed sexual violence or simply do not acknowledge the reality of sexual violence against men.

The complications of categorizing and coding sexual violence against men as torture, as elaborated above in reference to Leiby's work in Peru, constitute another factor contributing to the difficulty of measuring such violence. Even if and when we possess data and figures, as in the studies cited above, caution is nevertheless required. Methodologies vary across studies, or may be untransparent or unknown. As with sexual violence in general, the factual numbers of male-directed sexual violence may likely be higher than reported.

EXPLANATIONS FOR SEXUAL VIOLENCE AGAINST MEN

Departing from this overview on prevalence, I now proceed by scrutinizing different explanations for the occurrence of conflict-related sexual violence against men put forward in the literature. I show that specific explanations for sexual violence against men are not yet well established, frequently lacking empirically grounded data, but that feminist explanatory frameworks for the occurrence of sexual violence in general provide important insight into understanding these dynamics. Possessing a critical and sustained understanding of different attempts to explain conflict-related sexual violence, in general and against men in particular, proves necessary to determine the context-specific dynamics of such violence in northern Uganda in the following chapter.

Scholars such as Leiby and Cohen remind us that a "phenomenon as complex as wartime rape may have any number of conceivable causes" (Cohen 2016: 3) and that "even within the same conflict, sexual violence can serve multiple functions in different contexts and at different points in time" (Leiby 2009: 445). Reiterating that there is rarely ever one all-encompassing or mono-causal explanation to account for the dynamics of conflict-related sexual violence is therefore fundamentally important for this discussion of prevalent explanatory frameworks.

Furthermore, explaining the occurrence of sexual violence is inherently difficult without sufficient empirical data from the perpetrators' perspectives. Cohen (2016: 20) argues that to "determine the motivations for rape—and whether it is being used strategically—researchers must study the perpetrators themselves." Yet in spite of a few noteworthy exceptions, there is a persistent lack of data on perpetrators of conflict-related sexual violence, referred to as a "theoretical vacuum" in the literature. For male-directed sexual violence specifically, data from the perpetrators' sides remains almost entirely absent, despite some first attempts in Elise Féron's recent book (2018) to incorporate a perpetrators' perspective, hence constituting a prevailing lacuna in the literature. Conducting such research, however, would obviously imply various ethical, methodological and practical challenges and difficulties. Yet despite this lack of perpetrator-centric data, by analyzing patterns of sexual violence against men from a survivors' point of view, we can nevertheless begin to unravel and unpack some of the collective dynamics and infer arguments and explanations regarding potential causes from the outside.

Again, we can gain important insights from feminist scholarship on the gendered dynamics of conflict and violence more broadly and on sexual violence specifically, and from integrating masculinities and feminist perspectives. Although most of the existing research on male-directed sexual violence fails to sufficiently engage with feminist debates, Sjoberg's (2016) layered theoretical exploration of gender subordination and Eriksson Baaz and Stern's foundational work on sexual violence (2013) constitute novel contributions for bridging this divide. Their work will therefore be referenced extensively in this section.

Overall, existing explanations for conflict-related sexual violence are manifold and diverse, although most dominant explanatory frameworks broadly classify the occurrence of such violence as either *strategic* or *opportunistic,* with respective subsidiary precisions. For Wood (2014), strategic sexual violence broadly refers to "instances of rape [and sexual violence] purposefully adopted in pursuit of organization objectives," while opportunistic sexual violence is generally "carried out for private reasons rather than organization objectives" (47). According to Eriksson Baaz and Stern (2013), these two most common theoretical frameworks for explaining, understanding, and analyzing sexual violence during conflict can generally be categorized as "the sexed" (opportunistic) and "the gendered" (strategic) story respectively. Elisabeth Wood (2018) also adds a third manifestation to this classification, situated somewhere in between and in conversation with the two opportunistic and strategic categories: that of sexual violence as a pervasive policy or practice within armed groups. In this reading, sexual violence would not be officially ordered but nevertheless tolerated and perpetuated, thus occurring fairly regularly.

The "Sexed Story"

In essence, the "sexed story" proposes that conflict-related sexual violence can mostly be attributed to male perpetrators' unfulfilled sexual needs and can be "facilitated by a lack of command structure or norms against sexual violence within the armed group" (Henry 2009: 50). This explanation is based upon the (essentialist) assumption "that sexual release is a 'natural' need for men, exacerbated by the stress of battle conditions" (Sjoberg 2016: 188). At the core of the sexed story thus lies the "substitution" argument, according to which "sex by force occurs in military contexts because soldiers do not enjoy 'normal' access to women in other ways" (Eriksson Baaz and Stern 2013: 17). The sexed story and the related "opportunistic rape argument" have received considerable scholarly attention in relation to sexual violence against women, especially throughout earlier scholarship on the topic. The widely cited work on wartime rape by Susan Brownmiller (1975), for instance, largely pursues this line of argumentation, although partly phrased differently.

While the opportunism variable has been found to be of explanatory value in some cases of sexual violence against women and girls, it has also been heavily critiqued, as being sex essentialist and deterministic and for depoliticizing rape in conflict. The sexed story is also inherently heteronormative and relies on constrained categorizations of male perpetrators and female victims, and thus "overly negative towards men" (Eriksson Baaz and Stern 2013: 19). At the same time, the opportunistic rape argument has not yet been considered to explain the occurrence of male-directed sexual violence during conflict settings specifically, in part because of its hetero-normative foundations and expectations. Sjoberg (2016) therefore argues that purely relying on the sexed story is problematic because it takes away an explicit gender analysis, ignores elements of power, and thus oversimplifies the complexity of conflict-related sexual violence.

The "Gendered Story"

By centralizing a gender lens, the "gendered story" departs from this ascribed sex essentialism that characterizes the sexed story. Focusing on gender and militarization, this explanatory frame "sheds light on the power of gender ideologies as underlying rationales for the 'use of' sexual violence in armed conflict" (Eriksson Baaz and Stern 2013: 19). According to the gendered story, sexual violence in conflict constitutes an effective instrument of humiliation and intimidation in a gendered manifestation. For Sjoberg (2016), "Understanding sexual violence in war and conflict as gendered adds explanatory value not only for that sexual violence, but for understandings of war and gender" (188) more broadly.

It is indeed the gendered story that primarily "underwrites the dominant framing of conflict-related sexual violence" (Eriksson Baaz and Stern 2013: 15) throughout contemporary scholarship. Scholars and humanitarian practitioners alike have fostered the "weapon of war" narrative to appeal to international security actors and to motivate them to act. In light of this, the "rape as a weapon of war" framing has widely been accepted by civil society organizations, aid agencies, and governments. The United Kingdom's Preventing Sexual Violence Initiative, for instance, perpetuates this discourse (Kirby 2015), while the UN campaign "Stop Rape Now" explicitly focuses on preventing and ending the "use of sexual violence as a tactic of war." The majority of existing studies follow and/or reproduce this line of inquiry and consequently suggest that wartime sexual violence is primarily strategic and systematic, often portrayed as a weapon of war, aimed at punishing and intimating its victims, mainly through gendered subordination and disempowerment.

Taking these dominant framings into account, however, Eriksson Baaz and Stern (2013) themselves offer a compelling critique of the persisting narrative of sexual violence as a weapon of war, which too unilaterally frames sexual violence along gendered storylines, ignoring the intricacy and oversimplifying the complexity of gendered conflict dynamics more broadly, while specifically ignoring the explanatory power of patriarchy in understanding sexual violence (see Kreft 2019). Building on findings from extensive fieldwork in the Democratic Republic of the Congo, they caution that this exclusive framing sidelines the multiplicity of conditions under which sexual violence occurs, without sufficient consideration for its actual causes, manifestations, and actors. In concert with Eriksson Baaz and Stern (2013), Sjoberg (2016) also underscores that the gendered story fosters the essentializing and misleading assumption of male perpetrators and female victims.

Gendered scholarship on conflict and security in general also increasingly seems to neglect sexuality and sexual acts from discourse around sexual violence, instead exclusively focusing on gender (as separated from sex) while uncritically and unilaterally adopting the strategic rape-as-a-weapon-of-war narrative. Such is particularly the case for discussions about male-directed sexual violence that solely center around gender as linked to dominance and control without seriously considering how sexuality and sex are organically connected to power, and thus to gender, as convincingly demonstrated by Foucault (1978) in *The History of Sexuality*. In his contribution about wartime sexual violence against men, Sivakumaran (2007), for instance, claims that "rape is about power and dominance *and not sex*." Eriksson Baaz and Stern observe these "curious erasures" of the *sexual* in wartime sexual violence, which "has been seemingly theorized away as irrelevant, and even dangerously misleading in efforts to explain and redress conflict-related sexual violence" (2018: 2). Despite rigorous feminist scholarship on the interconnections between sex, sexuality, violence, power, and dominance more broadly (Brownmiller 1975; Millet 1970) and despite an arguably excessive (and often not particularly helpful) reliance on sexual and biological factors to explain wartime rape throughout earlier scholarship, it appears that more recently consideration of the "sexual" has largely been forgotten "or bypassed in our attention to *wartime* sexual violence" (Eriksson Baaz and Stern 2018: 2). This point is of particular significance for analyses of male-directed sexual violence, owing to heteronormative and homophobic assumptions, according to which same-sexual acts cannot possibly be about sex, sexual desire, pleasure, or opportunity—that is, the sexual—but must solely center on dominance and control as linked to gender. While gender must undoubtedly remain the cornerstone of any analysis of sexual violence, sexuality and sex similarly need to be foregrounded in any such discussions.

In light of this critique, it is therefore insufficient to exclusively rely on either of these dominant explanatory frameworks in illuminating wartime sexual violence. The dichotomizing distinction between sexual violence as *either* opportunistic (the sexed story) *or* strategic (the gendered story) is often essentializing and does not accommodate for the actual complexity of lived realities in (post)conflict zones. Frequently, sexual violence in any given case can be explained only by an alternating combination of the sexed and the gendered story, which often are more closely connected than commonly suggested. As emphasized by Leiby (2009b: 465), "Even with the same case, sexual violence can be used for multiple purposes."

Against this background, I concur with Sjoberg (2016), who convincingly argues that conflict-related sexual violence "is sexed, sexual and gendered, and all of these observations matter in theorizing it" (139). Undoubtedly, conflict-related sexual violence is a multifaceted phenomenon, and henceforth any mono-causal explanatory model is unlikely to account for its occurrence in all its variation and polyvalent complexity.

EXPLANATIONS FOR WARTIME SEXUAL VIOLENCE AGAINST MEN

Building upon these most common theoretical frameworks for wartime sexual violence in general, I now specifically scrutinize explanations for conflict-related sexual violence against men. As shown above, existing scholarship demonstrates strong synergies between male- and female-directed sexual violence, as both are part of the gendered dimension of armed conflict. Comparable to gendered violence against women, male-directed sexual violence frequently is an expression of aggression, power, and dominance over the enemy. Stemple (2011) argues that sexual violence (and in particular rape) is closely related to, and in many was constitutes a form of, the exercise of domination and subjugation of its victims, specifically in a gendered manifestation. Responding to common misrepresentations of conflict-related sexual violence as only (or almost exclusively) affecting women, Stemple (2011) posits that sexual violence and rape "is almost always about gender, which is not to say it is always about women" (825). These dynamics are effectively captured under the gendered story and compatible with the rape-as-a-weapon-of-war argument presented above.

Sexual Violence against Men: "Emasculate" and "Feminize"

Throughout the literature, a consensus prevails that "ideas about masculinity directly underpin the use of sexual violence against men" (Wright 2014: 14). An accurate understanding of the empirical reality of conflict-related sexual violence thus requires theoretical models to take into account the manifold ways in which masculinities feature in wartime sexual violence, and their intersections with constructions of ethnicity. Alison suggests that sexual violence against men "is no less gendered nor any less ethnicized" (81) than sexual violence against women. According to such arguments, sexual violence against men is a highly masculinized act of male-to-male communication, asserting the perpetrators' dominant (hyper)masculinities while subordinating and compromising the victims' masculinities.

In line with this, a dominant narrative explains sexual violence against men as aiming to "emasculate," "feminize," and/or "homosexualize" its victims. Surveying the relevant literature on this topic reveals that the vast majority of existing studies suggests that "emasculating" victims is among the most common, if not *the* single most prevalent, driver of male-directed sexual violence. It is thereby widely argued that "sexual violence against men involves forms of emasculation in which perpetrators seek to feminize their victims by rendering them weak, violated and passive, in contradistinction to stereotypical masculine ideals" (Auchter 2017: 1340). Lewis (2014) similarly attests that "the emasculation of the victim is widely recognized as being a motivation for the perpetration of male-directed sexual violence" (211). Deriving from a socially constructed premise that masculinities are incompatible with vulnerabilities, and that manhood is irreconcilable with victimhood, sexual violence is theoretically considered to compromise men in their masculine identities by foregrounding their gendered and sexual vulnerabilities.

Throughout the literature, it is widely presumed that when a perpetrator forcibly overpowers another man, the perpetrator humiliates the victim by perceivably subordinating him to the status of a woman or a homosexual man within a patriarchal gender hierarchy. The male victim is therefore considered subordinate to the perpetrator, who embodies a superior form of masculinity. Meger (2016) argues that in this way, "sexual violence is useful for delineating between 'man' and 'other,' with anything not approximating the social ideals of masculinity falling in the latter category" (179). The seeming paradox that male-on-male sexual acts only seem to cast "a taint of homosexuality" (Sivakumaran 2005) on the victim, but not on the perpetrator, can be explained through the gendered dimension of penetration in heteronormative societies. As explained more fully and context-specifically applied to gender dynamics in Acholiland in chapter 4, it is also the act of penetration that communicates, performs, and transfers power and dominance in a gendered manifestation, and not only the gendered body of the victim. Alison (2007) further argues that sexual violence in particular appears to be the preferred form of violence because it most clearly communicates gendered dominance, power, and control and thus demonstrates perceived gendered subordination while also highlighting the perceived hypermasculinity, and thus superiority, of the perpetrator.[18] Sexual violence against men within theaters of war can thus constitute a highly communicative and performative act.

Cases of male-directed sexual violence hence often (intentionally or unintentionally) compromise survivors' masculine identities. However, existing scholarship thus far has failed to critically engage with the conceptualization and associated terminologies of so-called emasculation and feminization. Borrowing from feminist critiques, in the introduction I argue that these concepts and terms are problematic in conceptual, analytical, and normative terms, while furthermore not being reflective of the highly fluid character of survivors' lived realities.[19] At the same time, mono-causal generalizations that universally portray the emasculation of victims as the sole or primary driver of male-directed sexual violence are often too reductionist and simplistic, failing to account for the messy complexities of conflict and violence. Crucially, conflict-related sexual violence needs to be analyzed context-specifically and circumstantially, rooted in conflict-related microdynamics of politics and violence, as well as localized gender constructions—as I intend to do in this book in the northern Ugandan context.

It therefore appears that previous attempts of explaining male-directed sexual violence during wartime thus primarily pursued the gendered story, arguing that sexual violence is often a strategic weapon of war. As a result, scholarship on sexual violence against men thus far turned a blind eye to the sexed story and the opportunism argument to explain such violence. This neglect of opportunism as a potential variable for understanding the occurrence and dynamics of male-directed sexual violence largely derives from heteronormative and heterosexual assumptions. According to such homophobic presumptions, same-sex violations can simply not be assumed to be opportunistic, but must instead serve a strategic and military objective, and male combatants cannot be expected to rape other men for sexual gratification.

Wartime Sexual Violence as Gender Subordination

Taking into account many of the above arguments and critiques, Sjoberg's (2016) recent application of gender subordination theory to sexual and gender-based violence in conflict zones advances an understanding of the dynamics of such violence, including against men, in all its complexities. Framing sexual violence as a form of hierarchical gendered subordination, Sjoberg's work accounts for male survivors or female perpetrators alongside the conventionally adopted categories of male victimizers and female victims, thereby moving beyond prewritten scripts. Effectively, gender subordination must be conceptualized as (dis)placement along gendered hierarchies by way of undermining victims' gendered and sexual identities. To cite Sjoberg (2016): "Gender subordination is fundamentally a power relationship in which those perceived as female/feminine are made less powerful than those perceived as masculine/male. This power relationship extends through the perceived possession of gendered traits and the gendering of perceived behaviors and actions" (39).

Crimes of sexual violence against men thus communicate a power relationship between the victimized, who in Sjoberg's (2016) terms are "perceived as female/feminine" and less powerful and thus displaced from their gendered personhood, and the perpetrator, or "those perceived as masculine/male" (39). These dynamics adeptly apply to male rape as one particular form of sexual violence against men among many.

Despite these previous attempts of explaining sexual violence against men, however, existing research has not yet provided sufficient explanatory models for amplifying the occurrence and complex dynamics of male-directed sexual violence within and across localities. The overview of existing explanatory frameworks in this section similarly showed that there is not one unilaterally applicable explanation to account for the occurrence of sexual violence, whether perpetrated against women or men.

CONCLUSION

This chapter critically reviewed the limited yet growing body of literature on conflict-related sexual violence against men, thereby situating this book within existing scholarship on gender and armed conflict. I have demonstrated that such forms of violence occur more frequently than popularly assumed and that such crimes are closely rooted in gendered patterns and dimensions of violence in general. This constitutes the overall backdrop for the analysis to unfold throughout this book.

While recent years have seen a shift toward including men and boys in dominant political conceptualizations of wartime sexual violence, male survivors and their perspectives nevertheless remain only of peripheral interest to policy-making and scholarship alike, and male survivors' lived realities are particularly underexplored. Situated within and in response to these broader epistemological gaps, in this book I integrate empirical data from the perspectives of male sexual violence survivors in northern Uganda into intersecting bodies of scholarship within gender and IR. This sheds important contextual light on male survivors' lived realities and carries implications for the growing body of literature on conflict-related sexual violence against men.

While wartime sexual violence against men in general remains underresearched, specific intersections between sexual violence against men and other areas remain particularly poorly explored. Survivors' gendered harms and vulnerabilities, the ways in which they exercise agency as well as the nexus between sexual violence against men and (transitional) justice are specific areas that warrant further study, as addressed in this book. Against this background, and following from these global reflections, the following chapter now turns toward portraying the locally specific and contextual dynamics of wartime sexual violence in northern Uganda in empirical detail.

3

Tek-Gungu

Wartime Sexual Violence in Northern Uganda

Once referred to as "the biggest forgotten, neglected humanitarian emergency in the world" by Jan Egeland, UN undersecretary-general for humanitarian affairs and emergency relief coordinator at that time, the northern Ugandan conflict between the Lord's Resistance Army (LRA) rebel group and the government of Uganda (GoU) between 1986 and 2006/2008 has received substantial international and academic attention.[1] The LRA's horrendous atrocities in particular have been subjected to extensive scholarly debate. Multiple human rights violations committed by the Ugandan government armed forces, on the other hand, have received significantly less attention. Within this context, crimes of sexual violence against men perpetrated by the government's National Resistance Army (NRA) in the early years of the conflict, between the late 1980s and early 1990s, are particularly poorly documented and remain almost entirely absent from academic analyses of the conflict, with only few noteworthy exceptions.[2] Although important scholarly and advocacy work by Chris Dolan and the Refugee Law Project (RLP) brought attention to these crimes in northern Uganda, arguably no *systematic* and *comprehensive* scholarly examination of male-directed sexual violence in this context exists to date.

Against this backdrop, this chapter sets out to paint a detailed picture of the dynamics surrounding conflict-related sexual violence against men in northern Uganda situated within their overall sociopolitical historical context and through a survivor's lens. Drawing on field research findings, I argue that sexual crimes against men, and specifically male rape, perpetrated by the NRA were widespread and part of wider systematic military operations against the Acholi population. By moving government-perpetrated crimes of sexual violence against men into the spotlight, the chapter thus offers a corrective to the predominant ways in which responsibilities for conflict-related human rights violations during the conflict in northern Uganda are typically allocated and distributed.

Before proceeding with the analysis, however, a brief methodological and source-critical note from a postcolonial perspective is required. While the northern Ugandan conflict is extensively researched and documented, the most widely cited studies are primarily written from an outside perspective and tend to privilege the viewpoints of external, Western academics over national Ugandan scholars. These dynamics mirror many of the previously detected problems of "white man's" scholarship in international relations and conflict studies (Lake 2016; Fanon 1963). In an attempt to counter this neocolonial "whitewashing" of scholarship on politics and conflicts in Uganda, I deliberately seek to combine Ugandan scholars with Western authors as much as possible.

HISTORICAL ROOTS OF THE CONFLICT

The historical origins of the conflict between the LRA and the Ugandan government can be traced back to colonial times, and to some extent the conflict's roots lie in Uganda's overarching and deeply rooted ethnic divides (Kasozi 1994). During colonial occupation (1894–1962), alleged tribal differences between Ugandans from the north and the south resulted in binary categorizations and a regional as well as ethnicized two-level classification: The British colonial administration recruited northerners primarily for the military, in part because of their physical appearances and stereotypical assumptions of northerners as warriors (Onyango-Odongo and Jamal Mikla 1976), and southerners mostly for the civil service and the economy because of their presumed intellectual superiority. The country's south consequentially hosted the majority of Uganda's educated class, whereas the north became poor and underdeveloped. Dolan (2009) argues that this north-south divide and the singling out of men from northern Uganda into the military "contributed to a reputation for militarism and violence" (202) specifically for the Acholis, one of the largest tribes in the country's northern region.[3] This reputation was simultaneously rooted in and further contributed to internalized ethnocentrism and racism and sat uneasily with Acholi men's self-perception.

The colonial administration's divide-and-rule policy consequently created a socioeconomic division between the north and south, generating a polarized nation ripe for conflict (Mamdani 1995). For decades this division was further intensified and exploited by (masculine) individual presidents who employed violence to rally one region against the other in order to catapult themselves into power and maintain their regime, generating a highly masculinized political climate marked by militarization and violence. Uganda's postcolonial history from 1962 onward is thus characterized by militarization and episodes of violence and counterviolence. Since colonial rule and after independence, the Ugandan state increasingly became a militarized instrument of violent retaliation. Anthropologist Heike Behrend (1999: 23) observes that "whoever took over state power was not only able to gain wealth, but also to take revenge—against members of other ethnic groups or religions" or populations of specific regions.

Following independence in 1962, Uganda experienced several exchanges of power. As Uganda's first postcolonial president, Milton Obote from the northern subregion of Lango continued to pit the country's regions against each other. Under his regime, northerners from Lango and Acholiland continued to be recruited into the armed forces. Obote's reign ended in 1971 with a military coup led by Colonel Idi Amin, from the West Nile region, who instituted a regime notorious for its political violence. One of Amin's first systematic violent acts upon acquiring political power was murdering numerous Acholi and Langi soldiers in the army. Following a violent regime toppled by an invasion from Tanzania, Amin was overthrown in 1979, with Milton Obote returning to power for a second regime. During the Obote II period, between 1979 and 1985, northerners once again dominated the armed forces.

Various political actors who already opposed Amin, including Yoweri Museveni, did not accept Obote's recapture of power. With his National Resistance Army (NRA), and alongside various other armed rebellions, Museveni waged a guerrilla campaign against the northern-led government and its Uganda National Liberation Army (UNLA). Museveni enjoyed immense support from his own region in the southwest, where a widespread antipathy prevailed toward what was perceived as (military and political) northern domination at the time. During this brutal civil war between 1980 and 1986, Acholi and Langi men mostly fought on the side of the UNLA government army under the ultimate command of Milton Obote. Eventually, rivalries and tensions within the UNLA—where Obote was accused of sacrificing Acholi soldiers in battle while protecting his Langi clansmen—resulted in a coup that installed Tito Okello from Acholiland as interim president. Fighting between the UNLA under Okello's command and Museveni's NRA continued, and despite a peace agreement between the two factions signed in Nairobi in December 1985, the NRA marched on Kampala. Up to this day, Museveni's violation of the 1985 Nairobi Peace Agreement is a source of deep-seated grievances among many Acholi and is interpreted as demonstrating that Museveni can never be trusted and does not want peace or reconciliation. In a turn of events over the following weeks, President Museveni effectively assumed presidential authority on 26 January 1986 and remains in power today—more than thirty-three years later.

Within the context of these pre-1986 episodes of violence and conflict, Acholi men in the state army were heavily involved in fighting Museveni's guerrilla movement, which was mostly composed of soldiers from the country's central, southern, and western regions and from Rwanda. Most of the fighting was concentrated in central Uganda, in particular around the town of Luwero, about an hour's drive north of Kampala. Across the Luwero triangle, "appalling atrocities were perpetrated by what was officially the national army, the UNLA" (Allen

1991: 371), primarily composed of Acholi soldiers, who are reported to have killed an estimated three hundred thousand civilians. These historical developments are fundamentally important for situating and contextualizing cycles of violence and conflict within Acholiland following the NRA's acquisition of power (Otunnu 2002).

Early Conflict Years—Retaliation and Intimidation

As soon as Museveni and the NRA gained control over Uganda, thousands of Acholi (and Langi) fighters under the previous government(s) were forced to flee northward and seek protection in northern Uganda and southern Sudan. With growing unease about their complicated reintegration into civilian life and in opposition to the widespread violence perpetrated by NRA soldiers against the civilian population, substantial numbers of Acholi men soon joined the resistance movement. This armed opposition was primarily organized around the Uganda People's Democratic Army (UPDA), composed of former UNLA soldiers and formed in Juba, South Sudan, in March 1986.

Equipped with military and state power and thus with greater opportunity to commit acts of revenge against the northern population for previous crimes, NRA soldiers quickly advanced into northern Uganda. Various local and academic sources suggest that the NRA effectively took control of Gulu and Kitgum, the two largest towns in the region, in March 1986. The atmosphere during those first months was reported to have been largely calm, but it quickly changed as of May 1986, when the UPDA regrouped and attacked various NRA army barracks and outposts. Consequently, "stories of harassment and abuse of civilians by the NRA began circulating in mid 1986" (Branch 2010: 33). According to Adam Branch, "The paradoxical result would be that the NRA/M's wrong-headed strategy, in particular its violence against Acholi civilians, would give birth to the very rebellion the NRA/M had expected" (2010: 34).

During this time of political instability—a continuum of conflict and a spatial shift of violence from central to northern Uganda—spirit mediums began to play a significant role in relation to the conflict. As Allen and Vlassenroot (2010) observe, "Partly as a consequence of dramatic social changes, local understandings about communication with the spirit world had expanded in ways that helped make sense of what was happening" (7–8). Spirit mediums were particularly central to the LRA and the Holy Spirit Movement (HSM), led by a young woman called Alice Auma, popularly known as Alice Lakwena. In a complex chain of events, Alice was said to be possessed by various spirits, including one referred to as *Lakwena*—Acholi for "the messenger." "Initially formed as an egalitarian, gender-equal, non-violent religious movement" (Finnström 2003: 109), the HSM expanded rapidly, with the political intention of overthrowing Museveni's government. The military wing of the movement, the Holy Spirit Mobile Forces (HSFM), regularly engaged NRA battalions in combat and registered various military advancements, moving approximately one hundred kilometers east of Kampala, where in November 1987 Alice's army was defeated.

Following Lakwena's defeat, Joseph Kony soon assumed control over Alice's remaining and returning soldiers, as well as over other former UNLA cadres. Kony eventually "renamed his army the Lord's Resistance Army (LRA) and continued to fight against the government" (Esuruku 2012: 147). Kony, who is often reported to be a cousin of Alice, similarly claims to have taken over some of her spirits, including the Lakwena, and to be possessed by various other spirits. Divides within the UPDA over the political and military direction of the armed resistance led various soldiers to turn toward Kony, whose movement grew in size and importance. As noted by Allen and Vlassenroot (2010), "By 1990, Kony's force was the only significant armed unit still fighting in the Acholi homelands" (10) against the NRA and eventually against the Acholi civilian population.

Interpreting the existence of these multiple rebel groups as the ultimate proof of Acholi resistance against Museveni's government, the state's armed forces soon unleashed a violent military campaign against the population, including the code-named "Operation Pacifying North." For many observers, the NRA military operations must be seen as "part of a broader strategy implemented by the Government to target the Acholi population of northern Uganda for their links to the LRA and other rebel movements" (JRP 2013: 26) and for their alleged role in central Uganda in the 1980s. Various sources suggest that the NRA's violence occurred on the basis of accused rebel collaboration and as retaliation for previous crimes committed by Acholi soldiers against civilians in central Uganda, and in particular in the Luwero triangle region.

As summarized by a local cultural leader whom I interviewed in 2016, the NRA's "atrocities were also a payback and a revenge for what the Acholi soldiers did in Luwero, and they were a general punishment for all of Acholi." It is indeed a widely held belief, if not a conviction, among the Acholi population and among academic observers that NRA soldiers "exploited the opportunity to avenge themselves upon their former [Acholi] opponents by plundering, murdering, torturing and raping" (Behrend 1999: 25). Especially while searching for weapons taken by former UNLA soldiers and while tracing suspected and accused rebels or collaborators, NRA soldiers repeatedly attacked the Acholi civilian population. Men were particularly targeted by many (albeit not all) forms of violence, influenced by stereotypical assumptions associated with masculinity, violence, and aggression, and because of the common ethnocentric view of Acholi men as warriors. One community member commented that "the NRA thought that they will have to attack men because they thought that men are always the ones fighting and joining the rebels, especially the Acholi." It is within this context that soldiers of the NRA committed horrendous human rights abuses against the civilian population, including killings, torture, and sexual violence against women and men.

The LRA Conflict and Violence against Civilians

While the early years of the conflict were primarily characterized by the NRA's large-scale human rights violations against civilian communities, the Acholi population arguably suffered most heavily at the hands of the LRA during subsequent years and during most of the conflict-affected period. Nevertheless, during this early phase of the war, the Ugandan army continued to commit human rights abuses, such as sexual and gender-based violence, primarily against women, and attacks against suspected or accused LRA collaborators or former rebels. With regard to the rebels, however, throughout the course of the conflict, levels of violence by the LRA varied significantly. Indeed, the rebels' acute brutality fluctuated over the years before ultimately increasing again. Violent attacks, massacres, and mass abductions were often in response to military operations instigated by the Ugandan government, such as Operation Pacifying North (1991), Operation Iron Fist (2002), and Operation Lightning Thunder (2008). Overall, for more than two decades, between 1986 and 2006/2008, the conflict between the LRA and the government resulted in large-scale human rights violations with immense civilian casualties. An African proverb quite adequately describes this situation of civilians being affected by and trapped between warring parties: "When two elephants fight, it is the grass that suffers."

While much has been written about the LRA's initial motivations for taking up arms against the government, many studies seem to exclusively suggest religious reasons, often mystifying, demonizing, and depoliticizing the rebel group, as previously observed and critiqued by Finnström (2010). In fact, most analyses of the conflict center around religious and spiritual aspects, concentrating on the LRA's motivation to rule Uganda in accordance with the Ten Commandments, as well as the LRA's widespread (and often seemingly random) brutality, while the rebel group's extant political ambitions are often ignored. However, throughout the course of the conflict, and particularly in the early years, the LRA justified their actions by clearly stating their political objectives, which included overthrowing the government under President Museveni and ensuring the Acholis' political participation and overall development. The armed opposition against the incumbent government was thereby also largely connected to a somehow spiritual mission to "cleanse" the Acholi tribe.

As the conflict gradually unfolded, however, attacks against the civilian population increased, in part as retaliation for not supporting the insurgency or for allegedly assisting the enemy—the Ugandan government. For instance, parts of the civilian population formed citizen militias and local defense units (LDUs), locally referred to as arrow boys, which the LRA interpreted as a sign of civilian resistance against their rebellion. At the same time, the LRA grew largely dependent upon forcefully abducting civilians, especially youths, to generate a larger armed force to fight its cause. This tactic became particularly acute during the mid-1990s, when the LRA received significant support from the Sudanese government and was therefore able to expand their operations. According to UNICEF, approximately thirty-five thousand to sixty-six thousand children and youths were abducted by the LRA, forced to fight as child soldiers and/or serve as sex slaves. Data regarding scale and incidence of abduction, however, vary. Another widely quoted UNICEF figure refers to twenty thousand to twenty-five thousand abducted children.[4] Overall, during the more than two-decade-long conflict, tens of thousands civilians were killed, mutilated, tortured, raped, and otherwise sexually abused by both the LRA and government forces. Most of the region's basic infrastructure was destroyed, and social relations largely broke down.

At the height of the conflict in the early 2000s, more than one and a half million people, or up to 95 percent of the civilian population, were forced from their villages and homesteads into camps for internally displaced persons (IDPs) across the entire northern region. In these camps, civilians were supposed to live under the government's protection. In fact, however, the conditions in the camps were largely inhumane and IDPs suffered continuous human rights violations, including gender-based violence, often at the hands of the soldiers there to protect them. Civilians in the camps were similarly exposed and vulnerable to constant rebel attacks. Against this background, Chris Dolan (2009) appropriately describes the camps as a form of "social torture."

Throughout the course of the conflict, various political actors pursued different military and political attempts to put an end to the fighting, including military operations, mediations and negotiations, and an amnesty policy. Religious leaders and civil society representatives have also long been involved in attempting to find a mutual, peaceful end to the conflict, and therefore—often with support of the international community and regional stakeholders—initiated various rounds of peace talks and negotiations. Esuruku (2011) interestingly notes that although they were male dominated, these peaceful means were often regarded as feminine and incompatible with masculine ideas of resolving disputes militarily. Out of all the nonviolent means of conflict resolution and different attempts at negotiation, the 2006–2008 Juba peace talks were seemingly the most promising initiative. The talks led to the signing of various separate agenda items of a peace deal, although the final peace agreement was never signed by Joseph Kony and the LRA. The separately signed agenda items nevertheless provided a framework for a ceasefire deal, an Agreement on Accountability and Reconciliation (AAR), and an accord on Demobilization, Demilitarization, and Reintegration (DDR). The AAR eventually led to the development of a draft national transitional justice police, which forms the backdrop of the country's current attempts to deal with the past (see chapter 6).

Shortly after the signing of the AAR in February 2008, the Ugandan government set up a Transitional Justice Working Group with the aim of putting in place a concise policy of dealing with past atrocities. Essentially these developments provided the framework for Uganda's draft national transitional justice policy. Over the years, the drafting process has continually been delayed, largely attributable to an apparent lack of political will by the Ugandan government to initiate a holistic transitional justice approach. At the same time, the development of the transitional justice policy is heavily dependent upon external donor funds, much of which have been withdrawn in recent years. Under the auspices of the Justice Law and Order Sector (JLOS) of the Ugandan Ministry of Justice, the transitional justice policy sets out to provide "an overreaching framework of the Government of Uganda, designed to address justice, accountability and reconciliation needs of post conflict Uganda" (JLOS 2017: 3). Aimed "to ensure accountability, serve justice and achieve reconciliation" (ibid.), the policy proposes the implementation and utilization of the following: formal justice processes at the national and domestic level (the International Crimes Division [ICD] of the High Court of Uganda) and at the international level (the ICC); traditional justice processes; a truth-telling process; a reparations program; and an amnesty policy.

Prior to these developments, in late 2003, during a press conference with President Museveni and the ICC prosecutor at that time, Luis Moreno Ocampo, the government of Uganda announced the referral of the northern Ugandan situation to the ICC in The Hague. The court in 2005 issued five arrest warrants against the top LRA cadre, including its leader, Joseph Kony, and commander Dominic Ongwen, who in early 2015 surrendered and whose trial commenced in December 2016.[5] The ICC indictments in the Ugandan situation sparked much scholarly debate and political concerns and are illustrative for wider debates about peace versus justice in conflict-affected and transitional settings.[6] At the same time, the ICC faced much criticism for issuing arrest warrants only against LRA commanders, while failing to investigate crimes committed by NRA soldiers and instead heavily relying on support, intelligence, and information provided by the government.

By and large, Uganda therefore constitutes a poignant example of a relatively diverse transitional justice landscape, including international criminal proceedings by the ICC, national prosecutions by the ICD, traditional justice processes, and proposals for a state-driven and government-led draft national transitional justice policy. In chapter 6 I discuss to what extent and how these transitional justice mechanisms imply the potential to respond to male sexual and gendered harms. In brief, the analysis shows that all of these measures are characterized by various sociopolitical as well as gendered blind spots and are thus largely unresponsive to the experiences, needs, and priorities of large portions of the conflict-affected population in general and of male sexual violence survivors in particular.

In today's postconflict context, reports about the current status, activities, and whereabouts of the LRA vary but generally indicate that the group operates with limited human capital, mostly in the Darfur region of Sudan, parts of the Central African Republic, and the Democratic Republic of the Congo. Joseph Kony is still at large, reported to be in hiding in the Central African Republic or Darfur, and recent evidence shows that the group has fewer than a hundred fighters, many of whom were recently abducted, with only few Acholi soldiers left.

TEK-GUNGU—MALE RAPE IN NORTHERN UGANDA

During the early stages of the war, the government's National Resistance Army also perpetrated crimes of sexual violence against men, and in particular penetrative rape. These crimes were widespread and constituted integral components of a wider military campaign centered around interrogation, retaliation, and punishment of the Acholi population at large.

The vast majority of male-directed sexual violence in northern Uganda took place between the late 1980s and early 1990s in the context of military operations perpetrated by the NRA, composed of soldiers from mostly southern and central Uganda.[7] Although the NRA, and later the UPDF, continued to commit atrocities across Acholiland throughout the entire conflict period, the military operations against the Acholi population predominantly ceased by the early 1990s, and with it came an end to the widespread perpetration of sexual violence against male (and female) civilians at the hands of the government forces. Crimes of sexual violence against men within this context were also accompanied by other human rights violations, such as acts of torture, beatings, or degrading and heinous crimes— which included acts of defecating in cooking pots and granaries, and acts of urinating in the mouths of goats and cattle, perceived to be intended to humiliate the Acholi population—as well as sexual violence against women. As noted in the introduction, male rape in Acholiland is locally referred to as *tek-gungu*, which in Acholi language literally translates as "to bend over" (*gungu*) "forcefully" or "hard" (*tek*), or alternatively "the way that is hard to bend." According to my findings, this terminology specifically applies to male rape in this context and was not commonly used before.

Despite its prevalence, however, previous research on the war in northern Ugandan, although rich and diverse, has not yet sufficiently analyzed NRA-perpetrated violence in general, and definitely not sexual violence against men. Throughout the scholarship on the conflict, despite a few noteworthy exceptions, only occasional references to male-directed sexual violence exist, often lacking detailed information and analytical depth. For instance, Behrend's (1999) insightful account of the early years of the conflict only briefly refers to "the NRA's homosexual practices" of raping men (183). Finnström's (2009) extensive ethnographic research in the region likewise includes two brief cross-references to male rape, while demonstrating that up until recently, stories about tek-gungu only circulated as rumors across Acholiland. Dolan's groundbreaking research and influential advocacy work by the Refugee Law Project (RLP) and the Justice and Reconciliation Project (JRP) remain the only exceptions that go beyond solely mentioning male rape. Nevertheless, a holistic picture of sexual violence against men in Acholiland, including a deconstructed understanding of scope and prevalence as well as survivors' experiences, so far remains absent from the literature.

Prevalence and Dynamics of Tek-Gungu

In determining the scope and dynamics of sexual violence against men in northern Uganda, I rely on the qualitative empirical data underpinning this study, infused with secondary sources and literature where appropriate. Across time and space, determining the prevalence and scope of sexual violence during armed conflicts proves inherently difficult, conditioned by a general absence of numerical data, underreporting, and misrecognition (see chapter 2). Yet drawing on survivors' accounts, key informants' assessments, and numerous triangulated indicators, I assess that sexual violence against men in northern Uganda was common and widespread and occurred in many locations across the conflict-affected region. In this context, *widespread* primarily refers to the spatial extent of these crimes and their frequent occurrence in different places. I mostly utilize the expansive geographical occurrence of these crimes, coupled with respondents' assessments of the pervasive prevalence of sexual violence against men and the invention of the specific vocabulary of *tek-gungu* to attest this widespread character.

The research underpinning this study has documented the occurrence of male-directed sexual violence in various locations across Acholiland, including in the current-day districts of Gulu, Nwoya, Amuru, Kitgum, and Pader, suggesting that these crimes were geographically widespread. The majority of documented cases are scattered across subcounties and trading centers around Gulu town, the biggest urban center in the region and the epicenter of the conflict (*see* map 2). At the same time, villages along some of the major and militarily strategic roads connecting Gulu town with other regionally important locations (such as Anaka) or leading north toward southern Sudan (via Pawel or Palaro), where the majority of rebels and former UNLA soldiers were suspected to be in hiding, were particularly affected (*see* map 3). As indicated by the maps included here—which document the occurrence of male rape—various villages around Alero subcounty on the way to Purongo in the current-day Nwoya district were particularly targeted. Tim Allen observes that in Alero in general, "NRA anti-insurgency measures had been particularly violent" (1991: 375). Other examples are the major routes to Palaro and Awach subcounties, which witnessed widespread sexual violence and the particular targeting of men. Tracing these locations suggests strategic patterns, as expanded upon below, directly corresponding with movements of military operations and the involvement of specific NRA battalions, colloquially referred to as *gungu* battalions.

Map 2 documents all villages and subcounties across the conflict-affected north where cases of sexual violence against men reportedly occurred.[8] Due to the

MAP 2. Map of Acholiland documenting cases of tek-gungu.

absence of reliable quantifiable data, the map does not indicate prevalence within respective localities but instead illustrates the variety of locations in which NRA soldiers reportedly raped men.

Map 3 then zooms into specific areas and roads where sexual violence against men was particularly prevalent. Again, this map shows that some of the most important and militarily strategic roads, for instance northward in the direction of southern Sudan or toward Anaka (a traditional opposition stronghold), were especially targeted and affected, corresponding with NRA troop movements and wider conflict dynamics at that time.

Various respondents also referred to the period between the late 1980s and early 1990s, which was characterized by dynamic political developments and intense human rights violations, as the "gungu period." During a focus-group discussion with male elders, one respondent attested that "it was almost only men during that time who were raped—this is why people call it the gungu period." Such illustrative references and connotations suggest that these crimes must have been relatively widespread and/or perceived to be so extraordinary as to make them

MAP 3. Perpetration of tek-gungu along major and military-strategic roads.

stand out from the extensive catalog of other human rights violations perpetrated by government soldiers during this turbulent period.

Furthermore, compelling evidence exists to suggest that the LRA's top command was well aware of the perpetration of these crimes and used it in its favor politically, in part to mobilize the population against the government. This awareness partly stems from the fact that some of these acts were perpetrated in public and in front of entire communities, as explored further below. Figure 1, from an early rebel manifesto (ca. 1991) that was circulated by the LRA in the early years of their insurgency includes a graphic illustration of an act of tek-gungu, showing two clearly marked NRA soldiers raping a man (see Finnström 2009).[9] The LRA used this to signal and communicate to the Acholi population that Museveni's government was attempting to destroy them, and acts of male rape appeared to constitute a poignant example to demonstrate the NRA's perceived extraordinary cruelty.

Similarly, during the 2006–2008 Juba peace talks, LRA commander Joseph Kony referred to the government soldiers' violent and common practice of raping

FIGURE 1. Illustration of tek-gungu from Rebel Manifesto (unpublished, untitled, and undated, ca. 1991). (Finnström 2009: 64). Reused with Finnström's approval.

Acholi men. Baines (2014) notes that Kony specifically addressed the peace talks delegation by stating that "the elders should not act like they don't know what caused the war. For instance, in 1990 during Operation North, there were cases in which men who were captured were reportedly sodomized (*tek-gungu*) by the NRA—don't you know about *tek-gungu?*" (6).

Overall, the extensive geographical coverage, the communities' statements and assessments, the invention and application of the specific vocabulary of tek-gungu, the gungu period as a time indicator, and the labeling of specific gungu NRA battalions all suggest a widespread occurrence of sexual violence against men by the NRA between the late 1980s and early 1990s. Some informants, including male survivors themselves, explained that during this period "men were heavily affected by rape." Mirroring the findings presented throughout this section, both Esuruku (2012) and RLP (2014) previously attested that male rape was widespread. The field-based material presented here therefore serves as additional evidence for such prior assessments. While it remains inherently difficult to quantify the extent and scale of tek-gungu, including numbers of victims, the evidence presented here suggests that sexual violence against men within this specific context and during this particular period must have been common and widespread.

Forms of Male-Directed Sexual Violence in Acholiland

Forms of sexual violence against men in northern Uganda are quite varied. As conceptualized in chapter 2, I employ a broadened understanding of conflict-related sexual violence against men, which Carpenter (2006) categorizes into three main types: (1) rape and direct sexual mutilation or torture; (2) civilian men being forced to actively rape or commit sexual violence; and (3) connected harms, referring to situations in which the sexual abuse of women "forms part of a psychological torture against men" (Eriksson Baaz and Stern 2013: 34). Empirical evidence from northern Uganda draws attention to all these forms of sexual violence perpetrated against Acholi men. Male civilians were forcefully raped; men, and in particular youths, in the LRA were forced to have sexual intercourse, either with family members as linked to abduction or in the context of forced marriages; and men were forced to witness their wives, daughters, sisters, or mothers being raped in front of them by either rebels or government soldiers.

While all of these forms of SGBV against men occurred during the conflict in northern Uganda, I specifically focus on penetrative anal rape, perpetrated against civilian men. I employ this focus specifically because male rape was arguably the most common and prevalent form of sexual violence against men during this period in northern Uganda, and certainly the most prevalent form of such violence committed against the vast majority of survivors who participated in this study. Other forms of sexual violence against men—such as genital beatings, stabbings, or sexual humiliations—often accompanied crimes of penetrative anal rape, but mostly did not occur in isolation. Although I am therefore primarily concerned with acts of male rape, the analysis of course also takes into account other sexual violations and harms experienced by the male survivors who participated in this study.

In addition to the vocabulary of tek-gungu, many male survivors commonly described their experiences of sexual violence as *butu tek-tek*. Interestingly, this is how rape is commonly translated in Acholi and how female victims often refer to their sexual abuse. Porter (2017) writes that this common translation of rape literally means to "sleep strong strong" (223). As argued by Porter, to "sleep with" "is the most common way of referring to having sex in Acholi" (ibid.), and the descriptor *tek-tek,* "strong strong," refers to the forceful and coercive character of the sexual act. The fact that most male survivors therefore directly refer to their sexual violations as rape, and chose the same terminology as female victims, stands in contrast to some previous studies arguing that men commonly refrain from employing this terminology and instead describe their experiences of sexual abuse as torture without any sexual(ized) specification (see chapter 2).

Localities of Tek-Gungu: Private and Public Spheres

Crimes of sexual violence against men in northern Uganda occurred within both the private and the public sphere. At times, crimes of male-directed sexual violence were perpetrated by "small groups of two to four soldiers in the bushes or even in the men's own homesteads" and therefore in the private sphere, "out of sight of the rest of the community" (JRP 2013: 22, 23).[10] Various survivors were indeed raped by multiple perpetrators, suggesting a prevalence of gang rape, which across time and space generally constitutes the vast majority of reported wartime rape cases. Cohen notes that "gang rape is a form of public, sexualized violence, which serves to communicate norms of masculinity, virility and strength between fighters of both sexes" (2016: 36).

Other acts of male rape occurred in the public sphere, sometimes in front of the victims' families and communities. For instance, in one subcounty, NRA soldiers separated the men from the women, locked the men into granaries as holding cells, individually singled them out, and then raped them publicly in front of other community members. In other locations, men and women, including husbands and wives, were raped in front of the wider community as a form of public dehumanization and humiliation through sexual violations. One male survivor described that "the rape was done in public, and so many people from here knew about it because they witnessed it." In another instance, as narrated by a survivor: "In the year 1991, government soldiers arrested us. Then they took us and dumped us in the hole in the trading center. The hole was dug by the soldiers and they would use it as a cell. Then in the morning, they would pick us one by one and would tie us on the tree and you were beaten. Then under the tree, there were always spears pointing at you. They beat us seriously, then took us back to the hole and started raping us. We were many, and we were given allegations that we were rebels."

The distinction between public and private spheres matters when seeking to understand male survivors' harms and how they experienced the violations and their aftermath. Specifically, these differing locations shape how the violences are perceived to impact male survivors' masculinities, as different gendered dynamics play out in the private and public sphere respectively, which will be explored more fully in the following chapter. The locations of violence likewise influence survivors' attitudes toward talking about their violations, and their willingness to talk about them, which in turn links to their justice-related concerns and priorities.

Explaining Sexual Violence against Men in Acholiland

The survivor's narrative above also illustrates that crimes of sexual violence against men during the conflict occurred as integral components of punishment and retaliation attacks against the civilian population at large. Based on these dynamics, below I scrutinize different context-specific explanations for the occurrence of sexual violence against men in northern Uganda, thereby drawing on established theoretical explanatory models introduced in chapter 2.

To fully explain conflict-related sexual violence, however, perpetrator-centric data is needed. Yet, despite a few noteworthy exceptions, there is a persistent lack of data from the perspectives of perpetrators of conflict-related sexual violence.

For male-directed sexual violence, this lack of perpetrator-centric data is particularly striking, and existing research has not yet explored the motives of these perpetrators. By analyzing patterns of sexual violence against men from a survivors' point of view, we can nevertheless begin to unpack some of the collective dynamics and infer potential causes.

Explanations for conflict-related sexual violence, including against men, are manifold and diverse. As noted in the previous chapter in relation to global dynamics more broadly, conflict-related sexual violence is undoubtedly a complex phenomenon and "any mono-causal theory is unlikely to account for the observed variation" (Wood 2014: 463) in its causes. Most studies suggest that sexual violence against men is primarily strategic and systematic, often portrayed as a weapon of war, aimed at punishing and intimidating its victims, primarily by way of humiliation through gendered subordination and disempowerment.

Although criticism has been directed to the universal framing of sexual violence (primarily against women) as a strategic "weapon of war" (see Eriksson Baaz and Stern 2013), the findings underpinning this study generate convincing empirical evidence to argue that in northern Uganda, sexual violence against men qualifies as a tactic, or at least as a policy, of wider systematic and strategic warfare operations. While I do not necessarily intend to squarely position these crimes within either of these different categories as laid out in chapter 2, as either exclusively opportunism, strategy, or a policy, here I nevertheless tease out the obvious strategic elements and dimensions surrounding these crimes.

Indeed, the geographically widespread acts of tek-gungu perpetrated by the NRA occurred within the context of wider military campaigns and systematic human rights violations against the civilian population at large. As contextualized above, these military operations are locally understood as retaliation and revenge attacks against the Acholis and/or as interrogation and punishment for suspected rebellion or rebel collaboration. A male community member asserted that "the NRA decided to rape men to revenge against the Acholi for what happened in Luwero, and because they accused the population of supporting Kony's rebels." Numerous survivors reported that they were raped on accusation of supporting the LRA or because they were suspected to be former UNLA soldiers. Various survivors were also explicitly accused of "being a father to the rebel" and were told that "this is what you get for supporting Kony." Wood (2014) asserts that sexual violence qualifies as strategic if perpetrated against particular populations and, for instance, "as a form of collective punishment" (472).

Previous research has documented that state armed forces in particular perpetrate sexual violence "where and when rebel forces are visibly active but not strong enough to engage the State in frequent combat, using rape against communities of purported insurgent supporters . . . but also to punish and terrorize [the civilian population]" (Wood 2014: 472). For both Leiby (2009) and Wood (2014), if sexual violence conforms to these dynamics, it qualifies as strategic. These patterns certainly apply to general violence, including male rape, perpetrated by the Ugandan state army against Acholi civilian communities as a form of punishment and retaliation. As shown above, many acts of male rape were committed as punishment for accused rebel collaboration. The geographical patterns of the occurrence of tek-gungu, related to military troop movements similarly suggest a widespread and strategic perpetration of male rape (see maps 1 and 2). These crimes also occurred during the early phases of the conflict, when LRA rebel forces were visibly active although not yet strong enough to engage the state army in frequent combat.[11]

Key informants similarly suspected that the "raping of men was a deliberate strategy as part of wider deliberate attempts to discourage and destroy the Acholi, by humiliating and weakening them through rape." Various male survivors stated that during the sexual abuse, the perpetrating soldiers frequently said (mostly in Kiswahili, the lingua franca of the Ugandan army) that they "wanted to finish the Acholi people" or that these acts were intended "as a payback for what happened in Luwero." Most survivors themselves indeed suspected that collective revenge and retaliation as well as the intention to prevent the male Acholi civilian population from rebelling against the government were among the main reasons for the government soldiers to sexually violate them.

As articulated by one survivor, "They chose to sodomize men because men are the ones known to be military strong and they were in the previous government and army. The NRA wanted to show that the Acholi were defeated because they are now weak." A male elder further explained that "men were sodomized and they are now like women because they are also powerless. They targeted men because they were security provider. They were sodomized to prove that they are now powerless." Research by the Justice and Reconciliation Project (JRP) similarly suggests that "the sexual abuse of men was utilized as a way to further humiliate the people . . . by stripping the men of their dignity" (2013: 23) and manhood. The community's interpretations upheld that "men who have been raped are considered to have lost their status as men" (ibid.). Sexual violence therefore is perceived to render Acholi male survivors subordinate to the (non-Acholi) male perpetrators. This gendered devaluation of individual male victims is expected to translate and transfer across the local population more widely. The motive of revenge against and to punish the Acholi, as explored above, therefore played out on a collective and communal level, in a gendered manifestation and with strong ethnicized dimensions.

Another widespread belief regarding the causes of male rape is that these crimes deliberately aimed to infect the Acholis with HIV/AIDS. Olara Otunnu, former undersecretary general of the United Nations and special representative for children and armed conflict and himself a Ugandan, noted that during the conflict "rape and sexual exploitation, especially by government soldiers, have become routine" and "HIV/AIDS is being used as a deliberate weapon of mass destruction" (2009: 1). He further alleged that "government soldiers [were] screened, and those who test HIV-positive [were] deployed to the north, with the mission of wreaking maximum havoc. . . . Consequently, the rate of HIV infection [in Acholiland] has exploded . . . to staggering levels of 30 to 50 percent" (ibid.).[12] Behrend (1999) similarly notes that "a high percentage of the soldiers [were] HIV positive," and therefore "many of the rapes result[ed] in infection and thus in death" (183). According to Finnström's (2009) observations, it was locally alleged that the NRA's raping of civilians of both sexes aimed to spread the deadly HIV virus as a way of targeting the Acholi population. Linked to these secondary assessments and speculations, my empirical findings evidence HIV/AIDS infections among the physical consequences of sexual violence against men in northern Uganda (see below). For instance, the data underpinning this study include references to male survivors who died due to HIV/AIDS or who are currently HIV-positive as a result of having been raped by government soldiers. That being said, however, it is of course immensely difficult to verify if the government soldiers purposefully aimed to spread HIV/AIDS among the civilian population, or if this was rather a by-product of these crimes. In light of this, my discussion of these concerns does not intend to agree with or support the claim that male rape purposefully aimed to spread HIV/AIDS among the civilian population.

Taken together, however, all of these intersecting aspects lend strong empirical support for the argument that sexual violence perpetrated by the NRA against the civilian population, including against men, during the northern Ugandan conflict was a deliberate and strategic tactic, conforming with theoretical explanatory models of sexual violence as a strategy, or at least as a policy (see chapter 2). At the same time, however, it remains inherently difficult to verify whether these crimes were specifically ordered by the army's top command, including President Museveni, or whether military orders were issued at lower ranks. As emphasized by Wood, "Organizations that explicitly order combatants to rape are probably rare (but do exist). Probably more common are organizations where some form of sexual violence by combatants is a *strategy* authorized not by explicit orders but by 'total war' or other permissive rhetoric" (2014: 471, emphasis added).

Various male survivors themselves also suspected that the NRA soldiers specifically chose to rape civilians of both sexes "because they stayed for too long in the bush without seeing their women so they took women and men to have sex with." According to another male survivor, "I think these were soldiers who were so long in the bush without sex so I think this is why they decided to rape me." According to such interpretations, the large-scale occurrence of rape would at least in part be attributed to the fact that, immediately after the guerilla war in central Uganda (1980–86), many NRA soldiers were posted to northern Uganda and thus spent considerable time away from civilian life and their wives or other female sexual partners. Within this context and deprived of sex, NRA soldiers are thought and accused to have raped civilian women and men in order to satisfy their sexual needs. Research by Eriksson Baaz and Stern (2013) demonstrates that many people in general, including military staff and soldiers, "understand conflict-related rape in this way" (19).

Such an alternative interpretation would lend empirical support to the opportunistic rape thesis, referring to "rape carried out for private reasons rather than organization objectives" (Wood 2014: 470). Cohen (2016) explains that according to the opportunism argument, which heavily relies on essentialist and dichotomized categories of male perpetrators and female victims, "rape, then, may be the result of a lack of access to sex that would normally take place within combatants' peacetime relationships with their wives and girlfriends" (47). Scholarship on sexual violence against men, however, has almost entirely neglected this explanatory framework. This neglect of opportunism as a potential variable for explaining the occurrence and dynamics of male-directed rape derives from heteronormative and heterosexual assumptions regarding gender relations and the nature of sexual violence.

However, by presenting these survivor viewpoints, I also do not intend to suggest that male rape during the war in northern Uganda should in fact be unitarily qualified as opportunistic violence. To ultimately determine these causes, we must study the perpetrators. At the same time, the evidence too strongly suggests systematic and strategic patterns. The opportunism argument in this context would also downplay the violations' gendered components, and would thus not allow for a sophisticated analysis of sexual violence as sexed and *gendered,* underpinned by patriarchy and clearly rooted in gender inequalities. Instead, my discussion of these divergent survivors' interpretations aims, first, to contrast male survivors' diverse and individual subjective interpretations regarding the reasons for their sexual violations with conceptually driven scholarly analyses; and second, to underscore that mono-causal explanatory models cannot sufficiently account for the causes of and establish explanations for sexual violence. While the occurrence of male rape in Acholiland thus suggests clear strategic patterns, this does not preclude that individual soldiers at times opportunistically sought sexual satisfaction and gratification out of these acts and that they nevertheless remain closely connected to power. Indeed, "even within the same conflict, sexual violence can serve multiple functions in different contexts and at different points in time" (Leiby 2006: 445) and can have manifold explanations and causes.

CONSEQUENCES OF MALE RAPE
IN NORTHERN UGANDA

Drawing on this wider discussion regarding the dynamics of sexual violence in northern Uganda, it is important to also explore the consequences of such crimes for Acholi survivors, which can broadly be categorized into physical, psychological, and physiological impacts. One male survivor affirmed that "the effects of the violations were really many: many health complications, physically and also psychologically."

Physical Consequences

Various survivors stated that "our biggest challenge is our physical health." Survivors frequently described abdominal pain, waist and back pain, body aches, rectal prolapse and anal ruptures, and anal itching and bleeding, among other symptoms. As a compounded result of many of these health complications, numerous survivors also reported physical difficulties in urinating or passing stool. As described by one survivor, for instance: "I started developing a lot of complications in passing urine and stool with a lot of pain. Every time I go to pass stool, my rectum collapses and at times I discharge blood when passing stool and also when passing urine, I get a lot of pain."

These medical complications affecting the male survivors reflect the limited existing accounts of physical consequences of sexual violence against men during armed conflict as discussed throughout the literature.[13] Interestingly, several male survivors related their physical injuries to women's experiences and cataloged the consequences as typically female harms. For instance, one male survivor explained that he "experience[d] waist pain like a woman during pregnancy," while another survivor said he would "always get waist pain which is a thing that happens to women but not to men." Another male survivor described his problems of anal bleeding—a result of rectal prolapse—as "menstruating."

Many of these physical consequences persist into the current postconflict period, up to thirty years after the violations occurred. "I am still feeling the pain up to today," a survivor attested, while another survivor described that "to date, I still have problems; I am still affected up to now." For numerous male survivors, the continuous consequences and harms can be attributed to the lack of medical treatment in the aftermath of the violations. "It was not easy to access medical services in that period of time," a survivor attested. According to yet another survivor, "Unfortunately during that period there was no hospital that was operational here so they were using only warm water to treat me. That is why it has brought me a lot of weakness up to now, because I think that if there would have been an operational hospital that would have been better than now."

While the conflict was ongoing and particularly in the early years of the war, the provision of medical care and the availability of hospitals and health centers were severely limited. Not only male sexual violence survivors, but the entire conflict-affected community with diverse injuries at large was unable to access sufficient medical treatment. The high degree of militarization in the region and insecurities caused by intense rebel activities also prevented civilians in rural areas from traveling longer distances—for instance, to Gulu or Kitgum town, where medical treatment was available, although in a highly restricted capacity.

At the same time, the situation for male rape survivors was particularly difficult due to fear, shame, and stigmatization underpinned by notions of masculinity and because of health professionals' internalized stereotypes of who can be a victim of sexual violence within a highly heteronormative societal setting. Because of social constructions of Acholi hegemonic masculinity, which disallow men to be vulnerable and dictate that they be strong, the majority of male survivors refrained from reporting their violations and from seeking services, because they were ashamed or because they perceived that "they should be able to cope as men." For instance, an Acholi male survivor described his experience: "I went with the physical complication to [Saint Mary's Hospital] Lacor in 1995.[14] Reaching Lacor, instead of being seen by a man or at least a mature person, they sent me a young lady to examine me. I refused to undress and went back home so I just bought drugs from the clinic and I have just been taking drugs ever since, but the problem of pain in my anus, waist, and back continues."

Studies across various contexts have previously documented that male survivors face inherent challenges of accessing medical treatment and refrain from reporting the sexual violations committed against them because of these factors. According to another Acholi male survivor, "It was not possible for you to go to the clinic with this violation and explain what happened. They would have laughed at you, called you a homosexual or even reported you to the government."[15] For feminist scholar Leatherman (2011), this lack of adequate health care and support structures constitutes a clear form of revictimization.

Furthermore, and as described above, the sexual violations often occurred in combination with a variety of other forms of violence, such as torture or severe beatings. The injuries and physical consequences of these (nonsexual) violations frequently intersect with the sexual harms. As a result of these manifold and intersecting physical consequences, various male survivors were unable to work.[16] Several male survivors also attested to having been infected with HIV/AIDS as a result of the sexual violations, and participants explained that some former members of their support groups have died as a result of HIV and other sexually transmitted infections and diseases, most probably caused by the sexual violations.

Psychological Consequences

The psychological consequences experienced by male sexual violence survivors extend from shame, fear, and stigmatization to nightmares, reported symptoms of depression, and social isolation and exclusion as well as feelings of anger and powerlessness, among others.

For one Acholi male survivor, "The immediate impact that the rape brought was fear. I was living under extreme fear that they will come again and either do the same or even do worse." For another male survivor, "Even up to now when I look at a soldier, I start shivering and shaking." According to one survivor, "Because of fear and anger, some victims deliberately joined rebel forces in those early years," primarily in an attempt to retaliate against the NRA and to take control (back) into their own hands. Further, according to various survivors, in localities where the sexual violations occurred in the public sphere or where community members otherwise got to know about these crimes, there is "a lot of stigmatization of us by the members of the community and that has really broken our hearts because everywhere we go, people are pointing at us." As narrated by yet another survivor, "From the people here, I feel stigmatization. When people are drunk they will stigmatize me, and that will undermine my dignity as a human being." One male survivor described that he "decided to stay isolated and not in public places, because if I stay with other people there is the problem of stigma. People are calling us the wives of the government or homosexuals because of what happened to us and that is really stigmatizing."

This stigmatization in turn often results in social isolation and exclusion. Because of the humiliation and stigmatization, coupled with fear, various survivors reported that they fled their homes, mostly to Gulu town or other (semi) urban centers across the region. The prevalence of social stigmatization as one central psychological implication of male-directed sexual violence during war and armed conflict has previously been documented in the literature (see Onyango and Hampanda 2011). Most existing studies indeed argue that one of the most common and most severe social consequences for male survivors is the social stigmatization attached to their violations.

Conditioned by a variety of intersecting factors, including shame and social stigmatization, various male survivors were also excluded or expelled from their families and communities, and thus frequently live(d) in isolation. As deconstructed in more depth in the following chapter, a considerable number of male victims were left by their wives or wider families due to the stigma attached to the sexual violations committed against them. Comparable to the absence of medical treatment, there similarly was a striking lack of psychosocial support, further exacerbating survivors' psychological problems. For instance, one male survivor said, "Psychologically, we were also greatly affected because of many troubling thoughts but we had nobody to share our experiences with and get any emotional support."[17]

Physiological Consequences

The majority of male survivors moreover reported physiologically conditioned inabilities to achieve or sustain an erection and attributed this to their sexual violations. "Ever since the rape, I cannot get an erection anymore," one male survivor attested. As Edström, Dolan et al. (2016) point out, "One of the most common physiological dimensions of the impact on male victims of sexual violence appears to be its almost universal numbing of their capacity for sexual arousal. An inability to achieve or maintain erections—so central to their relations with their wives or female partners—is the visible symptom" (26).

"My desire for sex vanished and diminished ever since the rape," one survivor similarly described. Research on male-directed sexual violence outside the context of war—for instance, in prison settings, male fraternities, or the military—documents similar effects on male survivors' desire for sexual intercourse or on their physiological abilities to achieve an erection. Specifically focusing on sexual violence against men within the setting of war and armed conflict, only few existing studies have paid particular attention to these physiological consequences, including their gendered implications.[18] Against this background, in the following chapter, I more closely examine how the inability to erect, to have sex, and thus to procreate—which is so central to the Acholi model of hegemonic masculinity—impacts male survivors' gendered identities.

SEXUAL AND GENDER-BASED VIOLENCE AGAINST WOMEN AND GIRLS IN NORTHERN UGANDA

Crimes of sexual violence against men must also be positioned in relation to other forms of sexual and gender-based violence perpetrated during the conflict more broadly. Okello and Hovil (2007) note that gender-related crimes during the conflict have been pervasive, while Finnström (2009) similarly observes that during the course of the conflict, "sexual violence and rape have . . . become common in war-torn northern Uganda" (63). From the early to mid-1990s, crimes of sexual violence were primarily directed against civilian women perpetrated by government soldiers, LRA rebels, and civilian men alike (Baines 2014; Porter 2017).

The breakdown of social relations (Porter 2016), catalyzed by the conflict in general and the massive forced displacement in particular, contributed to growing rates of domestic violence and spousal abuse. Sexual and gender-based crimes committed by civilian men against their partners or against other women are often linked to changing gendered power relations. Okello and Hovil (2007) observe in this regard that in the camps "men, unable to support their families, feel impotent, which leads them into a vicious cycle of anger and abuse" (442). Because women often became the main recipients of aid distributions within the camps and were thus (temporarily) the main provider for their families, men's identities and roles as household heads were threatened, producing a context in which some men reverted to (sexual) violence to (re)gain power and dominance and (re)assert their masculinities. Further, high insecurities, constrained income-generating activities, and inhumane living conditions in the camps often left women dependent on "survival sex" in exchange for food or security, often offered by the soldiers stationed within the camps.

Women and girls abducted by the LRA were also subjected to various forms of sexual and gender-based violence. Although a strict sexual conduct prevailed within the LRA, young female recruits were given as servants and wives to male commanders within the context of "forced marriages," and senior commanders often had several wives (Baines 2014). Some men—especially younger, less senior recruits or abductees—were also forced into these marriage arrangements, which can therefore also be seen as a form of gender-based violence against men in a broadened conception, although this constitutes a subject of further study. Based on statements by Joseph Kony and other top LRA commanders, Baines (2014) considers forced marriages to be a component of the LRA's political project of imagining a new Acholi national, by way of "reproducing—literally giving birth to—the [new] nation" (2). Baines therefore explains that "the vision of the 'new Acholi' was operationalized through the institution of forced marriage and recreation of the familial unit" (6).

Within the rebel ranks, sexual relations outside the context of these arranged marriages were strongly prohibited, and violations of these rules, including the rape of civilians or (forced) sex with other LRA abductees, were punished, often in the form of severe beatings or death (Amony 2015). Baines (2014) quotes a former female abductee who explains that "the rape of civilians did not happen. There was a rule among the Holy (the LRA) that no one was to be promiscuous. This meant that when you abducted a civilian you were not to sleep with her recklessly" (8). As explained by Baines (2014), such rules primarily aimed to protect "the moral purity of the new Acholi as a chosen group" (6). Despite these regulations, however, there clearly were cases of sexual violence against civilian women by the LRA. Based upon research with 187 female rape survivors in Gulu district, Holly Porter (2013) notes several incidents of female civilian rape by the LRA. Baines in her research furthermore "encountered dozens more incidents" (2014: 8). According to Baines, "The LRA undoubtedly carried out civilian rape even if reported in smaller numbers, but likely these were incidents that took place without the knowledge of more senior commanders" (ibid.), thus suggesting opportunistic causes.

At the same time, many former LRA "bush wives" continue to face numerous gendered challenges and experience diverse forms of sexual and gender-based violence and discrimination upon return to civilian life. For instance, returnees are often exposed to violence by family or community members and experience highly gendered discrimination in terms of limited access to education, income-generating activities, or, crucially, agricultural land for themselves and their children. In the sociocultural context of Acholiland, children born of war face additional hardship. For instance, they often do not have a relationship to their paternal clans. This is especially problematic, as in Acholi's patrilineal and patrilocal culture, a child's identity is linked to his or her father's family and clan. Knowing one's paternal home village is a paramount aspect of social belonging and identity formation.

Sexual Violence against Men within the LRA

Although the overwhelming majority of sexual violence crimes against men in northern Uganda were committed by government soldiers, and most forms of sexualized and gender-based crimes perpetrated by the LRA targeted women, a few isolated cases of male-directed sexual violence by the LRA exist. While studies on NRA-perpetrated sexual violence against men are generally scarce, research on such violence within and by the LRA thus far remains almost nonexistent.

My research, in the form of coincidental findings, has uncovered at least two cases of male-on-male rape within the LRA. In both cases, senior male commanders raped young male LRA recruits, and the dynamics of these instances suggest opportunistic motives rather than strategic causes. While "sexually immoral behavior" (Baines 2014: 1) in the form of sexual violence against women was prohibited and often punished by severe beatings, the former forced wife of a rebel commander explained to me that the rape of men within the LRA was "considered unimaginable" and indeed punishable by death. This harsh punishment of male sexual abuse within the LRA may be linked to the group's and Kony's spiritual beliefs and their heteronormative (and homophobic) conception of family and society. In one of these reported cases, the commander, who also had several forced wives, was shot immediately when the LRA leadership found out he had sexually abused a male recruit. In another instance, the sexual abuse stopped when the victimized abductee threatened to report the commander to the LRA leadership, which inevitably would have resulted in the commander's execution. In addition to these sporadic cases of male-on-male rape, a group of counselors of a psychological-support service provider working with former LRA abductees similarly reported a rare instance of continuous sexual abuse of a young male recruit by a senior female commander. These few isolated reported cases of male-directed sexual violence are likely not the only instances of sexual violence against men within the LRA, and hence warrant further research.

CONCLUSION

In this chapter I have painted a detailed picture of the extent and dynamics of sexual violence against men during the conflict in northern Uganda, situated within wider conflict dynamics and in relation to gendered forms of violence more broadly. This chapter thereby provides the contextual groundwork for the analysis in the following chapters.

Based on original empirical field research findings, I demonstrated that crimes of sexual violence against men committed by government soldiers of the NRA between the late 1980s and early 1990s against Acholi civilian men were geographically widespread, resulting in the application of the new vocabulary of tek-gungu. I have shown that sexual violence against men in Acholiland, situated in relation to wider conflict dynamics, suggests clear strategic motives and rationales behind the perpetration of these crimes.

While this chapter already included an exploration of the gendered and sexual manifestations and consequences of male rape, a sustained, empirically driven yet theoretically grounded understanding of how sexual violence against men compromises male survivors' gendered identities remains thus far only insufficiently explored. Against this background, the following chapter proceeds by unpacking how sexual violence against men impacts male survivors' masculinities to aid our understanding of the gendered harms experienced by survivors.

4
_____

"I used to be a strong man, but now I am not"

Gendered Vulnerabilities and Harms

Sexual violence against men during armed conflict is commonly theorized to compromise male survivors' masculine identities. What throughout the literature is almost exclusively labeled as the "emasculation" and "feminization" of male survivors is frequently portrayed at once as a motivation for the perpetration of such violence as well as its primary consequence and harm. Yet how exactly such perceived processes of gender subordination and the compromising of masculinities unfold, and what they entail, is only poorly understood.

To this end, in this chapter, I empirically deconstruct the gendered effects of sexual violence on Acholi male survivors' masculinities, drawing directly on their experiences and guided by their views, voices, and perspectives. While most existing studies treat the effects of sexual violence on male survivors' masculinities in static terms and as one-time events, I argue instead that gender subordination is a dynamic and manifold process, initiated by acts of penetration and further exacerbated by myriad layered harms that subordinate male survivors through gendered disempowerment. Challenging dominant assumptions in the literature, this chapter thereby demonstrates that the impact of wartime male rape is a fluid and compounded process, perpetuated over time through social interactions, health implications, and a lack of gender-sensitive medical service provision.

Throughout the growing literature on the topic, such processes are frequently conceptualized and portrayed as "emasculation" by way of "feminization" and/ or "homosexualization." Male survivors' experiences, however, are much more fluid and nuanced than these seemingly static concepts and their associated terminologies suggest. In light of these discrepancies between dominant conceptual assumptions and survivors' empirically grounded lived realities, I avoid reproducing this language, and instead think and speak of these dynamics and of survivors' experiences as forms of "displacement from gendered personhood" as laid out in the introduction. In unpacking these dynamics, this chapter departs from "thick descriptions" of Acholi masculinities as a conceptual premise, because understanding the effects of violence on gender needs to depart from a contextualized understanding of relational gender identities in the first place.

COO-PEE—WHERE "MEN ARE NOT THERE"

Before proceeding with theoretical reflections about masculinities constructions and a deconstructed analysis of survivors' gendered harms, I begin by introducing the case of *Coo-Pee,* the village where men (*coo*) are considered not to be there (*pee*). I introduce this case study to illuminate the manifold ways in which armed conflict can impact men's gender identities and to illustrate how the effects of war and sexual violence against men are understood and perceived locally in northern Uganda.

Coo-Pee is a small rural trading center in Bungatira subcounty, approximately fifteen kilometers north of Gulu town along the road to Palaro (see figures 2 and 3 in chapter 3). In Acholi language, *coo* is the plural for men, while *pee* refers to something or someone not being there. *Coo-Pee* can therefore be translated and understood as a place where "men are not there," or at least are considered not to be there. Throughout the course of my research, I heard different explanations regarding the origin and meaning of this name. However, one interpretation in the contemporary environment appears to dominate the contextual understanding of the meaning of the village's name, at least among my respondents. Given the multiplicity and ambivalence of existing attributed meanings, however, my aim here is not to determine the *actual* meaning of the name Coo-Pee, which appears to have been in circulation from at least the 1950s, as demonstrated, for instance, by the archives of anthropologist Paula Hirsch Foster, and appears to have varying connotations and interpretations. Rather, I aim to explore how the community makes sense of the name, in Coo-Pee and in Acholiland more broadly, as well as among my respondents in the contemporary context in particular against the backdrop of recent developments during the protracted armed conflict and in its aftermath.

The most prevalent explanation of the meaning of the name Coo-Pee among my respondents goes as follows: During the early stages of the conflict, in the late 1980s and early 1990s, the civilian population, and especially males, suffered most heavily from violence perpetrated by government soldiers (see chapter 3). Acholi men were particularly targeted because of stereotypical assumptions linked to masculinities and ethnicity, and because they were suspected of fighting the state army and joining rebel groups, or as retaliation attacks for previous episodes of conflict linked to the country's troubled political history. As a consequence, in Coo-Pee, as in many other places across Acholiland, men were arrested, tortured, and killed in large numbers. Therefore, during that time, some men were physically

FIGURE 2. Coo-Pee.

absent from Coo-Pee. Other men remained in the village but were considered spiritually, symbolically, and psychologically not to be there. Confronted with the hardships of conflict and contextualized in a continuum of severe discrepancies between socially constructed and homogenized expectations and heterogeneous phenomenological lived realities, some of these men did not perform in their socially conditioned masculine roles and were thus displaced from their gender identities. At the same time, various other men were considered not to be there because they were "turned into women" as a result of having been raped by government soldiers, which was thought to have heavily impacted their masculinities and to displace them from their gendered personhood.

Kenneth, my research collaborator, and I regularly passed through Coo-Pee on our numerous trips to other villages in the surrounding areas, many of which were heavily affected by tek-gungu cases (see chapter 3). However, I learned about the apparent interpretation of the name as described here only during the latter part of my fieldwork. During an interview with a male elder in another village in Bungatira sub-county while writing down the name *Coo-Pee* in my notebook, I noticed the translation of the name and asked about its meaning and origin. Both Kenneth and the elder explained that it means "that men were thought not to be there, because of this thing of tek-gungu." On our journey back to Gulu, Kenneth elaborated in more detail the meaning of the name and his interpretation of it, reflective of the narrative offered above.

A few days later, Kenneth and I embarked on yet another trip that once again led us through Coo-Pee. Soon after we departed from Gulu town, it began to rain heavily, and due to the quickly worsening road conditions caused by the heavy downpour, we decided to seek shelter under the protective crown of one of the many large mango trees covering the road, just a few miles outside of Coo-Pee. A male elder on his bicycle followed our lead, and we began to talk— about football, the elections a few months earlier, and Ugandan politics in general—while sharing a few sweet and juicy mangoes from the trees protecting us. As it turned out, the *Mzee* was from Coo-Pee and without yet having told him about my research, I asked him about his interpretation of the meaning of the village's name. He elaborated:

> Coo-Pee has been known like this among the local people since a long time already. It is even the official name now. But as far as I know, it is nowadays called like this among the people, even from town, because when the Lakwena [referring to the rebels] conflict started, and the NRA mobile units were active in this place, many men were arrested, tortured, and killed, and they used the three-pieces method.[1] Many other men were made to suffer like women because [the soldiers] would even rape them, and so they were not seen as men anymore. That is why people now say Coo-Pee is the place where men are not there.

Identical versions of this story have thereafter been repeated to me, by others in Coo-Pee and Gulu town alike and independent from each other, even though I have heard at least one alternative explanation linked to the contemporary context. According to this alternative explanation, Coo-Pee would be short for *Coo mono pe kwene?*, which can translate as "Where do you think the men are" or "Do you think the men are not here?," which was subsequently shortened into Coo-Pee. According to this version of the meaning of the name, in the mid 1990s men in the village formed a local defense unit to protect themselves from increasing rebel attacks, as communities all over Acholiland did, which the community here provocatively called *Coo mono pe kwene?*, later on shortened into Coo-Pee.

This variety of possible explanations goes to show that there most probably is not one singular interpretation of the name, but that its meaning might be subjective as well as shaped by recent sociopolitical events. According to the apparently more common interpretation, however, which I am adapting here, the example of Coo-Pee illuminates the many ways in which Acholi men were impacted during the conflict while also illustrating how socially constructed expectations surrounding masculinities can render men vulnerable. The case furthermore exemplifies that sexual violence against men in this local context is predominantly experienced, theorized, and perceived as compromising male victims' gendered identities.

CONCEPTUALIZING MASCULINITIES

An important theoretical premise for my argument is that processes of (perceived) gender subordination are highly contextual in nature and must therefore be positioned in relation to local and temporally contingent constructions of gender. Any attempt to understand what it means to be considered "less of a man" thus needs to be firmly rooted in a prior conceptual and empirical understanding of what it means to be a man in the sociocultural context in the first place. Before conceptualizing locally contingent constructions of Acholi masculinities further below, I begin more broadly by reflecting on the multiplicities and contingencies of masculinities across time and space, particularly focusing on inherent hierarchical power structures and hegemonic forms of masculinity, which ultimately fuel unequal gender relations.

In more general terms, masculinities are socially constructed gender norms that refer to "anything which is associated with being a man in any given culture. Interpretations of what is considered to be masculine, and what constitutes being a man, vary across time and space, as well as between and within cultures" (Wright 2014: 4). The groundbreaking work by R. W. Connell (1995, 2005) provides particularly useful and applicable theoretical frameworks for conceptualizing the inherent power relations within and between masculinities and gender hierarchies more widely as well as for understanding the multiplicities and variations of masculinities, which encourage us to speak of masculinities in plural. Important historical and anthropological works similarly lay open the vast geographical and cultural differences across and between various masculinities conceptions and expectations (Gilmore 1990; Ratele 2007). Some key developments of masculinities theorizing hence arguably include the realization that masculinity is not unitary, and that different forms of masculinities exist across time, place, and space, marked by clear power differences and hierarchies.

Masculinities are also dynamic and imply the capacity to evolve over time and within spaces. Masculine gender constructions are therefore far from being universally applicable or static, but vary across and within cultures and contexts. Gilmore's (1990) extensive ethnographic collection of cultural concepts of manhood across a variety of settings evidences that masculinities are characterized by spatial and geographical contingencies. In particular historians and anthropologists have convincingly demonstrated that what it means to be a man and to perform and embody masculinities varies over time, context, and culture, and most often even within spaces. It is therefore necessary to acknowledge that "masculinities are configurations of practice that are accomplished in social action, and therefore, can differ according to gender relations in a particular social setting" (Porter, A. 2013: 488). Masculinities must thus be understood in comparative and regional terms.

Hierarchies of Manhood: Hegemonic Masculinity

In addition to these spatial, temporal, and cultural contingencies, significant power differences between and within gender relations in general and within masculinities constructions exist, and not all forms of masculinities are valued equally.[2] Within these multiple versions of manhood, some interpretations of being a man are prized as being more valuable to aspire to than others. The conception of manhood that appears as culturally dominant is labeled as hegemonic masculinity, in relation to which various subordinate and subversive notions of manhood exist (Connell 1995; Kronsel 2005). Masculinities are therefore relational within and among themselves, as well as in relation to the gender order as a whole. Gender scholars in fact emphasize that masculinities cannot exist but in contrast to femininities.[3] As stated by Michael Kimmel, an influential sociologist focused on men and masculinities, the "masculine identity is born in the renunciation of the feminine" (Kimmel 1996: 63). In his incredibly insightful investigation of military masculinity in the US military, sociologist Aaron Belkin takes this juxtaposition forward by further specifying that in almost all contexts globally, the ideal of masculinity "depends on a disavowing practices which position masculinity in opposition to its unmasculine foils: weakness, subordination, queerness, and so on" (2012: 26). Gender constructions in general, including masculinities conceptions, furthermore relate to and intersect with other social characteristics, such as class, race, sexual orientation, and age.

Within these relations and in most societal contexts globally, the hegemonic model of masculinity is seen as "an expression of the privilege men collectively have over women" (Connell 2002: 15) as well as over less powerful men and certainly over sexual and gender minorities. In this reading, hegemonic masculinities stand at the top of the gender hierarchy, above other complicit, subordinated, and marginalized masculinities, and certainly above femininities, let alone gender nonconforming, trans, or queer identities. The theoretical frame of hegemonic masculinity is therefore important in dealing with relational and power aspects of masculinities and gender. At the same time, and although culturally dominant and most aspired to, the hegemonic form of manhood does not necessarily need to be, and rarely is, the most common form of masculinity. In light of these assessments and observations, South African masculinities scholar Kopano Ratele (2014) has advocated for "marginality within hegemony" as an important prism and framework for advancing a critical understanding of the hierarchies of masculinities, with particular application to the diverse interpretations of manhood in a sub-Saharan African context. As summarized by Isaac Dery, Ratele's approach effectively argues that "any intervention that seeks to progressively approach and study African boys and men ought to be alert to the complex interplay between dominant notions of masculinity and political, economic, and social realities that circumscribe the daily life of men and boys in a deeply classed society" (Dery 2019: 175).

Just as masculinities in general develop and alter over time, the particular nature and characteristics of hegemonic masculinities change too. When ideas of hegemonic masculinities change over time, so too must the attributes and behaviors to achieve such hegemony adapt. In this vein, Myrttinen et al. reiterate (2016: 5) that "what counts as hegemonic is not fixed but is constantly subject to contestation and alteration." This potential for hegemonic ideas of masculinities to evolve can be particularly pronounced in postconflict contexts and in times of transition, for instance from war to peace, due to the variety of potential external influences and the often radically changing nature of society. At the same time, the forms of hegemonic masculinity, including their attributes and traits, are often aspired to but less frequently actually realized, therefore suggesting a discrepancy between masculine ideals and the daily lived realities of most men, especially during great economic, political, and social upheaval. Widespread violence, militarization, and displacement make it almost impossible for most men to realize a hegemonic state of masculinity (Dolan 2002), which nevertheless prevails, and which most men are socialized to aspire to. These discrepancies expose a seeming paradox between strongly pronounced and homogenous expectations vis-à-vis heterogeneous lived realities.

Critical Perspectives on Hegemonic Masculinity

While the concept of hegemonic masculinity has "influenced gender studies across many academic fields" (Connell and Messerschmidt 2005: 829) and is utilized by most existing masculinities scholarship, various scholars have nevertheless articulated a number of critiques, highlighting different shortcomings of the concept and especially its applicability.[4] Most critiques in the literature seem to refer to the application of the hegemonic masculinity frame in a globalized world (Morrell et al. 2012), or relate to conflating notions of hegemonic masculinity with narrow understandings of the concept, rather than to Connell's concept directly.[5]

Firstly, critical scholarship has evidenced prevailing conceptual and analytical gaps associated with the hegemonic masculinity frame and its Western-centric conceptions of manhood, especially "as the term goes global" (Beasley 2008: 91) and is increasingly employed in non-Western and conflict-affected settings. Hollander (2014: 417) proclaims that "Connell's classification of masculinities is inadequate for the analysis of clear crisis situations," losing "some of its analytical value in situations of extreme distress" (419). According to Hollander, Connell's theorization of hegemonic, complicit, subordinate, and marginalized masculinities furthermore "inadequately captures the complexities of situations of enduring crisis" (ibid.). Hollander therefore argues that new subcategories of manhood conceptions need to be added. In concert with this critique, Myrttinen et al. (2016) similarly emphasize that particularly in conflict-affected contexts, the notion of hegemonic masculinities "needs to be re-examined and re-articulated in more nuanced ways' (103). In recent years, a growing body of scholarship on non-Western, and often African, conceptions of masculinities has uncovered these context-specific differences and particularities of the positioning of hegemonic masculinities within hierarchies of manhood and gender (Ouzgane and Morrell 2005; Ratele 2014).

I agree that indeed caution is required not to uncritically and universally apply Connell's framework, particularly because it was developed in Western peacetime contexts and is based upon the lived realities of mostly white, Western (and economically relatively well-off) men. I therefore concur with Hollander (2014) that Connell's framework *may* under certain circumstances be inapplicable to *some* situations of crisis, extreme distress, and conflict. At the same time, however, the concept may prove to be applicable in other situations if qualified and applied with sensitivity to the context (Morrell, Jewkes, and Lindegger 2012). Depending on the circumstances, the hegemonic masculinity frame might be even more stratified in non-Western and conflict-affected settings. The mixture of repressive and patriarchal gender orders, combined with insecurity and armed conflict, can in some contexts imply that "the possibility of multiple, parallel and equivalent masculinities collapses" (Dolan 2011: 127), which in turn can cement new and contextually relevant notions of hegemonic masculinity. There is indeed evidence to suggest that this seems to be the case in northern Uganda, as I seek to demonstrate further below. In other words, Connell's classification cannot necessarily be applied wholesale to all (conflict) situations across the globe, but may be applicable in certain conflict settings, depending on contextual and circumstantial factors.

Secondly, although the concept of hegemonic masculinity is intended to highlight which forms of masculinities take on a dominant character at any given time and place, the concept is frequently misused to simplistically foreground "negative 'types' of violent and/or militarized masculinities" (Myrttinen et al. 2016: 107). This severely undermines the concept's applicability and utility. Indeed, the frame of hegemonic masculinity is often used imprecisely with regard to conflict-affected situations, thus often reproducing a false premise assuming that violent, military, and hypermasculinities are hegemonic. This misleading association results in a false conflation of hegemony with violence and militarization, often presenting the relationship between violence and masculinities as natural. Most scholarship therefore focuses on men's violence, leaving out nonviolent masculinities and the men and boys embodying such nonviolent masculinities. Connell (1995) clarifies, however, that it is "the successful claim to authority, more than direct violence that is the mark of hegemony" (77). Violence and militarization thus do not ubiquitously qualify as hegemony in any given context. With my examination of the model of normative hegemonic masculinity in Acholiland below, I likewise show that in this particular social and cultural context, hegemony in relation to manhood does not necessitate violence but is instead centered around other attributes and behaviors, including most importantly the ability to protect, provide, and procreate.

ACHOLI GENDER IDENTITIES

Drawing on these overall theoretical reflections regarding masculinities constructions across time and space, I now proceed to provide "thick descriptions" of Acholi gender identities and (hegemonic) masculinities, positioned in relation to contextual gender relations and constructions more broadly. I argue that despite some of the more general critique regarding the adaptability and utility of the concept, as articulated above, a model of normative hegemonic masculinity prevails in northern Uganda to which the majority of men are taught to aspire. The ideal of Acholi hegemonic masculinity is primarily characterized by men's responsibilities to protect and provide for their families and is centered around notions of heteronormativity, patrilocality and patrilineality. Even though significant variations exist between different conceptions of manhood in northern Uganda—defined by class, ethnicity, socioeconomic background, and locality (urban versus rural)—and despite sociopolitical developments over time, influenced by among others colonialism, modernization, and armed conflicts, one dominant ideal of civilian Acholi manhood continues to prevail. This form of hegemonic masculinity stands at the top of the hierarchical gender order, which in its hetero-patriarchal manifestation is inherently unequal, implying clear benefits and advantages for men aspiring to a sense of hegemonic masculinity vis-à-vis other subordinated men and, of course, women.

Dolan's influential work on this topic evidences the prevalence of common denominators of hegemonic ideals of manhood for Acholi men, setting clear parameters for what it means to be (or considered to be) masculine in a hegemonic manifestation in the northern Ugandan context. Further building on this, Rebecca Tapscott in her insightful work on the contrast between civilian and militarized masculinities in Uganda likewise identifies commonalities of "ideal types" of Acholi manhood. The majority of Acholi men are socialized into this model and judged and evaluated against it, by themselves, their families, and their communities as well as by the state and wider society. Especially during conflict, however, "the possibility of multiple parallel and equivalent masculinities collapse[d]" (Dolan 2002: 127), with a hegemonic form of masculinity manifesting itself above a ladder of lesser-valued masculinities. This empirical observation indeed suggests that the analytical and theoretical frame of hegemonic masculinity, although developed outside the context of violence and war and based upon Western men and masculinities, might be even more stratified and pronounced in non-Western and conflict-affected settings, as theorized above. Although Acholi gender constructions and understandings of masculinities are nonstatic and developed over time, among others shaped by colonialism, modernization, and militarization, as well as partly differ between rural and urban settings, this hegemonic conception of masculinity largely remains intact in the contemporary context. This status quo considerably fuels growing discrepancies between homogenized expectations and heterogeneous lived realities.

Gender Relations in Acholiland

Comparable to other societies in East Africa and sub-Saharan Africa, conceptions of manhood in northern Uganda must be situated within wider heteronormative, patriarchal, patrilineal, and patrilocal gender orders. These relationships are structured by clear gendered power relations among and across multiple gender identities, with a hegemonic masculinity model at the top of the hierarchy. These relations are especially pronounced between masculinities and femininities, resulting in vast gendered inequalities.

Acholi gender identities and related conceptions of manhood also need to be situated in wider social relations, which in turn depend on contextual constructs of personhood. Building on Acholi poet-scholar Okot p'Bitek (1986), Baines and Rosenoff-Gauvin (2014) emphasize that "conceptual categories of personhood and sociality, while fluid, necessarily impact human practice and social organization through time" (286). In the case of Acholi identity, such personhood and sociality is relational and rests upon social collectivism and communal structuring. In essence, an individual's existence and humanity emerge from their connections to others (p'Bitek 1986: 19–20). Okot p'Bitek writes that one can only answer the question of "Who am I?" about self and identity by first understanding the relationships in question (p'Chong 2000: 85; Baines and Rosenoff-Gauvin 2014: 286).

These relational and collective constructions of personhood are captured by the Acholi cultural concepts of *dano adana* and *bedo dano*. As contextualized by various informants, these cultural concepts imply that a singular person can only exist in relation to a community of people, while at the same time also dictating certain forms of normative behavior. In addition to the relational and communal aspect of society, the concept of *dano adana* specifically also refers to "a real human being" who knows his or her duties, including with regard to gender roles, identities, behaviors, and expectations. In Acholi language and within the context of these concepts, *bedo* refers to "being" or "to be," while *dano* circumstantially refers to a person in singular or people in plural. *Bedo dano* thus refers to the ways of being a person, or of constructing personhood. Anthropologists Sverker Finnström (2008) and Holly Porter (2017) both respectively discuss and apply these ideals of personhood to the Acholi idioms of *piny maber*—or "good surroundings' in Finnström's case, and "good existence" in Porter's case—referring to what it means to be human and to be in relationship with one another. Ultimately these concepts emphasize the cultural centrality of subjectivities and personhood constructions in the Acholi context, which in turn are central to my conceptual framework of "displacement from gendered personhood," as offered in the introduction, for understanding the effects of violence on gender identities.

Holly Porter's (2017) insightful discussion of "good existence" in the context of Acholi personhood, subjectivities, and relationalities also explicitly incorporates a gender focus, relating to ideal types of manhood and womanhood that make up and shape personhood and subjectivities. What it means to be a (good) person or a "real human being" (dano adana) for Acholi women and men respectively therefore shapes how femininities and masculinities are defined. A cultural leader representing the Acholi cultural institution Ker Kwaro Acholi (KKA) explained to me that "what it means to be a good person, *dano adana*, for a woman and for a man in Acholi influences how femininities and masculinities are constructed." Deriving from these conceptual and empirical observations, it appears that one dictated or hegemonic premise of being a good person in Acholi society prevails for women and men respectively. Such constructions and expectations of gendered personhood thereby result in normative hegemonic models of gender identities in general, including of masculinities, which (at least in part) impede the emergence of alternative constructions.

Acholi Femininities

Various gender scholars emphasize that masculinities cannot exist but in contrast with femininities. Therefore, to conceptualize Acholi masculinities, a prior relational understanding of "what women are (supposed to be) like" (Dolan 2009: 192) in northern Uganda proves necessary. In many ways, external influences in Acholiland, including colonization, the armed conflict, and globalization have shaped how Acholi womanhood is constructed. Acholi femininities are therefore dynamic and manifold and differences exist, among others, between classes or urban and rural settings. Nevertheless, despite these variations, a hegemonic premise of "being a woman" appears to dominate both the traditional as well as the contemporary context.

In Acholiland's patriarchal, heteronormative, and patrilocal society, a widely held assumption prevails that women differ from men in that they are "weaker, incapable and a burden" (Dolan 2009: 61). Across historical and contemporary Acholiland, it is relatively widely believed "that women cannot perform to the level of men, and must conform to the culture of their husbands" (Dolan 2009: 192). Indeed, through marriage and once the full bride-wealth has been paid via an elaborate *cuna* process, the woman is expected to leave her parental family and move to the husband's home, "where she is considered the subordinate and the property/asset of the husband" (Dolan 2009: 193), evidencing the patrilineal and patrilocal character of Acholi society.[6] Following the bride-wealth payment, the man's lineage agrees to politically and legally include the woman into their family or lineage and to properly provide for her (e.g., through the provision of land, a kitchen hut, granaries) (Porter 2016).

In Acholi language, the word for woman, *dako,* is closely linked to the verb *dak,* which loosely translates as "to migrate," reflecting the relationalities between men and women, the movement character defining Acholi gender relations and the expectation that women will migrate to their husbands' homes. Movement indeed quite clearly defines feminine identity constructions: In Acholi culture, women are expected to move, or to migrate, from their paternal home to their husbands' compound (and in the case of separation or divorce, back into their paternal home). Once a woman marries, she de facto loses her own clan identity, without fully assuming or inheriting her new husband's clan identity either, further evidencing the patriarchal and patrilocal system.

Acholi femininities are furthermore closely linked to motherhood and marriage. Baines and Rosenoff-Gauvin (2014) emphasize that a woman's "process of 'becoming a person' is assumed through the birth of children within a formalized marriage" and that a "woman's status as mother, therefore, defines her social role in her (adopted) home village" (288–289). Motherhood can thus be seen as embodying the Acholi female dano adana: the attainment of gendered personhood. In addition to motherhood, female personhood is furthermore defined by caretaking responsibilities and feminized activities designated for women, such as cooking, cleaning, and the day-to-day management of the family compound. Characteristic of patriarchal gender orders, women are therefore reduced to the private sphere, while men occupy and dominate public spaces, setting the political, social, and cultural parameters for the social order while simultaneously asserting male dominance.

Acholi (Hegemonic) Masculinities

The dominant notion of manhood in northern Uganda rests upon and constitutes a *normative hegemonic* model of masculinity. This social construction is hegemonic in that it prevents alternative forms of masculinities from emerging, while also being underpinned and sustained by significant forms of societal and political power. At the same time, the model qualifies as normative in that men (and women) are socialized into it. Society at large is taught that men should strive to achieve these defining components of masculinity. Not only men themselves, but also their families, communities, the state, and wider society judge, evaluate, and assess men's behavior and performance against this framework of hegemonic masculinity (see Dolan 2009). According to this normative hegemonic model of Acholi masculinity, men are expected to protect themselves, their families, and homesteads, provide for their families, and procreate.

Among a variety of factors, the recent LRA conflict (and related postconflict dynamics) in northern Uganda contributed toward manifesting this hegemonic model, preventing alternative forms of masculinities to emerge. In this capacity, Acholi hegemonic masculinity constructions also constitute a political construct and weapon at the disposal of national political forces (Tapscott 2018), the state, the military, and churches in Uganda. As argued by Dolan, "The Ugandan state severely aggravated the collapse of potential multiple masculinities through its simultaneous practices of militarization and forcible internal displacement" (2009: 128). Christian churches, and in particular the Catholic Church, further cemented this hegemonic ideal of manhood by holding it static and enforcing associated stereotypical assumptions about gender roles and relations in Uganda (see Alava 2016).

Colonial influences, Christianization, and globalization have also influenced Acholi gender identities in general, including how masculinities are constructed and related expectations placed on men. For instance, the colonization of the region, and with it the growing influence of Christianity, significantly shaped how young men and boys were socialized into manhood and adulthood. Traditionally and historically, informal education and socialization—primarily for boys, who are considered smarter and brighter than girls and who are given better access to education—were provided by male elders in the community. Through the rise of the formalized education system accompanying colonization, however, this largely changed. Culturally, male elders' roles included educating their sons, but when schools take over this role, this can be seen as "under[mining] the masculinity of adult fathers" (Dolan 2009: 198). In relation to formal and informal education, it is interesting to note that formalized education was by no means universally considered positive. Dolan's influential work demonstrates that some traditional and cultural authorities and male elders initially viewed formalized education as undermining informal and traditional socialization, thereby contributing to a process of cultural dilution. In a context where culture and education are greatly intertwined, "the rise of the formal education model made it difficult if not impossible for a boy to become a man" (Dolan 2009: 198). Such views are metaphorically reflected in the cultural writings of Acholi artist and academic Okot p'Bitek, and in particular by this poem from 1985:

> For all young men
> Were finished in the forest,
> Their manhood was finished / in the class-rooms
> Their testicles / Wer' smashed
> With large books!

Constructions of Acholi masculinity must also be positioned in relation to a mixture of precolonial, colonial, and postcolonial influences that resulted in what can broadly be referred to as a hybrid-hegemonic form of normative masculinity. Comparable to, for instance, developments in the eastern DRC, the influence of colonization in northern Uganda did not necessarily result in the holistic collapse of indigenous gender orders, but rather "induced a hybridity between traditional and modern notions of hegemonic masculinity" (Hollander 2014: 421).

Africanist gender theorists and ethnographers have previously observed colo-nizers' attempts to shape gender identities.[7] Throughout most of colonized sub-Saharan Africa, colonial administrators endeavored to construct an African masculinity that remained subordinate and colonized to the imperialists' and colonialists' notions of manhood. Dolan (2009) similarly notes that in construct-ing contextual masculinities, "it is important to pay due heed to the undermining of men's sense of self in the colonial period" (128) by the imperial administration. At the same time, the growing influence of Christianity and especially the Catholic Church—a by-product of colonialism and in itself intensely male-centric and patriarchal—furthermore entrenched heteronormative patriarchy in Acholi soci-ety, rooted in a hegemonic model of masculinity. Drawing on empirical research on the role of religion in Kitgum, Alava (2016) concludes that the heteronormative and patriarchal gender order of the Catholic tradition "found a fertile ground in customary Acholi gender notions" (45).

In light of these external influences and dynamics, a common set of respon-sibilities and roles dominates not only historical constructions of manhood in northern Uganda but also current idea(l)s and expectation, thus construct-ing the model of Acholi normative hegemonic masculinity in the contemporary context. This model of hegemonic masculinity originates from constructions of sociality and personhood, dictating a male dano adana, for a masculine gen-dered personhood.

If masculinities are defined in contrast with femininities, then it logically fol-lows that men in northern Uganda are "supposed to be richer, stronger, more capa-ble, knowledgeable and skilled [and] trustworthy" (Dolan 2009: 194) than women. As is characteristic for patriarchal societies in general, men enjoy clear benefits in various dimensions of social life, including access to land and education, and men and boys are generally regarded as brighter and better in most aspects when compared to girls, representing and reproducing gender inequalities. Being a man also entails being responsible, patient, moderate, respectful, serious, and effective, but also reproductive and sexually active, among others.

Constructions of masculinities and the hierarchical gender order as a whole are furthermore naturalized through social practice. Ethnographic research by Finnström (2009), for instance, demonstrates that according to Acholi sociality, "men are more able to resist," while "women are weak" (64). Finnström illustrates this by referring to funerals, "in which women are allowed to cry and publicly express their agony while men are discouraged from doing so" (ibid.). My own observations confirm these gendered behavioral patterns: At the funeral of my friend's sister, mourning female relatives of the deceased cried intensely at the grave, while my male friend and other male relatives made sure not to display any emotions in public. "I have to remain strong and cope like a man," my friend said, while obviously struggling to withhold tears and control his emotions for the sake of remaining, or rather appearing, masculine.

Male elders on the community level furthermore repeatedly emphasized that "men must be strong, wise, knowledgeable, and respected, and they must provide and protect for their families." This observation is echoed by the assessment of a male cultural leader who confirmed that "the cardinal roles and responsibilities of men in Acholi are to provide and to protect and defend the family." While a whole variety of external factors and influences arguably influenced the means to provide and protect, which further differ between urban and rural localities, the responsibilities for men to do so prevailed over time and remain intact today. In addition to protecting and defending their families and wider communities, Acholi men are also specifically expected to provide protection for the family's homestead, which is the center of Acholi cosmology and therefore supposed to be impenetrable, private, and secure. In this capacity, men are primarily expected to ensure physical protection, from violence, attacks, and armed robberies.

The primary social requirements for achieving hegemonic masculinity are therefore the provision for and physical protection of the household, following the attainment of some level of financial independence, wealth, and preferably employment, coupled with marriage and starting a family (p'Bitek 1986; Porter 2017). As explained by one of my interlocutors, in Acholi, "The accumulation of wealth is the central epitome of manhood," as it allows men to provide materially and economically for their family and to offer physical protection. "Accumulating wealth constitutes an integral step toward achieving and fulfilling your responsibilities and duties as a man." These defining characteristics of Acholi manhood correspond with constructions of masculinities on the African continent more widely. African gender theorists have outlined how self-sufficiency, financial independence, and familial provision and protection are paramount characteristics for and among the most consistent measures of sub-Saharan African masculinities (Baker and Ricardo 2005; Ouzgane and Morrell 2005).

Acholi manhood is also constructed in contrast with youth, and an integral component of being a man is marriage. The full achievement of masculinity is "impossible without making the transition to adulthood by way of marriage and thereby making the difference between youth and adults" (Dolan 2009: 196). In fact, merely being a provider is insufficient for the comprehensive realization of hegemonic masculinity: "a man has to be a *married* provider" (ibid.), preferably formalized with children. During my fieldwork period various friends and colleagues often jokingly yet somewhat critically remarked that even though I was able to provide for myself, I was not yet considered a real man because I was not yet married nor did I have children. When in April 2017 I phoned one of my close friends and research collaborators to share with him the happy news of the birth of our daughter, and then later of our marriage, he seemed relieved: "You are a real man now—congratulations."

An Acholi proverb, captured in the writings of Okot p'Bitek (1985), colorfully illustrates this interdependence between marriage and masculinity: *Labot kilwongo ka dek wi kot*—"A bachelor is called to a meal in the rain." According to p'Bitek (1985: 7), this particular proverb "reflects the attitude of the Acholi towards unmarried young men." p'Bitek explains that "to be seen running through the rain to go for a meal was considered undignified. But since unmarried men lived in the boys' hut, *otogo*, they had to go for their meals wherever they were prepared" (ibid.). Unmarried men, the proverb asserts, are not yet considered to be real men in the hegemonic and normative sense.

During the conflict in northern Uganda, however, men were confronted with substantial challenges that hindered their paths toward marriage and thus manhood. The conflict made it almost impossible for young men to become financially secure enough to marry. Dolan (2009: 199) observes that "the economic basis of the hegemonic combination of marriage and the subsequent provision and protection of the household was substantially worsened by the war." In particular, the large-scale forced displacement of up to 95 percent of the Acholi population into IDP camps, characterized by a considerable lack of income-generating and agricultural opportunities, significantly constrained men's capacity to accumulate wealth and thus afford marriage. Neither Dolan (2009) nor Finnström (2008), who both have conducted extensive research in northern Uganda since the late 1990s, witnessed or came across even a single wedding inside the protected villages.

This inability to marry during the conflict heavily affected the ability of men to achieve the defining requirements of adulthood and manhood, and thus negatively impacted their masculine identities. Masculinities constructions and associated expectations, however, did not rigorously change as a result of these impediments to marriage, and during the conflict as well as in the current postconflict phase, marriage remains closely connected to hegemonic Acholi masculinity. Although there is a lack of systematic research on the rates and frequency of weddings in the postconflict setting, my own observations seem to suggest that in the contemporary context, more than ten years after the war, wedding rates have increased significantly. While working in northern Uganda between 2011 and 2012, I attended four weddings. During my research in 2016, I attended three, was invited to several more, and heard of countless more weddings taking place across the subregion, including both traditional and religious ceremonies (see Alava 2016).

Comparable to constructions of manhood elsewhere globally, notions of Acholi masculinity are furthermore shaped and enacted by heterosexuality and sex. Based on ethnographic research in Acholiland, Porter (2013) notes that "sexual relationships with women [are] a medium by which [men] establish and perform their own masculinity in relation to their peers" (183). Porter further observes that sex "is an enactment of gender relationships and what it means to be a man or to be a woman through social practice" (ibid.: 184). The centrality of sex and reproduction to Acholi relationships and specifically to love and intimacy is furthermore reflected in Okot p'Bitek's essay "Acholi Love" (1964). Sex thereby plays an important role in men's relationships not only to their female partners but also to each other, and among themselves men frequently speak about heterosexual relations. Porter describes that one of her male respondents estimated that sex "was usually about 90 percent of what he and other Acholi men talk about when they get together" (2013: 183). My own observations and interactions with male Acholi colleagues and friends mirror Porter's assessment regarding the centrality of sex and sexuality in embodying and enacting masculinity in relation to male peers, often through sex being the primary topic of conversation. Interestingly, however, at least in my company, men seldom spoke about sex with their wives but more often about sex with their numerous "girlfriends" or "side-dishes," how casual female sexual partners were often referred to. Overall, masculinity is thus shaped by foregrounding and highlighting one's heterosexuality and sexual virility—often in relation to others.

Throughout much of the gender studies literature, hegemony in relation to manhood is also often falsely equated with physical violence, and Acholi masculinity in particular is frequently portrayed to be inherently violent, both within Ugandan society and throughout the literature. Esuruku (2011) for instance classifies "risk-taking, physical toughness, aggression and violence" (26) as defining elements and ingredients of hegemonic masculinity in the Acholi context. Such portrayals, however, are in part based upon and simultaneously responsible for ethnocentrism and stereotypical portrayals of Acholi men as warriors and war prone. These misleading portrayals sit uneasily with Acholi men's self-identifications and perceptions (Dolan 2009) and are influenced by colonial and postcolonial policies of playing out the country's regions against each other—as detailed in the previous chapter. Even though providing physical protection occupies a prime role in the construction of Acholi manhood, the use of violence is in fact not a defining element of the model of hegemonic Acholi masculinity.

As reflected upon earlier, across time and space "hegemony does not necessarily require violence," and "the use of physical violence is often not viewed societally as a hallmark of respectable or hegemonic masculinity" (Myrttinen et al. 2016: 108). Mirroring observations from other cases, in the civilian Acholi context, being a member of the military or a military-like institution or behaving particularly violently is not necessarily the most hegemonic, nor the most accepted or respected, form of masculinity. Violent men, and especially soldiers and combatants, are often equated with lower levels of education and thus in some ways occupy subordinate masculinities. At the same time, members of different vigilante groups are comparatively poorly remunerated (Tapscott 2018) and frequently not paid for months, thus often lacking the financial means to provide for their families in a hegemonic sense. In contrast, bureaucrats, businessmen, and staff and representatives of international organizations, for instance, are seen as the epitome of the ability to provide financially and materially for (and thus also to ensure the protection of) one's family, thereby striving for hegemony.

To an extent the contemporary and customary homogenized expectation of masculinity thus stands in stark contrast to the heterogeneity and vast diversity of most men's gendered lived realities. Comparable to many developing and post-conflict contexts globally, the hegemonic aspirations of manhood are extremely difficult to attain in conflict-ridden northern Uganda, conditioned by a variety of internal and external factors, including most prominently the more than two decades of armed conflict. Dolan (2002) argues that "in the northern Ugandan context of . . . war, heavy militarization and internal displacement, it [was] very difficult if not impossible for the vast majority of men to fulfill the expectations of husband and father, provider and protector which are contained in the model of hegemonic masculinity" (64).

Noncombatant civilian men (constituting the overwhelming majority of men in northern Uganda) faced extensive difficulties, which left them unable to achieve "some of the key elements [of] the normative model of masculinity into which they have been socialized" (Dolan 2002: 67). At the same time, during the conflict and in the contemporary context, economic constraints prevented many families, as headed by men in a patriarchal domain, to pay school fees and therefore for their children to receive an education, and boys were thus confronted with difficulties in living up to societal expectations of being educated in order to become a man. On a more structural level, the increased militarization of the region in the context of war also meant that there were very few secondary schools available in rural areas and outside the district capitals.

Among a variety of conflict-related factors, in particular the forced displacement of up to 95 percent of the Acholi population into internally displaced persons camps at the height of the conflict furthermore "contributed to a loss of social control" (Baines and Rosenoff-Gauvin 2014: 289). Constituting a form of enforced infantilization, the conditions of the camps installed significant barriers for men to live up to socially constructed expectations surrounding masculinities, and effectively incapacitated men in their masculine roles and responsibilities. Severely limited income-generating and agricultural opportunities largely rendered men unable to provide. Instead, women often became the primary breadwinners of their families, both through greater access to food aid and camp regulations that at times allowed women to maintain small gardens surrounding the camps. At least in some camps, some women (in certain age segments) were allowed to leave the camp during curfew hours and to cultivate their fields and gardens, and were thus able to provide at least some food.

According to some respondents, only women were allowed to leave the camp because they were erroneously deemed to be at lesser risk of abduction or violent attacks by the rebels than men. Evidence shows, however, that young girls were also abducted in large numbers and frequently exposed to sexual violations (Okello and Hovil 2007; Okot, Amony, and Otim 2005). Men's social responsibilities to protect were also largely (yet unsuccessfully) taken over by the state, and the army specifically. In the IDP camps, therefore, temporarily "men became women and women became men" (Hollander 2014: 420; Lwambo 2013). Nevertheless, and despite this overall inability of the majority of men to live up to the hegemonic notions of Acholi masculinity, the most important and prevalent expectations regarding this model—that is, men's abilities to protect and provide and to remain strong and invulnerable—are applicable in the contemporary context.

DECONSTRUCTING MALE SURVIVORS' HARMS

These contextual reflections on Acholi hegemonic masculinity constructions were necessary because any attempt to understand the impact of violence on manhood must be firmly rooted in a prior understanding of what it means to be a man in each socio-cultural context in the first place. Therefore, and building on these theoretical and contextual reflections, I now proceed with the analysis by unpacking Acholi male survivors' sexual and gendered harms.[8] I specifically argue that the impact of male-directed sexual violence is characterized as a process, rather than a singular event as it is most commonly treated in the literature.

This process begins with perceived gendered subordination through acts of penetrative rape but is further manifested and cemented through a variety of gendered harms extending far into the postviolation period. Throughout the expanding literature on sexual violence against men, the impact of these crimes is frequently theorized as compromising survivors' masculine identities, which in turn is most often linked to perceived gendered subordination as the result of penetrative rape. In the literature these processes are frequently labeled as "emasculation" by way of "feminization" and/or "homosexualization." Yet, despite initial conceptual insights, how exactly the compromising of masculinities unfolds empirically remains only poorly understood, both in general terms and context-specifically in northern Uganda. At the same time, scholarship has not yet sufficiently scrutinized the conceptual categories and associated terminologies of "emasculation" and "feminization," which imply analytical and normative limitations and ultimately do not do justice to survivors' dynamic lived realities. Recalling my critique regarding the emasculation-feminization-homosexualization conceptualization and terminology offered in the introduction, I therefore instead think of and refer to these processes as forms of "displacement from gendered personhood."

In essence, I seek to demonstrate that within a heteronormative and heterosexual context such as northern Uganda, male-directed sexual violence in general, and penetrative anal rape in particular, is considered as subordinating male survivors within a gendered hierarchy. During a focus group discussion, various respondents, for instance, stated that "men were sodomized, and therefore they are now seen as women because they are powerless and have been slept with." A former service provider explained that "the process of male victims losing their manhood has to do with them being subordinated through the penetration. Only women are supposed to be penetrated, so if a man is raped he becomes like a woman." Within the Acholi cultural context and according to corresponding constructions of gender and sexuality, men are expected to actively penetrate and women to be passively penetrated. If a man is forcefully penetrated, however, he involuntarily assumes a female sexual role or character and is therefore rendered feminine, and thus subordinate in the gender order. To reiterate Sjoberg's argumentation (2016: 39), "Gender subordination is fundamentally a power relationship in which those perceived as female/feminine are made less powerful than those perceived as masculine/male. This power relationship extends through the perceived possession of gendered traits and the gendering of perceived behaviors and actions."

Applying this to the context of male rape in Acholiland, a key informant explained that "through penetration, you subordinate the man. Male victims are helpless and give in to other men and are being subordinated through penetration."

Crimes of sexual violence thus communicate a power and dominance relationship between the victimized, who are "perceived as female/feminine" and "less powerful," and the perpetrator, or "those perceived as masculine/male" (Sjoberg 2016: 24). Rendering someone (or something) as female through acts of penetration, often referred to as "feminization" throughout the literature, can conceptually be understood as placement along gendered hierarchies. According to Sjoberg, femininity "is associated with rejection, devalorization, immobility and limits" (ibid.), while Cynthia Enloe (2004) explains that to marginalize the female implies to infantilize, ignore, or trivialize, among others. In contrast, to masculinize someone (or something) is associated with affirmation, potential, success, and valorization. For Peterson (2010), the ultimate effect of rendering someone (or something) female is a reduction in legitimacy, status, and value. Sjoberg (2016) further argues that "gender relations are not power relations that just happen between men and women" (26). Instead, "gender relations happen among parties in war and conflict" (ibid.), including between war-affected civilians and armed combatants.

These (perceived) processes of compromising masculine identities as a result of male-directed sexual violence similarly rest upon the theoretical premise of a socially constructed discrepancy between masculinities and victimhood (chapter 1). Across most patriarchal societies, the notion of vulnerability arguably sits uneasily with "social expectations of what it is to be a man . . . —as strong, tough, self-sufficient and impenetrable" (Weiss 2008: 277). Within a heteronormative environment in particular, this disjuncture becomes further exacerbated if the victimization takes on a sexual(ized) dimension. Concurring with Fineman's (2008) theoretical work on vulnerabilities as inevitably human, and based on a feminist premise, Gilson argues that vulnerability is a feminized concept, "associated both with femininity and with weakness and dependency" (71). Precisely because of these feminized characteristics, vulnerability is constructed as incompatible with manhood, and men are therefore socially conditioned not to be vulnerable if they wish to remain masculine.[9] Sexual victimhood in particular clearly signifies (sexual) vulnerability, which in turn is irreconcilable with manhood, and male sexual victimization thus implies perceived compromises of masculinities.

From Bodies to Acts—The Gendered Performativity of Penetration

While compromising the survivors' sense of manhood, sexual violence (perpetrated against women or men) is also often seen as enhancing the perpetrator's masculinity and equipping him (or her) with a sense of hypermasculinity. Conceptually, however, it may seem contradictory and even paradoxical that acts of same-sexual penetration between men are theorized to cast "a taint of homosexuality" (Sivakumaran 2005) only on the victim but not on the perpetrator. Why is the perpetrator who actively penetrates another man not also (or even more so) regarded as homosexual and thus as less of a man, but instead seen as even more of a man and hypermasculine? We might assume that he who actively and consciously engages in same-sexual acts between men might also (if not even more so) be considered gay and thus in hetero-patriarchal terms as less of a man.

As poignantly argued by Edström, Dolan, et al. (2016), however, it is not exclusively gendered bodies but rather *acts* of penetration that most effectively communicate and transfer power and dominance and thus masculinity within the context of male-directed sexual violence. "It is the subjection to an act of penetration (i.e. being penetrated), rather than the body of the victim, that renders the victim feminine, a woman, and therefore subordinates" (ibid.: 36). Drawing on empirical research on male-male rape in the US military, Aaron Belkin similarly argues that "penetration is associated with masculinity and dominance while penetrability is a marker of subordination. . . . The penetrator is masculine while the penetrated is feminine" (2012: 83). Being penetrated, Belkin writes, "is a marker of weakness, subordination, and a lack of control" (80). Taking these gendered markers of penetration into account, feminist scholar Laura Sjoberg (2016) further attests that "both the enactment and the experience of sexual violence in war and conflict is an embodied practice, where people's bodies (as victims and as perpetrators) are both the sites of inscribed violence and the site of the inscription of messages of gendered subordination" (196).

A systematic examination of sexual violence against men and penetrative rape in particular thus contributes to a shift of the "basis of gender essentialism from bodies to acts" (Edström, Dolan, et al 2016: 36). Understanding the sexual *act* of penetration as effectively communicating masculinity, power, and dominance helps us to resolve the seeming paradox of why victims' masculine identities seem to be compromised, but perpetrators seem to gain masculinity within the context of male-on-male rape. This is because of the powerfully gendered performativity of penetration as linked to masculinity and gender (see Butler 1990; Drumond

2018). Sjoberg (2016) similarly emphasizes the need "to focus on *what happens* when sexual violence is committed" in terms of gendering and that "*acts* of sexual violence . . . can be understood as gendered" (177).

Crucially, an analysis of penetrative acts is inherently linked to the thwarting, compromising, and awarding of masculinities thus (re)connects elements of sexuality and sex, as linked to gender, power, and dominance, to discourses around sexual violence in general and against men in particular. Recent research by Eriksson Baaz and Stern (2018) has demonstrated and critically questioned that gendered scholarship on conflict and security increasingly seems to write out and neglect sexuality and sexual acts, instead focusing solely on gender (as separated from sex). Such is particularly the case for discussions around male-directed sexual violence that center only around gender as linked to dominance and control (Schulz and Touquet 2020). Sivakumaran, for instance, claims that male "rape is about power and dominance *and not sex*" (2007: 272)—thereby directly ignoring sexuality and sex as contributing causes to male-directed sexual violence, and neglecting how sex itself is also inherently linked to power. Sara Meger likewise explicitly states that "women may experience CRSV borne out of opportunism, bolstered by ideas of masculine virility . . . , and the male sex right . . . , as well as for strategic purposes. Male victims, on the other hand, are targeted for this violence not out of patriarchal constructions of the male sex right, but for their particular strategic value" (2018: 114).

Scholarship on male-directed sexual violence thus evidently fails to seriously consider how sexuality and sex are organically connected to power (and thus to gender) (Foucault 1987). While gender must crucially be the cornerstone of any analysis of sexual violence, an examination of penetration within the context of sexual violence and its gendered effects reminds us that sexuality and sex similarly need to be foregrounded in any such discussions. Sjoberg (2013) argues that "sex, sexuality and violence are more closely linked than traditional analyses [of sexual violence in war] might acknowledge" (196). Sjoberg therefore concludes that conflict-related sexual violence, including against men, is sexed, sexual, and gendered—and urges us to analyze these crimes as such as well.

The literature on sexual violence against men moreover suggests that such violence not only renders the victim female, but also/alternatively potentially "homosexualizes" male survivors. Acts of anal penetration by another man are theorized to render the male survivor homosexual, which in Acholis' heteronormative society is similarly seen as incompatible and irreconcilable with manhood, in addition to being socially unacceptable and criminally punishable. However, none of the survivors who participated in this study expressed that they perceived themselves as "homosexualized" (see Sivakumaran 2005) following their sexual violations. As evidenced above, survivors regularly articulated that "they turned men into women" or that the soldiers "made us to suffer like women" as a result of the rapes, but never that they were turned into homosexuals. In northern Uganda's highly heteronormative society, where homosexuality is regarded as an abnormality and outlawed, ascribed homosexualization as a result of male-directed sexual violence thus appears to be less prevalent among survivors' experiences and lived realities, at least in terms of how they spoke about and categorized their harms. Speculatively this may well be due to the exacerbated and immense stigmatization attached to homosexuality in northern Uganda, which may be intensified by the government's criminalization of same-sex acts. In this social context, being considered by others and perceiving oneself as homosexual may be even more harmful and damaging than being symbolically "turned into a woman." At the same time, however, society at large, and in fact various service providers and health professionals, nevertheless frequently confused male rape with homosexuality. To illustrate, when I interviewed a potential research assistant (with extensive prior experience) to work with me on this project, he responded to my explanation of my project on male rape with: "Ah, you are studying homosexuals". Needless to say, I did not end up collaborating with him.

"I used to be a strong man, but now I am not"—Gender Subordination through Disempowerment

Most of the literature's theories and analyses regarding the gendered effects of sexual violence against men center on the subordination of male survivors through various sexual acts, and therefore most analyses stop here. My fieldwork findings, however, evidence that survivors' displacement from their gendered personhood frequently is a layered process, revolving around myriad intertwined gendered harms rather than a one-time event solely linked to penetrative rape or other sexual crimes. Essentially the gendered impact of sexual violence is further compounded by the sexual violations' gendered aftereffects. These different and intersecting harms signify male survivors' inabilities to protect, render them unable to provide for their families, and imply effects on their abilities to erect and procreate, which in turn further compromise survivors' gendered identities. The analysis offered in this section is structured in accordance with these most common gendered harms that holistically contribute toward survivors' (perceived) displacement from their gendered identities and personhood.

First, sexual violence against men communicates and is perceived to symbolize male survivors' inabilities to protect themselves and, often by association, their families as they are expected to according to the model of normative hegemonic masculinity. One male survivor explained that "admitting the violation would admit that I have not been able to protect myself, which means I am no longer a man." A key informant likewise confirmed that according to survivors, "if they admit to the violation, they admit to being less of a man because they failed to protect themselves." This perceived inability to protect themselves furthermore embodies what many survivors frequently referred to as "helplessness" and "powerlessness" or as "being forced to give in." In relation to this, a male community member said, "What makes you less of a man, in Acholi it is cultural norms, it is about power. If I take your woman and you cannot protect, you are not a man. Men are expected to provide and to protect. So if you do not have the power to protect either your wife or yourself, you are not a real man."

As this statement evidences, it is commonly assumed that if a man is not capable of protecting himself, he will likewise not be able to protect his family, thus significantly failing in one of his cardinal masculine roles as protector of the homestead. As a result of this perceived inability to protect themselves and the assumed incapacity to protect their families, various male survivors have been left by their wives (as examined in further detail below).

A spatial analysis of where the sexual violations took place offers further insights: As documented in the previous chapter, sexual violence against men in northern Uganda occurred both in the public as well as in the private spheres. When perpetrated in public, deliberately visible to other family or community members, the sexual violations were highly symbolic, communicative, and performative, as they publicly demonstrated the men's gendered subordination and their inability to protect themselves. On the other hand, when the sexual violations occurred within the men's own homesteads and therefore in the private sphere, the male survivors considered themselves and are perceived to be unable to provide for the protection of their homestead, considered the epicenter of Acholi cosmology (p'Bitek 1986). Male survivors are thus seen as failing in one of their primary masculine responsibilities of protecting themselves and the home, and sexual violations within the men's own homesteads signal clear intramale communication and an establishment of masculine hierarchies between the hypermasculine male perpetrator and the subordinated male victim. Their (perceived) inability to live up to the model of hegemonic masculinity thus (at least temporarily) displaces them from their gendered personhood.

At the same time, the physical consequences of sexual violence frequently affect men's capacities to work and thus their abilities to provide, as is expected of them as male breadwinners and heads of households. Many respondents reported that the health complications caused by the violations, including significant waist and back pain and rectal injuries, prevented them from carrying out any manual labor or agricultural work.[10] Most respondents indeed attested that as a result of their violations and the related health complications, they are too weak to conduct any work. As one survivor explained, "I have many scars and injuries that I got as a result of the rape and this has weakened me and it cannot enable me to do any hard labor. I am not performing as a man." Another survivor attested that the sexual violation "has also affected my ability to work and my productivity." The majority of survivors who participated in the study reported that the physical injuries caused by the sexual violations rendered them "unable to perform any farm work as men are expected to do." Many respondents indeed described that they felt less of a man because of this: "I started feeling useless and not man enough," a male survivor said, while another complained that the "was not having the ability to work like a man." Yet another survivor articulated it this way: "I am not a real man anymore because ever since the violence, I cannot do any work anymore and I cannot dig in the gardens so I cannot provide for my wife and for my children and my family. I cannot raise enough money to pay my children into school. So that is why I am now no longer a man."

These layered gendered and sexual harms further challenged the survivors in their masculine roles and responsibilities as providers, thereby (at least temporarily) displacing them from their masculine personhood. As Onyango (2012) attests, "For the Acholi, men feel they are 'not men' when they cannot provide for their families' (217). In addition to the physical implications of the violations, the psychological effects also prevent male survivors from working and thus from providing for their families. As a result of diverse psychological consequences, many male survivors have disengaged from many community activities, including agricultural work.

Yet this displacement from the survivors' gendered identities can be temporary. Some male survivors have regained their physical strength and thereby their ability to work. Some, following medical treatment, are experiencing improved health conditions and are therefore in a position to work again and thus to adhere to masculine expectations compared to the immediate aftermath of the violations. These improvements are often connected to their engagement in survivors' groups as well as their conceptions of postconflict justice, as will be explored in more detail in the following two chapters.

Another consequence of the sexual violations is survivors' difficulties in achieving or maintaining an erection. Edström, Dolan, et al. (2016) note that the "almost universal numbing of their capacity for sexual arousal" (26) constitutes one of the most common and most prevalent physiological aftereffects of male-directed sexual violence. Several survivors I engaged with indeed reported not only difficulties in achieving an erection, but also a lack of interest in sexual interaction. As one male survivor put it, "Without the ability to have sex I feel like a castrated bull. Due to that pain that I experience I have no urge for sex." Survivors feel the impact of this physical impairment on their masculinities.

A service provider working with male survivors contextualized these common experiences: "The inability of manhood in relation to [sexual violence against men] is psychological and physiological. He cannot perform his sexuality and functioning of sex anymore and is thus no longer a man, according to him and his wife." As further argued by Edström, Dolan, et al. (2016: 26), "One of the concerns around this is, of course, centred on the absence of sexual pleasure and joy in a person's private life. . . . But it is also linked to fundamental issues around masculinity and identity, not to mention serious concerns over reproductive health and choice."

The service provider quoted above also referred to another male survivor for whom "sex was useless because it reminded him of his own rape all the time. His erection goes and his feelings of being a man are completely lost." Being sexually active and the ability to father children (and preferably boys as firstborns) constitute central markers of Acholi manhood, and being unable to fulfill this translates into an implied inability to be a "real man" and thus a compromising of their masculine identities and a displacement from their gendered personhood. Yet, over time, several survivors (following group-based therapy) have regained their sexual potency, thereby repairing and remaking their gendered self and personhood.

A combination of these layered gendered and sexual harms likewise heavily impacts male survivors' relationships to their partners, families, and communities. The empirical findings underpinning this study suggest that these impaired and aggravated relationships constitute significant harms, often resulting in communal isolation, social exclusion, and stigmatization. As a result of survivors' inabilities to have sex, procreate, and reproduce, further compounded by the inabilities to protect and to provide, numerous survivors have been left by their wives. "I cannot stay in the house with a fellow woman" is a statement and a lived reality that several respondents were confronted with by their wives. Keeping in mind that having a family and being married constitute cornerstones of the Acholi model of normative hegemonic masculinity, such experiences—in addition to causing much emotional and mental distress—further undermine male survivors' masculinities within this local context. One survivor attested, "I am less of a man because now nobody is with me. My wife left and I am not a real man anymore." This mirrors previously documented dynamics of female sexual violence survivors being left by their husbands or boyfriends due to the stigma attached to their sexual violations, both in northern Uganda as in other conflict settings globally (Coulter 2009).

Furthermore, in Acholiland men and especially elders are culturally and socially expected to attend and actively participate in community meetings and consultations. Respondents explained that taking on a leadership role in the community is one of the integral responsibilities and requirements of being a man in northern Uganda. Out of fear of being stigmatized, however, many survivors purposely decide not to engage in any such meetings. "It is better to stay alone and not to attend these meetings, because they might stigmatize or name-call you," one survivor explained. By not participating in these meetings, male survivors are seen as neglecting and ignoring their masculine duties and responsibilities within their wider communities, which in turn negatively impacts their gender identities.

Clearly, the inabilities to provide and to protect as undermining manhood within the context of a protracted conflict are neither unique nor exclusive to male survivors of sexual violence. The example of men's forced infantilization in the context of displacement camps shows that these experiences are representative for large parts of the male Acholi population. Similarly, throughout the conflict, countless civilians suffered horrendous atrocities, leaving them with a variety of untreated wounds and physical and psychological health complications impacting their abilities to work and provide and thus also their gender identities. For instance, a man who was beaten by the rebels and suffers from medical complications, or who was shot by government soldiers and has bullet fragments in his body, is equally, if not even more so, unable to conduct physical labor and thus to provide.

However, when initially conditioned and caused by sexual violations, which affect male survivors' masculinities in the first place, these layered gendered harms can become further gendered, compounded, and intensified. The experience and process of displacement from gendered personhood must thus be conceptualized as an intertwined process, originating from the sexualized, sexed, and gendered nature of initial violations in the first place and further exacerbated through layered gendered harms experienced in the aftermath of the violent acts.

As my analysis here shows, these sexual and gendered harms are never static but rather fluctuate over time and are malleable by different socioeconomic and political interventions. These key insights, to be gained from this deconstructed understanding of the impact of wartime rape on masculinities, ultimately prevents me from wrongly freezing dynamic experiences into time and space, which the commonly employed conception of "emasculation" often does. Instead, and as described in more detail in the introduction, I apply the frame of "displacement from gendered personhood" to analyze these dynamics, which more accurately captures the fluid and variable character of survivors' experiences.

CONCLUSION

In this chapter, I have offered insights into the phenomenological lived realities of male sexual violence survivors in northern Uganda. My findings foreground that the impact of wartime rape on male survivors' masculinities is not a static one-time event, but rather a dynamic process of layered gendered harms unfolding over time. The impact of sexual violence on survivors' masculinities is initiated through acts of penetrative rape, which within a patriarchal and heterosexual context "turned men into women." This perceived gendered subordination is further compounded by the violations' layered gendered harms, which render male survivors unable to protect (themselves and their families), to provide, and at times to perform sexually and procreate, thereby significantly challenging their masculine roles and responsibilities and hence impacting their gender identities. Male-directed sexual violence during armed conflict thus strikes at multiple levels of what it means to be a man. The compromising and reifying of male survivors' masculine identities must therefore be understood as an evolving and unfolding process, rather than an event, necessitating the more fluid and dynamic understanding of the "displacement from gendered personhood" frame.

This deconstructed understanding of male survivors' experiences enables us to better theorize and grapple with these gendered harms, therefore setting the foundations for the next chapters to explore how survivors in northern Uganda engage with the gendered harms. Against this background, the following two chapters carefully take into account male survivors' phenomenological experiences and their gendered harms when analyzing survivors' agency and quests for justice in relation to these crimes and their impact.

5

Exercising Agency

Survivors' Support Groups

It was about seven p.m. and the sun had just set as Okwera—whose case study narrative opened this book—and I sat by the pool and shared a cold Anchor beer at a small boutique hotel in Cambodia's capital, Phnom Penh. We talked about the tiring journey he had taken from Uganda to Cambodia and the jetlag he experienced for the first time ever in his life. We then moved on to mostly discuss different farming strategies—a topic I admittedly had (and continue to have) very little knowledge of, much to Okwera's amusement. We were both in the country for the 2015 South-South Institute (SSI) on Sexual Violence against Men and Boys, joined by numerous male survivors of sexual violence as well as practitioners and activists from around the globe, including several colleagues from the Refugee Law Project (RLP), who co-organized this groundbreaking event.

Earlier that week, Okwera had shared with the institute's participants his experience of forming the Men of Courage survivors' support group that he coordinates as the chairperson. The day thereafter he gave an incredibly inspirational and motivational speech as part of the closing ceremony of the institute, which included excerpts of the testimony opening this book. As part of our conversation about farming strategies, Okwera explained to me how group members engage in collective agricultural activities, and that this helps them to jointly generate an income to support themselves and their families—something that many survivors up to that point struggled with on their own, because of the numerous injuries and health complications as a result of the sexual violations, as explored in the previous chapter. "The group is so important because it allows every one of us to be free and to support one another," he elaborated further. "It also helps us to better understand what has happened to us, and to find solutions for how to move forward," he added. The institute in Cambodia was indeed a perfect stage to reflect on the transformative and agentive potential of the group, which over the years has empowered Okwera to be where he was and to advocate for male survivors' needs.

When I returned to northern Uganda about half a year later, for the longer spell of my field research and had a chance to engage with the Men of Courage group more closely and regularly, almost all of its members on different occasions agreed with Okwera's views about the group. They all explained how the group "has helped us come together and be one," and how their activities "make people aware about the violations and suffering we had undergone so many years ago." For the survivors I engaged with, the group was therefore an important piece in a broader and procedural puzzle of engaging with their experiences, by way of coming to terms with their gendered harms. In light of this, in this chapter I focus on the Men of Courage survivors' group as an important avenue for survivors to exercise agency.

This analysis thereby reveals that despite being confronted with a myriad of gendered harms and vulnerabilities (chapter 4), male survivors over time also actively engage with their harmful experiences in a number of ways, and by exercising differing forms of political agency. In the literature, however, sexual violence against men is almost exclusively portrayed through the frame of vulnerabilities, representing male survivors as ever-vulnerable victims without a voice and without any agency, and as indefinitely stripped off their manhood. In this chapter, I seek to refute these essentialist portrayals, by outlining how survivors exercise different politicized strategies and choices in order to come to terms with their experiences in different ways. Although I take into account different instances of survivors' agency, such as strategically navigating silence and disclosure, I specifically set the focus on one particular avenue for survivors to exercise agency and engage with their experiences: The example of male survivors' support groups, and in particular the Men of Courage survivor association in northern Uganda. In response to the gendered impact of wartime rape, and in the absence of formalized support avenues, numerous male survivors across the conflict-affected territory began creating their own spaces to advocate for their needs, in the form of survivors' support groups.

Founded in 2013 and exclusively composed of and led by Acholi male sexual violence survivors, the Men of Courage group offers an avenue for them to collectively respond to their sexual and gendered harms. In this association, male survivors exercise agency in ways such as these: by engaging in joint agricultural activities, thereby providing an income for them and their families; by organizing storytelling sessions among members of the groups, thereby collectively making sense of their harmful experiences and their contemporary challenges; and by carrying out national and international advocacy work on sexual violence against men, thereby seeking recognition of their otherwise silenced and marginalized experiences. Essentially, such an examination of agency challenges the static and essentialist ways in which sexual violence survivors are commonly portrayed as exclusively passive, vulnerable, and helpless, instead showing that survivors can act as active agents in their quests to respond to their suffering and harms.

This chapter proceeds with a brief examination of the ways in which crimes of sexual violence against men in general and male survivors' lived realities are commonly portrayed, in essentialist and infantilizing ways, depicting male survivors as ever-vulnerable victims in need of protection, rather than as potentially agentive subjects. In doing so, I draw on feminist IR scholarship that in recent years has brought increased attention to women's and girls' agency in times of war and postconflict settings. I then offer a brief attempt to theorize the understanding of political agency that underpins my analysis, before proceeding with an empirically grounded overview of the role of victims' associations in postconflict northern Uganda in general, and an introduction of the Men of Courage support group specifically. The analytical core of the chapter then homes in on the ways in which survivors exercise agency, primarily in the context of support groups, but also in many other ways, for instance by navigating "engaged silences." I round off the chapter with an examination of how through this agentive capacity, groups simultaneously create pathways to justice on the microlevel, thereby linking this chapter with the next.

SEXUAL VIOLENCE, VICTIMHOOD, AND AGENCY

Despite the prevailing marginalization of male-directed sexual violence throughout scholarship and praxis, important political, empirical, and conceptual inroads have been made into recognizing men and boys as victims and survivors of wartime sexual violence. As the overview in chapter 2 shows, most studies argue that sexual violence against men is employed strategically and systematically, often portrayed and framed in the "rape as a weapon of war" narrative (Eriksson Baaz and Stern 2013), aimed at terrorizing, punishing, intimidating, and humiliating its victims. Emerging scholarship has also begun to examine the manifold vulnerabilities and harms experienced by male sexual violence survivors, and different studies, complemented by the previous chapter in this book, have focused on the gendered consequences of sexual violence.

However, as per this focus, crimes of male-directed sexual violence and survivors' experiences have thus far almost exclusively been analyzed with attention to, and through the frames of, vulnerabilities. As a result, existing studies—whether willingly or unwillingly—fall into a tendency to represent "survivors as victims without a voice," resulting in a victimizing and "disempowering narrative of silenced, isolated, and wholly marginalized male survivors" (Edström and Dolan 2018: 176) indefinitely stripped of their masculine identities and without any agency. Even though agency is considered a masculine trait, male survivors—who are believed to be robbed of their masculinity as a result of sexual violence—by association are also seen as deprived of their agency. But, as argued by Baines, "one's vulnerability in one relationship does not define the person as ever vulnerable" (Baines 2017: 14), as I seek to further illustrate throughout this chapter.

Thus far, however, how in spite of their manifold vulnerabilities, male survivors also actively engage with their experiences and exercise myriad forms of agency has not yet been analyzed. This in turn results in incomplete and essentialist scholarly representations of the dynamics of wartime sexual violence in general, and of male survivors' lived realities in particular. Potential forms of agency in this context can include navigating the silence surrounding one's marginalized experience or the choice of joining (or not joining) and engaging in a survivors' support group.

In the context of a move toward a more global international relations (IR) (Acharya 2014) and growing attention to peacebuilding "from below" and at the local level, different studies increasingly emphasize the importance of recognizing conflict-affected communities' agency, to facilitate more sustainable peace, to challenge (neo)colonial representations of international politics, and to construct more holistic analyses of the lived realities within armed conflicts. Focusing on victims' and local agency during wars comes at a poignant moment, as questions around victimhood, culpability, and responsibilities have been subjected to increasing scrutiny in the growing literature on conflict studies. Indeed, the existing bodies of literature frequently fall into a (wrongful) tendency to construct an "ideal" type of victim, as a person without agency and as ever-vulnerable, vis-à-vis a perpetrator whose unrestricted agency must be brought under control. In addition to reinforcing a dichotomous victim-perpetrator binary, these assumptions produce essentialist representations of victimhood and survivorhood. Specifically, such portrayals reduce victims as apolitical subjects in need of external (and mostly white, masculine, and patriarchal) protection, rather than as political actors with the potential to analyze, engage with, and respond to their harms on their own terms.

Yet growing evidence shows that conflict-affected populaces are not merely passively subjected to violence and war; instead they actively resist, cope, survive, display remarkable resilience, and "strive to create a meaningful world in the midst of chaos" (Bolten 2014: 21; see Das 2007). Indeed, recent years have witnessed increasing "interest in the political agency of human beings whose agency is often seen to fall outside the realm of politics, or whose political roles and actions are considered when prompted by contingencies such as war or social unrest" (Häkli and Kallio 2013: 182).

With some exceptions, however, much of this research is narrowly focused on resistance, resilience, and survival, but does not fully comprehend the manifold ways in which conflict-affected populaces and communities position themselves as political actors and execute a variety of politicized choices and acts, often in quotidian and mundane ways—a gap that the examination here seeks to address, but that also warrants further research. For instance, in Sri Lanka, Walker (2010) discusses the agency of vulnerable populations, exercised in subtle and quotidian ways. Anthropologist Carolyn Nordstrom (1997) further shows that civilians in war-torn Mozambique in myriad terms endeavored to keep life as "normal" as possible, while political scientist Koloma Beck (2013) examines how civilian populations in Angola enforced and reassured the "normality" of civil war. Focused on northern Uganda, Sverker Finnström (2008) unpacks the manifold ways in which individuals seek to deal with the physical, psychological, social, and moral destruction of a protracted war, primarily by way of reasserting their ties to the spiritual realm.

At the same time, constructions of responsibility, victimhood, and agency during times of war are also heavily gendered, frequently based upon dichotomous constructions of male perpetrators and female victims. In her groundbreaking analysis of the gender politics of militarism, Cynthia Enloe (2004) critically exposed these essentialist binary categorizations of "all the men are in the militias and all the women are victims." All too often, this (re)produces an unreconstructed view of men as universal aggressors and women as universal victims during armed conflict. In addition to ignoring masculine vulnerabilities in conflict settings—including the widespread empirical reality of sexual violence against men—such prevalent assumptions fail to explain for women's roles in conflict, and they obscure female agency during and after war.

As noted by Erin Baines, however, the study of gender-based violence "would do well to incorporate a conceptualization of victim agency, and to avoid reducing men's and women's experiences of sexual and gender-based violence to acts solely done to them" (2015: 320). Seeking to dismantle these essentialist views, and guided by feminist curiosity to challenge the hetero-patriarchal manifestations of gender violence, scholars across disciplines—but in particular in anthropology and feminist IR—have attempted to "collapse the often gendered opposition of agency and victimhood that typically characterizes the analysis of women's coping strategies in war zones" (Utas 2005: 403). In light of this, different studies have begun to complicate gendered notions of victimhood and to bring attention to women's agency, focusing on how women and girls resist, subvert, and navigate the opportunities and constraints that characterize their everyday lived realities of war and coercive relationships (Amony 2015). This growing body of literature reveals that women's experiences and roles during war cannot be reduced to the passive and ever-vulnerable status of "bush wives" and/or "sex slaves." Instead, women and girls frequently stage acts of resistance or at times take on active combat roles (MacKenzie 2012), thereby operating as "active agents" (Utas 2005) in multiple ways and domains.

For example, countering reductionist and essentialist portrayals of women as passive victims of conflict, Utas (2005) shows that women's actions and their agency are a matter of constantly adjusting tactics in response to the opportunities and constraints that characterize situations of armed conflict. Utas argues that women's agency "represents a range of realizable possibilities," qualifying women as "tactical actors engaged in the difficult task of social navigation" (2005: 426). Chris Coulter's (2009) anthropological study of "bush wives" in the Revolutionary Armed Forces (RUF) in Sierra Leone similarly moves beyond the essentialist portrayal of women as exclusively vulnerable, by paying attention to the active roles played by many women during the armed conflict. In Sierra Leone—as in northern Uganda and indeed elsewhere globally—female combatants, and especially those who were forcibly abducted, are almost exclusively portrayed as weak, vulnerable, and passive, often referred to as "bush wives" or "sex slaves." Challenging such essentialist representations, Coulter instead evidences the diversity of women's experiences and their agency during the war and in the postconflict period. Megan MacKenzie's (2012) work on female soldiers in Sierra Leone likewise pays attention to the active participation of women during the war and its aftermath, thereby debunking the prevalent myth that women do not (and cannot) fight and countering the general picture of women and girls exclusively as victims of conflict. MacKenzie's examination empirically contributes toward a better understanding of female soldiers' experiences of and involvement in and after conflict, including their agency, which is important for crafting effective postconflict policies.

In postconflict Peru, Kimberly Theidon (2012) similarly illustrates the numerous ways in which women give meaning to their harms, which she refers to as "womanly narratives of heroism" (2007: 474). In her work on East Timor, Kent (2014) also describes that the lived experiences of women in forced relationships are much more complex than commonly portrayed by liberal human rights approaches. While narrowly presented as caught in relationships of coercion and violence, the women, Kent notes, often staged acts of resistance to reassert their independence within these relationships. And in one of the few existing cross-national and multicase studies on this topic, Denov (2007) traces the experiences of women and girls as participants and resisters of violence and as agents during the conflicts in Angola, Sierra Leone, Mozambique, and northern Uganda. Arguing that "girls in fighting forces are not simply silent victims, but active agents," Denov shows that women and girls made remarkable "efforts to bring about change for themselves and by themselves" (2007: ii). Denov likewise shows that the obstruction of women's and girls' agency in conflict zones leads to their frequent discrimination in the context of postconflict measures, having problematic implications and consequences for their postwar recovery (also see MacKenzie 2012).

Specifically focused on northern Uganda, the autobiographic accounts of Evelyn Amony (2015), who was forcibly married to LRA leader Joseph Kony, and of Grace Acan (2015), both of whom spent more than ten years with the rebel group, contribute to a more nuanced and detailed understanding of women's agency in conflict and postconflict settings. These personal narratives challenge stereotypical ideas of war-affected women, unearthing instead the complex ways in which female survivors navigated life inside and outside the LRA and politically engage as human rights activists. In the introduction to Amony's account, Erin Baines acknowledges that "previous studies highlight the diverse roles women and children play in rebel armies . . . , yet we know little about how persons within such groups perceive, experience, and bear witness to war over time. We know even less from the perspective of women' themselves" (2015: xvii). Together, Amony's and Acan's narrations of their experiences refute numerous stereotypes, "thereby repainting the picture of women in the LRA as not just vulnerable and passive victims but also empowered agents and actors" (Schulz 2016: 312).

Drawing on extensive and long-term research with women and girls formerly abducted by the LRA, Erin Baines (2017) further explores female political agency in northern Uganda. She argues that abducted women were not just passive victims, but instead navigated complex social and political worlds, both during captivity in the LRA as well as upon return to civilian life postconflict. Baines's work illustrates how women and girls who returned from LRA captivity in the postconflict period sought to rebuild "a web of relations that constitutes mean-ingful life" (2015: 328), and how these acts of rebuilding relationships constitute aspects of victims' political agency.

In combination, these different studies challenge essentialist portrayals of gen-dered victimhood in situations of armed conflict, evidencing that women and girls instead frequently exercise political acts of agency to come to terms with their harmful experiences. Despite this much-needed attention to the agency of female victims, however, the manifold ways in which male survivors of sexual violence—who are similarly portrayed as helpless and ever-vulnerable—also engage with their harmful experiences and exercise agency have not yet been sufficiently exam-ined (see Touquet and Schulz 2020). Taking inspiration from this growing body of critical feminist IR scholarship, this chapter offers a necessary examination of the different strategies Acholi male survivors employ to come to terms with their gendered harms.

THEORIZING POLITICAL AGENCY

Before introducing the survivors' associations as a particular space for exercising agency and proceeding with the analysis, I offer a few notes on theory in order to provide a brief but hopefully coherent conceptualization of political agency that will underpin the analysis to follow.[1]

In its broadest sense, agency refers to the human capacity to act, "a capacity that is not exercised in a vacuum but rather in a social world in which structure shapes the opportunities and resources" to act (Björkdahl and Selimovic 2015: 170). In this reading, agency is centrally composed of autonomy and intention and is dependent on structural factors. Here, however, the focus rests specifi-cally on *political agency* in a widened sense, "located in the social world that the embodied individual encounters in multiple different subject positions, averting, accepting and altering them through individual and concerted action" (Häkli and Kallio 2013: 191). As further emphasized by Björkdahl and Selimovic (2015: 171), political "agency should not only be understood as overt political (re)action, but may also be enacted through 'life projects' that may not necessarily be formulated as [formal] acts of resistance but that still have transformative effects in the gendered everyday."

Throughout most political science and IR scholarship, the "political" is commonly conceptualized in a formal and public sense, focused on states or institutions and necessitating a degree of autonomy enjoyed by rights-bearing individuals and guaranteed through liberal nation-states. But such a confined conception of the "political" excludes a range of politicized activities, actions, and choices, and assumes "that subordinate groups essentially lack a political life" (Scott 1990: 199). By departing from narrowly formalized understandings of "politics," I instead focus on forms of the "political" and agency that do not only emerge on the macrolevel and in (semi)institutional settings, but instead more widely in myriad "interactions and relations among and between persons" (Baines 2017: 14).

This broadened conception of political agency is underpinned by a relational understanding of politics as an integral part of people's everyday lives that requires attention to the phenomenologies of politicized action. The political is therefore conceptualized in an Arendtian tradition as "a form of activity concerned with addressing problems of living together in a shared world of plurality and difference" where "the space of this sharing is constituted by active agents" (Barnett 2012: 679). According to this relational understanding, a whole variety of actions and gestures can enter the realm of the political when individuals recognize and assert "themselves as particular subjects, in relation to others, to the structures in which they are situated, and to subject positions that may be imposed on them" (Elwood and Mitchell 2012: 4). Arguably, this relational approach to political agency is particularly applicable to the collectivist society of the Acholi in northern Uganda, where personhood and sociality rest upon social collectivism and communal structuring in a relational sense, framed within the categories of *dano adana* and/or *bedo dano* (p'Bitek 1986), as covered in the previous chapter.

Political agency as employed here thus broadly involves a wide range of choices, actions (or nonactions), and strategies within the public and private spheres, employed by individuals and communities aimed at remaking a world and reconfiguring their lives and relationships, as well as at reasserting their personhood, identity, and self, including in the aftermath of violence and injustices. Such a conception of political agency broadens much of the IR and conflict-studies literature's (neoliberal) treatment of agency as equated with resistance or survival strategies (see Mahmood 2001) and recognizes more broadly the manifold and relational ways in which survivors exercise political choices to come to terms with their war-related experiences.

This wider and open-ended theoretical understanding, however, implies the danger of potentially overpoliticizing everything and inevitably raises the analytical question of when and where to detect political agency. Ultimately, "agency [is] not a general characteristic which actors either have or lack, but a quality that actors' doing may have *in a specific context*" (Menzel 2018: 4), indicating the existence of spatially and temporally contingent structural factors and conditions for agency. For Menzel, a measurable conception of agency thus necessitates a differentiation between motivational (or intentional) and effective dimensions, which specify "that actors consciously want to do something (motivational dimensions), and are able to achieve at least somewhat desired effects (effective dimension)" (ibid.: 10). These contingencies and the contextual openness of political agency also imply that it is inherently difficult—if not impossible—to predetermine which activities or actions are or become political (and which are not) under any given circumstances. The particularities and specific understandings of the *political* may therefore often be unknown in advance and "thus need to be worked out empirically" (Häkli and Kallio 2013: 195).

To ultimately recognize specific instances as relational and political, Baines argues that "stories provide insight into a set of historical truths that otherwise slip from view in empirical and general theories . . . , enabling a more complex analysis of the living subject and opening space for consideration of the workings of power in the counters of life" (2015: 321). Stories in particular can offer meaningful interpretations of the complexities of harms and agency in wartime and can serve to illuminate "how people perceive of themselves and in relation to others" (Patterson and Renwick Monroe 1998: 317). After all, through the stories they narrate, "people locate themselves as agents in the various social worlds they identify with . . . or inhabit" (Fujii 2018: 3). To this end, I will draw on survivors' testimonies and stories to tease out the ways in which support groups offer avenues for male survivors to exercise different forms of agency.

An Example of Political Agency: Navigating Silence and Disclosure

Before proceeding with the case-specific analysis, I want to illustrate what is meant by political agency by referring to an example of a male survivor from northern Uganda who navigated what can be referred to as "engaged silences" as a form of political agency.

Throughout the literature on the nexus between gender, conflict, and silence, it is often argued that when externally imposed, silencing can further entrench gendered harms. Here, however, I want to focus on how (and under which conditions) silence can be agentive and can become a powerful political tool for survivors to deploy strategically. To examine the role of silence as a form of agency, it is important to recognize a distinction between being silenced (externally, involuntarily) and voluntarily choosing to be silent. I thus specifically employ Keating's (2013) framework of "engaged silences"—which broadly includes three forms: silent refusal, silent witness, and deliberative silence—in order to tease out the multiple forms and functions of silence. For Keating, silence can be a (collective and individual) form of resistance to power and must thus be understood as potentially agentive when deployed by politically marginalized groups (see Thomson 2019). For "silences are modes of being and self-representation which give individual social actors the active agency to reflect on, make sense of and represent their past experiences while simultaneously linking current predicament to the past and vice versa" (Dery 2018: 15).

To illustrate how silence can be(come) agentive, I refer to the case study of Okidi, a male survivor from the northeastern part of Acholiland. This example reflects the lived realities of numerous other male survivors whom I engaged with and who employ similar tactics and strategies of navigating silence and disclosure, thus constituting one particularly poignant illustration of my argument.

Okidi was arrested and taken captive by government soldiers of the NRA in mid-1986, just as the war in the north began. Like many other male survivors, Okidi was accused of being a former soldier fighting the newly instated Museveni regime. Because of his long, thick beard, he resembled one of the leading military opposition figures at that time who was previously a commander under Obote's regime. Okidi, who was a teacher at that time, was taken from the school compound where he worked to an NRA army barrack, where he was severely beaten, stabbed in the testicles with a bayonet, and anally raped by two soldiers. After two days of interrogation and torture, and while being transported to another army base on the back of a van, Okidi managed to escape and return home. However, he did not tell anyone about what happened to him. Due to shame and social stigma—coupled with the unavailability of medical services in rural northern Uganda during this time of the war—he did not seek any professional medical treatment. Instead, he nursed his wounds with warm water and traditional herbs by himself and chose to remain silent about his experience. More than two decades later, in 2013, he finally reported what had happened to him to the Justice and Reconciliation Project (JRP)—which conducted a study about incidents in this part of Acholiland during the war—and later to the Refugee Law Project, which offered medical treatment through rehabilitative support measures.

Following his much-needed medical recovery, he also decided to break the silence and report his experience to a broader audience. In 2014, at a specifically organized press conference in Gulu town supported by JRP and RLP, Okidi offered a thirty-minute account of his experience during the war, including the incidence of sexual abuse in 1986. This account was later published in the *Acholi Times*, an online English-language newspaper that focuses on sociopolitical developments in the Acholi subregion and that regularly features stories about the war and contemporary postconflict challenges. The article, published in September 2014 and thus twenty-seven years after the assault, describes what happened to Okidi in

NRA custody and includes his full name, his location, and even a picture of him. In his home village and even within his family, however, nobody knows about his experience. He explains that "from 1986 to 2013, I never told anymore what happened to me, and then I only disclosed it to JRP and to RLP in 2013 and later to the newspaper in 2014. But here I don't talk about it, I still keep it confidential because from the people here I feel stigmatization. When people here are drunk, they will stigmatize me and undermine me and that will undermine my dignity as a human being."

During a conversation we had in early 2016, Okidi explained to me that because the press conference was held in Gulu town—located about 150 kilometers from his home village—and the newspaper is published online and in English, he does not fear that community or family members in his village will ever get to know about it. In fact, the newspaper is primarily read by an urban-based, young, and largely educated elite, or by Acholi diaspora communities in Kampala, Entebbe, and other bigger cities in Uganda as well as abroad. It remains largely unknown, or at least unread, in rural parts.

This example poignantly illustrates the spatial-geographic dimensions of silence, as well as the ways in which survivors can exercise agency by choosing which stories to narrate in which spheres, and where to maintain what could be referred to as a "protective silence." In this case, Okidi broke the silence in the public sphere to attain a sense of social recognition of his otherwise silenced and marginalized experience. At the same time, however, he deliberately and in an agentive capacity maintains his silence within his private sphere and his immediate surroundings in fear of negative repercussions, such as stigma, shame, and humiliation. By both sharing his testimony and maintaining a protective silence, Okidi acts politically and relationally, towards his family and community in maintaining that protective silence, as well as towards JRP, RLP, the Acholi Times and its readership by way of sharing his testimony. He thus navigates his experience and vulnerability in different settings, thereby refuting the stereotypical representation of the ever-vulnerable survivor without a voice.

THE MEN OF COURAGE SURVIVORS' GROUP

In addition to navigating silence and disclosure in complex ways, as illustrated through this example, male survivors in northern Uganda also exercise differing forms of political agency in the context of survivors' groups. Departing from these conceptual reflections, here I focus on the roles of survivors' support groups and the spaces they facilitate for survivors to be(come) agentive by way of engaging with their experiences in multiple ways. To this end, I specifically draw on the Men of Courage survivors' group, composed of three subgroups located across Acholiland, which I will first introduce below.

Survivors' Groups and Dealing with the Past

Throughout the postconflict literature in general, survivors' groups and organizations are featured in different capacities. For instance, previous studies have analyzed how survivors in groups engage with wider processes of dealing with the past and postconflict reconstruction. To illustrate, Humphrey and Valverde (2008) show that victims' groups in Argentina aid survivors in demanding recognition from the state, while Rombouts (2004) unveils the manifold roles of survivors' forums in advocating for reparations in postgenocide Rwanda. Together these (and other) studies demonstrate that uniting individual survivors under the umbrella of an association can facilitate an environment that enables survivors to collectively engage with external and macrolevel processes in postconflict spaces.

Fewer studies have examined how groups can offer active coping strategies that may contribute to collective healing and recovery. In Nepal and East Timor, for instance, groups aid families in reconstructing their identities after having been impacted by conflict-related political disappearances (Robins 2009). Likewise, members of the Khulumani support group in South Africa, in a submission to the country's Truth and Reconciliation Commission (TRC), recommended the creation and maintenance of survivors' support groups as means to "address the ongoing problems resulting from the TRC and conflicts of the past [because] groups will serve as a living memory . . . while on the other hand mobilizing more resources for the empowerment of victims" (CSVR and Khulumani 1998).

Despite these positive aspects of survivors' groups, however, some challenges persist. Many victim–survivor associations are shaped by hierarchies among survivors, and there are often stark power discrepancies between different members exercising diverging levels of influence. Likewise there are frequently divisions between separate groups as well as between survivors who are members of groups and those who are not part of an association, further entrenching tensions within and between conflict-affected communities, such as in Northern Ireland. Similarly, in northern Uganda, various survivor-led groups stopped operating due to internal disagreements over what the group ought to concentrate on. The fact that groups are often established or supported by external actors can constitute an additional challenge, implying victim dependencies upon outside bodies. As argued by Kent in the context of East Timor, "the agency, autonomy and 'home grown' nature of victims' groups should not be overstated. . . . Victims' groups have been intensively cultivated by national and international NGOs. Without this support, it is likely that many of their activities would not be sustainable" (Kent 2011: 447–448).

Overall, however, across these diverse scholarly engagements, survivors' groups are primarily analyzed as precursors to wider macrolevel and state-led processes. Yet, the potential for survivors to actively exercise agency and facilitate healing or justice *through their participation in groups* has not yet been sufficiently

explored, especially within postconflict settings and through a gendered masculinities lens. The analysis pursued here thus aids our understanding of how conflict-affected communities can actively engage with their experiences on their own
terms and in agentive capacities in the context of survivors' support groups, particularly so in the absence of more formalized support measures, as is the case for
male sexual violence survivors in northern Uganda.

Survivors' Groups in Northern Uganda

Reflective of these global dynamics, in northern Uganda a variety of victims'
groups exist in different forms and with divergent mandates, objectives, and
foci, and variations in size, activities, and levels of organization. Most of these
groups unite survivors of the conflict between the LRA and the government of
Uganda and assist victims in advocating for their demands and pursuing their
quests for justice. Other groups also provide more practical assistance, including peer support, income-generating activities, and shared finance schemes, such
as Village Savings and Loan Associations (VSLA). Locally referred to as *bol cup*,
various forms of savings and farmers group existed prior to the conflict in northern Uganda (Allen 1987), and therefore, the current postconflict groups qualify as
a "continuation of local methods of self-help and income generation," although
their function "now extends to providing some form of non-material comfort too"
(McDonald 2014: 256). While smaller groups on the community level primarily
engage in these forms of immediate practical support for survivors, quests for justice and reparations have mostly been taken up by larger claimants' associations,
such as the Acholi War Debt Claimants Associations, thereby further entrenching
hierarchies between different types of groups.

On a more conceptual level, by uniting larger numbers of survivors under the
umbrella of an association, groups in northern Uganda also enable their members
to more widely disseminate their demands and needs. As articulated by a member of a victims' group, "When we organize ourselves we can raise our voices and
make them be heard by the government in order to receive help" (Akullo Otwili
and Schulz 2012: 2). The postconflict context in northern Uganda continues to
be characterized by restrained access to services for conflict-affected communities. Many survivors often do not benefit from any of the developmental programs
implemented by either the Ugandan government (such as the Peace and Recovery
Development Plan) or by the countless nongovernmental agencies, mainly due to a
lack of practical measures or their inaccessibility for rural communities in particular. This creates a vacuum of provisions and assistance for the majority of victims
of the conflict. In a variety of ways, such groups therefore constitute key avenues
"in which communities [are] coping with the legacy of the conflict" (McDonald
2014: 255). Despite these different positive aspects of survivors' groups, however,
many of the challenges pertaining groups in general as listed above also apply in
northern Uganda, including hierarchies between survivors within and outside the

groups, power discrepancies among members, and dependency on outside actors, particularly on NGOs.

Varying in their composition, some groups bring together different categories of victims within one association, while others primarily unite specific (sub)categories of survivors. Focusing on gender, some groups, such as the Women's Advocacy Network (WAN), provide a platform for conflict-affected women who have returned from LRA captivity with children born as a result of rape, in addition to other groups of female as well as male survivors of sexual.

Male Sexual Violence Survivors' Groups: Men of Hope,
Peace, and Courage

Here I specifically want to focus on the groups of male sexual violence survivors in Uganda that receive support through the Refugee Law Project, alongside other support groups that RLP works with. In addition to one umbrella association in the north, RLP assists and collaborates with two other male survivors' groups in Uganda: the Men of Hope Refugee Association Uganda (MOHRAU) in Kampala, established in 2011 and composed of over 100 members who are refugees from East Africa's wider Great Lakes Region; and the refugee support group Men of Peace (MOP), established in 2013 and located in Nakivale in southwestern Uganda, one of the country's largest refugee settlements, uniting more than 230 members from neighboring countries across the region.

In these two groups, survivors' harmful experiences of sexual abuse intersect with their marginalized status as refugees living in Uganda, implying additional vulnerabilities and challenges, such as no (or restricted) legal status, limited access to income-generating activities, and insufficient social support networks. Both associations, although to varying degrees, advocate for the rights of male refugee survivors of sexual violence on the international, national, and communal level. The groups' activities "include community awareness raising, sensitization, advocacy, and documentation of sexual violence against refugee men and boys" (Edström, Dolan, et al. 2016: 1). While these two associations have produced audiovisual materials or annual reports, no such materials so far exist about the group from northern Uganda.

During the first meeting of the South-South Institute (SSI) in Kampala in July 2013, individual male survivors from Acholiland had the opportunity to engage with other male survivors from within and beyond Uganda.[2] Unlike their counterparts from other areas of the country, however, they were not yet systematically organized as an institutionalized group. Inspired by the recently established Men of Hope and Peace associations from Kampala and the Nakivale settlement, individuals from northern Uganda expressed their motivation to establish a group for male survivors in the Acholi subregion themselves. During the institute, the male survivors from northern Uganda were repeatedly referred to as men of extraordinary courage for openly coming forward and sharing their stories about government-perpetrated sexual abuse in this highly politicized context and despite their age. In relation to this, one service provider, who was present at the institute, explained that "when elders speak out about [sexual violence], it takes particular courage," thus coining the group's name, Men of Courage.

Composed of three subgroups scattered across the Acholi subregion, the Men of Courage umbrella group is less organized and centralized compared with its partnering associations in Kampala and Nakivale. Northern Uganda's vast geographical area and the widespread occurrence of sexual violence against men across large parts of the north (see chapter 3) imply organizational challenges of uniting survivors from different locations under the umbrella of one association. During one of the workshops, representatives from the different subgroups expressed their interest in further uniting the group and setting in place a more formal and centralized structure in order to provide members with better access to and benefits from developmental programs provided by the government and nonstate actors alike, a goal toward which the umbrella group is currently working. The chairperson of one of the subgroups clearly stated, "We want to transition our status as a group to become an association to be registered with the subcounty . . . so we can be assisted."

Varying in size, membership, structure, and activities, the three subgroups are called *Alany Pa Mony Lii* ("humiliation by combatants is painful"), *Kany Akanya* ("just persevere"), and *Ciro Areem Tek* ("it is hard to bear pain"). Established between 2013 and 2015, these are quite new groups, each with between ten and forty-plus members. In addition to these groups, another group, called *Tim Kikomi Wek I Cang* ("Do it yourself so that you can heal"), previously existed but now more or less dissolved following the death of their chairperson, demonstrating the dependency of such groups on strong (individual) leadership, which arguably constitutes a challenge in itself. The names of these groups in themselves indicate not only the harms suffered by male sexual violence survivors (e.g. humiliation, pain) and some of the obstacles they face as individuals and as groups (e.g. dependency), but also the ways in which they as survivors, individually and collectively, want to move forward (e.g. perseverance).

Overall the groups carry out a variety of activities, including most commonly peer support, and members have received basic training by RLP to provide psychological support for counseling one another. Additional activities include organized income-generating activities. One of the groups, for instance, cultivates beehives to generate a small profit by selling honey. The same group also organizes a saving scheme (under the umbrella of a VSLA) for members and collectively conducts agricultural work. Members of the groups have also received psychological and physical rehabilitation at Saint Mary's Hospital Lacor outside of Gulu town under the Beyond Juba Project previously run by RLP.[3] According to survivors, such activities have helped them to respond to their everyday postconflict challenges, including poverty and dependency. The Men of Courage chairperson explained that "the members of the group have decided that they should not be spoon-fed by others but that they can stay on their own and fend for themselves without living in poverty like before."

According to survivors, the groups also enable members to collectively deal with and respond to stigmatization. "We are now in a group and it is harder to stigmatize us," one male survivor explained, while another member attested that "prior to joining the group, there was a lot of community stigmatization, but now we know how to deal with it." While the stigma surrounding male-directed sexual violence persists (chapter 4), for those whose experiences of sexual abuse are known among the community and who are consequently stigmatized, the groups constitute a support network to cope and engage with these negative and often harmful community reactions. Similarly, various survivors believe that the groups' advocacy initiatives, as further explained below, and the comfort of being in a larger group with other survivors can potentially reduce the levels of stigma, including its psychosocial consequences.

Despite such benefits, however, the groups also face multiple challenges. For instance, and although the groups partially helped some survivors to deal with numerous social consequences and harms, stigmatization often prevails. One survivor explained that "even now that we are organized, the people in the community still name-call us and stigmatize us. We still have to meet in silence." Due to this, meetings are sometimes held in secret, and some of the groups exist more or less undercover. One of the groups, for instance, is officially registered as a VSLA and does not publicly identify as an association of male sexual violence survivors, and none of the groups' names includes specific references to sexual violence against men. Numerous survivors believe that a larger group of male survivors would draw attention and suspicion, thus having the reverse effect of what has been explored above and evidencing the ambivalent role and positioning of these groups and of male sexual violence survivors in Acholiland. Linked to these fears of stigmatization are security threats from community members and state agents, which some of the survivors were previously exposed to. Survivors who have broken their silence continually discussed such threats in workshops, saying they are often accused of sabotaging the government by publicly talking about government human rights violations, including sexual violence.

As with other survivors' associations in different contexts, certain differences among members within as well as across the separate groups exist. For instance, some members are more engaged and active as well as more influential than others, and they speak out more frequently. For instance, the umbrella association's chairperson, Julius Okwera, embraces a higher-profile role and regularly represents the groups in public meetings, while other members primarily engage internally or participate to a lesser extent in advocacy work. Another challenge is the groups' heavy dependence on outside actors, and especially on RLP. As articulated by one survivor within the group, "We were unsure about how to help ourselves until RLP assisted us." At the same time, survivors emphasize their motivation to mitigate this dependency and transition toward a more independent association. In many ways, this ambivalent situation illustrates the complexity of victim dependencies when survivors' groups are closely linked to or even established by civil society actors.

"HERE I CAN TALK FREELY ABOUT WHAT
HAPPENED TO ME"—EXERCISING AGENCY
IN SURVIVORS' GROUPS

But how do groups relate to agency?[4] Here I argue that the Men of Courage association enables male survivors to engage with their experiences and address their gendered harms, thereby creating pathways for them to exercise myriad forms of agency in four fundamental ways: (1) by helping survivors to renegotiate their gendered identities; (2) by (re)establishing relationships, thereby mitigating isolation, ostracism, and exclusion; (3) by providing safe spaces for survivors to share their narratives and experiences through storytelling; and (4) by aiding survivors in the struggle for recognition of their harmful but otherwise silenced experiences. From the perspectives of male survivors, these four functions respond to and begin to address (some of) survivors' sexual and gendered harms. In this reading, survivors' groups constitute a conduit through which survivors can exercise agency and ultimately through which a sense of justice on the microlevel can be conveyed, among survivors themselves and outside the purview of formal and state-driven institutions, as several survivor attested and as I will demonstrate toward the end of this chapter. In this vein the groups use the proverbial "short stick," of being close to a "problem" in order to contribute to a solution, as explained in the introduction.

Renegotiating Gendered Identities

First, groups aid male survivors in a process of renegotiating their gender identities as impacted because of the sexual violations (chapter 4). This constitutes an integral aspect of exercising agency and acting politically in relation to their communities as well as their own sense of identity in synch with the conceptual understanding of political agency laid out above. Survivors' groups thus begin responding to survivors' compromised masculinities as one of the most prevalent harms resulting from male-directed sexual violence.

The peer support that the groups engage in is loosely based on a theoretical-conceptual model of positive psychology that "takes into account the role of social interactions and support in how people process traumatic events" (Edström, Dolan, et al. 2016: 17). Through this collective peer-to-peer support, survivors develop "a critical awareness about their situation," which in turn can facilitate a mutual, collective process of "unpack[ing] the causes and impacts of these experiences" (ibid.: 28). Engaging with these effects "has a deep and liberating influence on [their] individual sense of personhood and self-worth" (ibid.) and is important in order for survivors to renegotiate their gendered identities, although clearly additional components and processes may be necessary to ultimately facilitate such processes.

Addressing the UK House of Lords' Committee on Sexual Violence in 2015, RLP director Chris Dolan, who works closely with these survivors' associations, explained that "those groups allow [survivors] to reestablish a sense of social identity and a sense of being respected again. . . . Being in a group helps to give back a sense of being recognized as an adult and as a man" (Select Committee 2016). As articulated by one survivor, "Before we came together, we had a lot of feelings of being less of a man, but since being in a group, the feelings . . . have reduced."

The groups' peer support and collective economic activities have, according to one survivor, "economically empowered us and psychologically rehabilitated us." For instance, because of the groups' income-generating activities, male survivors are reenabled to help provide for their families. The groups thus contribute to a longer and multifaceted process of reinstalling male survivors in their role as providers, one of the central components of the Acholi model of hegemonic masculinity. This immediately addresses their gendered harms and initiates a process of reversing the displacement from gendered personhood in a relational way.

Nevertheless, criticism can be raised, especially from a feminist standpoint, that the activities of the groups thereby risk (re)installing and enforcing patriarchal gender orders. Helping male survivors to regain traditional masculine roles, responsibilities, and positions could further entrench hetero-patriarchy and thereby further fuel gender inequalities. This would obviously stands in contrast to feminist projects of gender justice, which seek to dismantle these very patriarchal orders and relations. Critical feminist IR scholarship increasingly recognizes that redress, justice, and repair mechanisms for men impacted by conflict may often depend on a return to and restoration of masculine privilege that rests on hetero-patriarchal and oppressive gender orders. For instance, Megan MacKenzie (2012) has argued that throughout the postconflict literature, a "return to normal" in the aftermath of war often implies a return to particular forms of patriarchal gender orders. Drawing on empirical research in Israel/Palestine, MacKenzie and Foster theorize these dynamics as "masculinity nostalgia," "associated with a romanticized 'return to normal' that included men as heads of household, economic breadwinners, primary decision-makers and sovereigns of the family" (2017: 15). Assistance or redress for conflict-affected men that specifically seeks to repair old gender ideals can thus rely on oppressive and heteronormative gender norms, identities, and hierarchies, therefore potentially involving compromises with unintended consequences for gender equality.

As explored in the previous chapter, however, men across Acholiland are evaluated against the dominant model of hegemonic masculinity by themselves as well as their wives, families, and communities, and they are considered to be less of a man if they are unable to live up to and fulfill these social requirements. For male survivors to transition and "remake a world" (Das, Kleinman, et al. 2001), renegotiating their gendered identities is therefore critically important. As emphasized by survivors themselves, reenabling them to contribute to their families and communities is a crucial part of this process of reconnecting with manhood.

At the same time, research with the Men of Hope support group in Kampala finds that "the collective consciousness-raising within the group has also begun to challenge many members' stereotypical ideas around masculinity and manhood, as well as gender equality and views on women" (Edström, Dolan, et al.: 40). The engagement in the group and the sensitization and awareness-raising through the collective sharing of experiences often facilitate opportunities to forge new, alternative types of masculinities for male survivors. In the case of Men of Hope, for instance, "several members appear to reject many traditional inequitable norms and ideas" related to masculinities (ibid.).

This aligns with my own observations from northern Uganda, where male survivors at times demonstrated a rejection of traditional and often restrictive ideals of masculinities. For example, one survivor explained that "being a man in our culture means . . . that you cannot be weak. This meant that we could not admit to what happened to us and could not seek any support, which really made it worse for us." Through the groups, male survivors thus begin to renegotiate their own gendered identities shaped by new (and possibly more gender egalitarian) understandings of masculinity.

Overall, support groups thus aid male survivors in facilitating a process of renegotiating their gendered identities and thereby begin to respond to the violations' immediate gendered effects—enabling survivors to exercise agency in relational and politically relevant ways.

Reestablishing Relationships

The groups furthermore aid male survivors in (re)establishing relationships, primarily among themselves within an intragroup setting. Indirectly, and although to a lesser extent, groups also aid male survivors in renegotiating relations with their families, communities, and social networks, which were previously impaired because of the sexual violations and the resulting stigmatization. According to survivors, (re)establishing these relationships can mitigate the isolation that prior to joining the groups characterized their lived realities, thus constituting an important component of "a right way forward in the aftermath of wrongdoing" (Porter 2017). Especially in a highly relational and communal society such as the Acholis (p'Bitek 1986), relationships are integral and necessary for the preservation of highly valued social harmony, and thus constitute an important element of male survivors' agency.

As previously discussed, compromised relationships constitute a fundamental harm resulting from the sexual violations, and many survivors live in isolation, ostracism, and social exclusion. Finnström (2003) writes that in Acholi culture, "to be forced to live in solitude, a total restriction of the ordinary life, disconnected from family and relatives is very distressing" (70). During the workshops male survivors themselves emphasized that joining the groups helped to connect with other survivors and to establish relationships, and that some of the activities further helped them to (re)integrate in their wider communities.

According to survivors, these group processes also mitigate isolation and help them to escape loneliness, which prior to joining the groups was often characteristic of survivors' lived realities (Schulz 2018a). Based on research with members of survivors' associations in postconflict Peru, de Waardt (2016) argues that "a motivation for participating in the activities of the [victim-survivors' associations] has to do with being in the company of others who have experienced the same type of hardship" (445). This reflects the viewpoints of many male survivors in Acholiland, one of whom explained that "bringing us together like this helps us to understand that we are not alone but that others are also affected and that it also happened in many other places." Another participant similarly attested that "coming together in a group made us more courageous," and that "it helped us to come out and be comfortable among other people." A key informant who directly works with male survivors further explained that "male victims are not feeling safe in any spaces, except for sometimes in their homes, but especially in cases in which the violation happened in their home or compound, they even do not feel safe in their home. . . . As a result, they do not feel safe anywhere, with the only exception being the group."

By providing safe spaces and communities, the groups help mitigate isolation and "challeng[e] the reasons for marginalization and ostracism experienced by male survivors" (Edström, Dolan, et al. 2016: 6). Within the support groups, therefore, "feelings of isolation and hopelessness are countered by the building of relationships with other men that understand a shared reality" (28).

Discussing how conflict-affected communities in Sierra Leone "were able to find peace and justice by regaining a sense of normality . . . through everyday practices," Laura Martin (2016: 401) similarly shows how survivors' groups provided a space for rebuilding relationships and reestablishing social connections. Through "creating spaces where war-related experiences can be remoulded and relationships repaired" (400), the groups hence contribute to what Veena Das (2007) terms the "descent into the ordinary" in the wake of un-ordinary war-related lived realities, helping to remake and recover life. Communities that are transitioning out of armed conflicts often long for these everyday experiences and a sense of normality, and that desire for the ordinary often becomes a focus and locus of their agentive strategies and choices. Reflective of the sentiments expressed by male survivors in northern Uganda, Martin (2016) observed that "these seemingly mundane interactions aided people in moving away from feelings of isolation . . . towards feeling a greater sense of community" (409–410). These dynamics

illustrate that the everyday can be a crucial "space of negotiation and renego-
tiation of social relationships that make life meaningful" (Baines and Rosenoff-
Gauvin 2014: 282), and thus of social repair, which in turn becomes the focus of
survivors' agency.

Although the groups do address male survivors' harmful experience of social
invisibility, misrecognition, and humiliation, the previous experience of being and
feeling abandoned cannot be entirely negated. Political philosopher Stauffer (2015)
argues that "not being heard or being ignored impacts how the past resonates in
the present" (3). But Stauffer (2015) also suggests that to counter marginalization
and isolation, "a survivor will need broad social support that functions as a promise that, though she [or he] was once abandoned by humanity, that will not be
allowed to happen again" (7). Hence, victims' support groups can be instrumental for countering abandonment in an agentive, relational, and politically relevant
manner. As Stauffer argues, the "conditions of the surrounding world will make all
the difference to a person trying to create a livable present moment in the wake of
past harm" (ibid.: 129). She specifically notes the strength that survivors can gain
from groups and supportive environments in order to break out of the isolation
and loneliness. Edström, Dolan, et al. (2016) further echo such observations: "The
nature of peer-to-peer support helps build a sense of belonging that assists survivors of violence to overcome the resulting stigma, isolation and erosion of trust
and dignity" (28).

At the same time, different aspects of the groups, such as the communal income-
generating activities, reenable male survivors to provide for their families, which
sometimes also catalyzes a longer process of reestablishing relationships with their
families and wider communities. As theorized above, acting relationally toward
their families, communities, and themselves makes these instances politically relevant and therefore qualifies them as episodes of male survivors' political agency.

Agency, Voice, and Storytelling

In addition to facilitating these processes of renegotiating gender identities and
repairing relationships, the groups also create safe spaces for survivors to share
their stories, voice their concerns, and thereby exercise agency. Addressing the
Select Committee on Sexual Violence of the Britain's House of Lords, RLP director
Chris Dolan attested that "with the groups we are able to create platforms for them
to speak for themselves" (Select Committee 2016). Drawing on this, I additionally
argue that the groups enable survivors to exercise agency by way of articulating
their demands and engaging in a process of storytelling as a culturally appropriate component of dealing with the legacies of the past. In this capacity the groups
further address survivors' gendered harms of exclusion and isolation and respond
to the externally imposed silencing of survivors' experiences.

With regard to agency, one central concern for postconflict reconstruction
and transitional justice processes is that the professionalization of the field has led

to the emergence of postconflict and/or transitional entrepreneurs (Madlingozi 2010) who are speaking on behalf of victims. Potential risks associated with this include "resilencing victims, negating their potential for agency and reproducing the sense of powerless" (McEvoy and McConnachie 2013: 498). By encouraging survivors to share their stories and articulate their concerns, the groups stand in contrast to these problems of speaking for others, by offering survivors a platform to speak for themselves.

For one survivor, the group offers "a venue where I can talk freely about what happened to me and others listen to me and acknowledge my story." During group meetings, male survivors regularly sit together and talk about their experiences in an environment where they feel safe and protected. "When we meet and sit together, we can talk freely about what happened to us, because everyone understands and had the same experience," another male survivor said. The groups thereby facilitate safe spaces for acts of storytelling, which, according to anthropologist Michael Jackson, provides possibilities for subjective experiences to become social. As Jackson writes (2002: 245): "Stories make it possible for us to overcome our separateness, to find common ground and common cause. To relate a story is to retrace one's steps, going over the ground of one's life again, reworking reality to render it more bearable. A story enables us to fuse the world within and the world without. In this way we gain some purchase over events that confounded us, humbled us and left us helpless. In telling a story we renew our faith that the world is within our grasp."

In Acholiland, storytelling constitutes a philosophical act, and cosmology and morality are expressed most prominently through the oral tradition. Recall, for instance, the proverb presented and contextualized in the introduction to this book as an expression of this strongly pronounced oral and story culture. In their previous work on storytelling, gender, and justice in northern Uganda, Baines and Stewart (2011) further illuminate how the "Acholi communal practice of *wang-o* (telling stories around the fire pit) is an everyday practice of inviting discussions of social life" (248), thus constituting a culturally appropriate space to voice one's stories and experiences. In the context of male survivors' groups, meetings do not necessarily always take place within the context of wang-o. Nevertheless, for their gatherings survivors often choose the comforting shade of a mango tree or the seclusion of a grass-thatched hut as equally culturally resonating venues. Indeed, two of the group workshops were held in such localities in members' homesteads.

In this context, stories are not necessarily told for external purposes, such as breaking the silence, but more "for survivors to testify to other survivors" (Baines and Stewart 2011: 260). As theorized by anthropologist Fiona Ross (2003), stories in such contexts "are particular instances, synopses of experiences, told at particular times for particular audiences and located in specific contexts" (332). Linked to the process of renegotiating identities and reestablishing social relations, Baines and Stewart (2011) argue that "stories told among survivors, in informal

settings . . . provide a space in which survivors might renegotiate their social marginalization and insist on their innocence and self-worth" (247). In the wake of
violence, therefore, "storytelling restores humanity through the reconstruction
of one's life story" (ibid.). Storytelling thereby implies the potential to reconsti-
tute families, communities, and social relations, all of which are crucial aspects in
"remaking a world" (Das and Kleinmann 2001) and centralize as well as resemble
the relational understanding of politics that is required to analyze these processes
as instances of survivors' political agency.

In their study on storytelling in Acholiland, Baines and Stewart (2011) therefore
claim that "storytelling . . . becomes a form of justice making that restores the
imbalances of individual value" (258). Drawing on my own findings, I transfer their
claims to the situation of male survivors in support groups in northern Uganda,
which elevate survivors' voices, enable them to exercise agency, and share their
stories in safe spaces that are not sanctioned by the overall silencing of sexual
violence against men. Survivors getting together in groups thus qualifies as what
Das and Kleinman refer to as the "creation of alternate (public) spheres for articulating and recounting experience silenced by officially sanctioned narratives"
(2001: 3). The capacity of these groups to facilitate an alternative platform for
storytelling and articulating voices must thus be situated in the context of a vacuum of official forums or public spaces to talk about sexual violence against men.

Nevertheless, and despite these dynamics, narrating and recounting harm can
of course never be an easy task, either in official spaces, such as publicized truth-
telling initiatives, or in alternative forums on the microlevel. As emphasized by
Ross, stories "may render testifiers vulnerable" (2003: 332) and can indeed have
unintended consequences, such as long-term negative emotional and psychological implications. The safe environment of the victims' groups is therefore crucial
to lay the soil for supportive spaces where survivors can tell their stories on their
own terms, at their own pace, and for a particular audience within a familiar and
protected setting, to mitigate some aspects of the potential vulnerability arising
from narrating harmful experiences. Retaining the stories within the safe con-
fines of the groups also means that survivors can narrate their experiences without
necessarily having to fear negative repercussions, including social stigmatization,
shame, and further humiliation. Further, since the acts of storytelling are restricted
to an intragroup setting, not told for outside consumption, some of the previously
detected challenges of storytelling within the context of truth commissions, such
as the potential co-opting, external reproduction, and politicization of individual
testimonies, arise less prominently in relation to the groups. As articulated by one
survivor, "The group is a place where we can share our testimonies in dignity,"
while another survivor proclaimed that in the group, "I can talk freely about what
happened to me without having to fear any consequences or negative reactions."

Overall, and despite some potential drawbacks of intragroup silences and the
nature of testifying, Acholi male survivors' experiences suggest that storytelling

within the groups enables them to exercise agency and articulate their voices, to counter the silencing of male-directed sexual violence and survivors' experiences, thereby responding to prior harms and in part addressing their vulnerabilities. All of these are crucial aspects of survivors' relational and political agency in relation to themselves, the groups as institutions, and other members in the association.

The Struggle for Recognition

Situated in this context where male sexual harms are heavily silenced, survivors also want their harmful experiences to be recognized not only among themselves, but also by the wider society, outside actors, and the government.[5] Here I concentrate on how groups aid male survivors in obtaining recognition of their harmful experiences, among themselves and societally, and how this constitutes a significant aspect of survivors' agency by way of responding to the systematic marginalization of survivors' experiences.

In northern Uganda, recognition of sexual violence against men seems particularly important, certainly for survivors themselves, because of the severely silenced character of these crimes. At the same time, however, recognition of male survivors' experiences and harms can take on an ambivalent character, as it carries with it the possibility for negative social consequences, such as additional social stigma and communal isolation. In light of this, through the groups male survivors primarily seek wider societal recognition of their experiences and of themselves as survivors rather than merely localized and individualized recognition on the community level. These dynamics thereby resonate with Okidi's experience of navigating silence, disclosure, and recognition as presented in the case study above. At least to some extent, the survivors' groups enable male survivors to operate within and to actively navigate these spatial nuances and influence their respective levels and audiences for recognition.

For male sexual violence survivors in Acholiland, the overall silencing of their painful experiences can entrench further harms. A community leader from Awach, where male-directed sexual violence was particularly widespread, confirmed that "the rape is the first part of the violation from which they suffer, but the silence and not being able to talk also makes them suffer in isolation, even up to now." Reflecting the lived realities of Acholi male survivors of sexual violence, transitional justice scholar Frank Haldemann (2009) theorizes that by "silencing the victims, their personal and social grievances have no reality. Thus, one's suffering is reduced to a clandestine experience—overlooked and forgotten. This . . . adds to injury, and one can describe its devastating effects as 'the wounds of silence'" (693).

Various male survivors therefore emphasized that "we need our violations to be recognized." Edström, Dolan, et al. (2016) similarly quote a male survivor who "would wish that the issues of sexual violence against men be recognized in the entire world" (31). According to the survivors from northern Uganda, recognizing sexual violence against men and survivors' experiences necessitates breaking the silence surrounding these crimes. "If we keep the silence, we cannot move forward," one male survivor stated, as others vehemently agreed. The Men of Courage chairperson similarly emphasized the need for breaking the silence: "What we need is to open up, share our stories and create awareness. We must reach out to all powers that everyone can be a victim of SGBV" (RLP 2014: 6).

During the workshops it also became evident that for the survivors, "being in a group is a way to break the silence" in the public sphere and on a societal level. As outlined by the Men of Courage chairperson, the groups' "aims and objectives are to break the silence." Thereby survivors' groups imply the potential to initiate a procedural transition from silence to recognition. Arguing along those lines, during the sixth Institute for African Transitional Justice (IATJ) in June 2016, RLP director Chris Dolan emphasized the need to consider transitions from silence to acknowledgment as a microlevel form of dealing with the past. In this reading, male survivors' groups can initiate a transformation from vulnerability to agency, and by association also a process of attaining justice—as explored below.

According to the survivors, the groups' engagement in advocacy is thus expected to contribute to breaking the silence on a societal level and to some degree even nationally and internationally. The groups thereby enable and catalyze individual members to exercise various forms of political agency in different spheres to obtain a sense of recognition of their experiences. For instance, individual members have participated in meetings and forums like the South-South Institute or IATJ to raise awareness about male survivors' experiences and to advocate for their demands. As described above, survivors like Okwera have narrated their testimonies in different geopolitical contexts, ranging from Cambodia to Uganda's capital, Kampala, to regional spaces such as Gulu or Kitgum town in Acholiland—thereby attaining recognition in different spaces and spheres as well as from different audiences.

However, these meetings and gatherings are primarily attended by professionals or selected NGO or government representatives, but generally not by community members, with only occasional exceptions. Therefore, and in close cooperation with RLP, selected members have participated in community screenings of RLP-produced documentaries about sexual violence against men to raise awareness and break the silence among the community. For instance, in May 2016, a video screening of the 2011 documentary *They Slept with Me* in Amuru district was attended by approximately five hundred community members, which was an unexpectedly high turnout. The Men of Courage chairperson, whose narrative is featured in the documentary, was present at the screening and afterwards engaged in a discussion with community members.

Overall, however, and despite the groups' objectives of breaking the silence, sexual violence against men and male survivors' experiences continue to be marginalized and silenced on a societal level, by external actors, and in official discourses and local accounts of the conflict alike. According to survivors themselves, therefore, more and continuous work is needed to obtain societal recognition of their harmful experiences.

Nevertheless, one must not uncritically assume a linear process of recognition that is expected to come from "speaking out" and "breaking the silence." Empirically, "speaking out" and obtaining recognition are rarely unitary and coherent processes. Although acknowledgment and recognition are often assumed to be straightforward consequences of testifying, in reality such processes are much more complex and can involve unintended and potentially harmful consequences. Inspired by anthropologist Fiona Ross, I therefore refrain from "assuming an unproblematic link between 'voice' and 'dignity' and between 'voice' and 'being heard'" (2003: 327) and ultimately recognition. As Hamber and Wilson write in reference to the South African Truth and Reconciliation Commission, "It should not be assumed too easily . . . that 'Revealing is Healing'" (2003: 37). Simply speaking about these violations and experiences can thus not be expected to translate automatically into recognition and can likewise not be assumed to be a universally healing, redemptive, and liberating exercise. Rather, and as argued by Hayes (1998), what fundamentally matters is "how we reveal, the context of the revealing, what it is that we are revealing" (43), and how the revealed content is received and responded to.

At the same time, and specifically applied to the situation of male sexual violence survivors in northern Uganda's hetero-patriarchal context, publicly speaking out about their harmful experiences of sexual abuse can have unintended consequences. Male survivors often do not want their families or communities to know what happened to them, thereby indicating important spatial nuances with regard to where and by whom recognition is to be obtained. These geographical dimensions are illustrated through the case study of Okidi referred to above, who has sought wider recognition of his experience by publishing his account in an online newspaper. In his home village and even within his family, however, nobody knows about his experience. This example illuminates the ambivalent situation of survivors seeking recognition of their experiences on a societal level but not within their own communities or by their families. Speaking out as part of an intended therapeutic process thus implies the potential danger of having these shameful and degrading experiences (semi)publicly known, not only abstractly or confined to the groups, but also locally, which can risk further social stigmatization and exclusion. Likewise, although the motivation to speak about their experiences applies to various survivors who seek societal recognition, this cannot generally be applied to all members of the groups.

Survivors' incentives to speak up about their experience and therefore to break the silence also often only seem feasible and desirable in the contemporary post-conflict context. Many survivors emphasized that they are only hoping to obtain recognition now, for some of them thirty years after the violations occurred. While the conflict was ongoing and in the immediate aftermath of the 2006–2008 Juba Peace Talks, "the silence surrounding these crimes has also been protective," as one survivor put it. As noted by Erin Baines (2016), "Silence is often a strategy of sur-vival in violent times, and enables those threatened to navigate difficult situations to protect themselves and loved ones" (19), illustrating that preserving silence can also be a way of exercising agency (which also applies to the case study of Okidi). In relation to these temporal nuances of recognition, it is helpful to refer to anthro-pologist Veena Das, who reminds us of the "difference between the time of occur-rence and the time of telling, sometimes conceptualized as the difference between historical truth and narrative truth" (2007: 96). For sexual violence against men in Acholiland, this difference between the time of occurrence (1986–1992) and the time of telling (2011–present) is particularly striking.

"BEING IN A GROUP IS ALSO ONE SENSE OF JUSTICE"

To transition from this chapter to the next—focused on justice, recognition, and reparations—I conclude by teasing out how through their agentive capacities, groups also immediately link to questions of justice. By enabling survivors to engage with their experiences on their own terms and by addressing male sexual harms in myriad ways, survivors' groups also constitute a pathway, or a conduit, through which a sense of justice can be achieved among survivors and on the microlevel. In the absence of official, top-down, and state-administered justice avenues, groups thus constitute "alternatives to traditional institutional responses for harms that have too often gone unrecognized, unnamed and unaddressed" (Minow 1998: 4).

The vast majority of survivors who participated in this study indeed expressed that for them, "justice can be seen in a group like this." One survivor specifically said that "being in a group has been helpful to us . . . so that we can get the justice that we wanted and deserve." As emphasized by yet another male survivor, being in a support group "is one sense of justice in a way that we now are together and we are seen and recognized as those people who underwent the specific kind of atrocities, but we are together." Several service providers working with male sexual violence survivors similarly confirmed that "being in a group can be a sense of justice for most of the survivors" and that "coming together in a group is also about attaining justice at their level." In considering survivors' groups as a path-way to justice, I follow Baines's (2010) approach to justice as "a social project" that "include[s] the various strategies employed by the war-affected population to deal with the legacies of mass violence" (7). This broadened understanding of justice is laid out and conceptualized in greater detail in the following chapter.

In many ways, the group's potential to renegotiate survivors' identities and to repair broken relationships is underpinned by restorative conceptions of jus-tice. For instance, one of the survivors emphasized that "justice for us means reestablishing relationships, among us and with families and communities," while a key informant working with survivors similarly explained that one of the major justice-related concerns for male survivors is to "restore trust and rebuild relationships that were damaged because of the rape" and that the "groups can help with that." Although primarily employed to deal with the restoration of relationships between victims and perpetrators, and only to a lesser extent also between survivors and communities, restorative justice theories offer important conceptual insights to understand how the rebuilding of relationships in this context can link to justice. Restorative justice theories are primarily about addressing "the range of harms that violence causes to human relationships and . . . [restoring] relationships out of these variegated harms" (Llewellyn and Philpott 2014: 4), assuming human connections and relations, which survivors seek to rebuild, as "a starting point for thinking about what justice means" (ibid.). A restorative-relational conception of justice thus seeks to remedy the range of harms that violence and injustices can cause to human relationships.

In relation to "the struggle for recognition," survivors similarly emphasized that "justice is recognizing suffering" and that "for justice, we need our violations to be recognized." To conceptualize these linkages between recognition, agency, and voice, a recognition-theoretical understanding of justice as defined by Axel Honneth (1995) and as specifically applied to transitional justice processes by Frank Haldemann (2009) offer crucial theoretical insights.[6] According to this conception, violence, humiliation, and injustice can be measured as the absence or denial of recognition. Responding to and reversing this misrecognition and humiliation, in turn, requires due acknowledgement of survivors as human selves and of their harmful experiences. Haldemann specifically applies these conceptual linkages between recognition and justice to processes of dealing with the past, asserting that "giving public recognition to the injured and their sense of injustice should be one of the central concerns to transitional justice" (2009: 737).

While previous research examined how victims' associations enable their members to engage with external processes of dealing with the past, the potential for survivors to experience justice through their participation in groups themselves has been insufficiently explored. Such an interrogation of the peripheries or margins of transitional justice processes thus has important implications for our understanding of justice in transition, requiring us to think outside the standardized toolbox of possible justice mechanisms. Justice as approached here, and as conceptualized more fully in the following chapter, is not primarily about ensuring or protecting rights in accordance with rights-based liberalism; instead it is about responding to harms by way of renegotiating impacted identities, restoring broken relationships, and obtaining recognition in noninstitutionalized settings and among survivors themselves. Technocratic and prescriptive measures are often ill equipped to achieve these relational and social components of agency and justice and are often unavailable or inaccessible for conflict-affected communities. Such is certainly the case for male survivors of sexual violence in northern Uganda. This necessitates a broadened and widened conceptualization of justice, beyond legalistic and institutionalized measures (chapter 6), as well as a survivor-centric approach (chapter 7).

These findings about survivors' groups as an avenue for justice thereby also support Martin's (2016) assessment that "justice is not something that happens to or for post-conflict societies, but [that] individuals employ their own agency in facilitating these processes" (414). Lundy and McGovern (2008) likewise emphasize that "there is a need to foster agency by thinking imaginatively outside the 'prevailing transitional justice box,'" adding that "the first step to developing strategies is to create spaces for people to determine, shape and develop solutions for themselves" (292). Tapping into these larger debates about participatory and alternative avenues of attaining justice, I have sought to show how survivors' groups can foster agency and thereby create spaces for survivors to develop strategies for and by themselves—in line with a victim-centric approach of dealing with the legacies of wartime sexual violence.

By enabling survivors to engage with their experiences and by immediately addressing survivors' gendered harms, the groups therefore embody the metaphorical "short stick" (see the introduction), which emphasizes the importance of being close to the "problem"—which in this case are survivors' sexual and gendered harms—in order to contribute to a solution, which the groups certainly do in numerous ways.

CONCLUSION

Although groups can thus provide avenues for survivors to exercise political agency, and thereby also facilitate justice on a microlevel—which primarily focuses on survivors' needs and is concerned with relationships between individuals—additional justice-related needs on the macrolevel nevertheless prevail. As articulated by one survivor, "Groups are one way for us to get justice, but in the future other measures are also needed." In this reading, survivors' groups can be seen as one piece within a larger and procedural puzzle of justice, further necessitating different components of redress, recognition, and reparations—which constitute the focus of the next chapter.

6

Justice, Recognition, and Reparations

Although being in the support groups already sets in place a process of attaining justice on the microlevel by way of addressing some of the harms ensuing from the sexual violations, male survivors in northern Uganda also articulate diverse exogenous justice-related needs. Yet, whereas recent years have witnessed increasing consideration for redressing conflict-related sexual and gender-based violence against women and girls, specific attention to justice for male-directed sexual violence remains remarkably absent. Indeed, despite "a pressing imperative for accountability . . . that takes specific account of gender-based violence, [only] scant attention has been paid to the sexual integrity and dignity harms experienced by men" (Ní Aoláin et al. 2015: 99).

Therefore, and despite increasing efforts at the United Nations level "to ensure that transitional justice processes address the full spectrum of gender-based and sexual violence" and recognition that the "effective participation of victims . . . [is] necessary to address different needs and opportunities of women, men, girls and boys" (UN 2014: 2), male survivors' justice concerns remain remarkably absent, both from the scholarly literature and postconflict programming in northern Uganda as elsewhere globally. To date, barely a handful of studies have focused on the intersections between wartime sexual violence against men and transitional justice processes, characterized by an almost exclusive emphasis on retributive means and a ubiquitous lack of empirically grounded survivors' perspectives.

This chapter homes in on this empirical puzzle and seeks to deepen an understanding of how Acholi male survivors conceptualize justice and what their respective remedy and redress priorities are.[1] This investigation thereby forms part of the book's broader objective of painting a detailed and holistic analysis of the lived realities of male sexual violence survivors in northern Uganda, taking into account different aspects and phases of their lived realities, including contemporary postconflict quests for justice. To this end, the chapter discusses multiple gendered political, societal, and cultural barriers male survivors face in accessing the (secular) justice sector and standardized transitional justice processes in Uganda. I also analyze to what extent and how (existing and proposed) postconflict justice measures in northern Uganda respond to survivors' needs and demands, thereby evidencing a vacuum of gender-sensitive and harm-responsive justice for male sexual harms. Drawing on survivors' viewpoints and priorities, this examination thereby constitutes one of the first ever systematic and empirically guided analyses of male survivors' perspectives on justice, both in Acholiland as elsewhere globally, and so the findings presented here advance an understanding of how to deliver justice for male survivors of sexual violence, a subcategory of victims situated along the margins and peripheries of ongoing justice debates.

At the core of this chapter lies the observation that male survivors express different justice needs, which broadly center around recognition, acknowledgment, and reparations. In contrast to the often unitary focuses on international criminal accountability in redressing SGBV, including sexual violence against men, criminal prosecutions were presented as neither contemporary priorities nor feasible possibilities in the contemporary postconflict context. Instead, especially official government acknowledgment was seen to address the marginalization of survivors' largely silenced violations. At the same time, reparations, and especially material compensation and physical rehabilitation, are expected to reenable male survivors to provide for their families and thus live up to socially constructed gendered expectations and responsibilities. Based on these findings, I argue that most Acholi male sexual violence survivors seem to desire "justice as a better future" (Nickson and Braithwaite 2014: 449), in which they are able to fully participate in community life and renegotiate their previously impacted masculine identities. This requires and emphasizes the importance of a survivor-centric approach of dealing with and responding to wartime sexual violence, as included in UN Security Council Resolution 2467 and as laid out more fully in the concluding chapter.

I begin with a theoretically guided exploration of the multiplicity of meanings related to justice in contexts of transition, in general as well as context-specifically applied to northern Uganda, before presenting and systematically analyzing male survivors' empirically grounded views and perspectives on justice.

UNDERSTANDING JUSTICE IN TRANSITION

To analyze what "justice" means for male survivors of wartime sexual violence in northern Uganda, it is necessary to first establish a theorization of justice in contexts of transition. Across time and space, but especially in Western(ized) societies, justice is often understood as a shortcut for the law or for "legal," equated with judicial means at the level of institutions. Such conceptions of justice are focused on institutionalism and liberal values and "demand the presence of a sovereign state" (Sen 2017: 262). Despite the prevalence and dominance of these conceptions and assumptions about justice, however, scholars across disciplines, and especially in legal anthropology, have foregrounded the coexistence of multiple culturally and temporally contingent understandings of justice (Merry 1988; Nader 1965), which form the starting point for my thinking about justice.

In line with these approaches, I employ a broadened and thickened understanding of justice, recognizing "justice as an amorphous and elusive concept that can be interpreted and experienced in a myriad of ways" (Kent 2012: 33). As argued by Kent, justice "may have multiple socially embedded meanings," thus constituting a "contested concept that is constantly being negotiated within particular social and political constraints" (2012: 43). My understanding of justice, and the framework of this analysis, thus stem from the observation that there is not one universal concept of justice that can be applied across or within time and space. Rather than a distinct goal, justice thus ultimately exists more as a "notion," which "will probably never have a universal meaning" (McDonald and Allen 2015: 289). This coexistence of diverse understandings of justice can in part be attributed to the fact that demands for justice depend on individuals' prior subjective and diverse experiences and expectations, including of justice and harms. In fact, any quest and desire for justice was likely preceded by acts and episodes of injustice. At the same time, interpretations of justice are far from static but able to evolve and change across time and space.

This coexistence of multiple justice conceptions and understandings across and within societies is illustrated and captured by debates about legal pluralism and the plurality of justice systems. Legal anthropologist Sally Engle Merry defines legal pluralism as "a situation in which two or more legal [or justice] systems coexist in the same social field" (1988: 870). Legal pluralism is conventionally found where religious laws play a role in the justice system, and/or where a "legacy of colonial interaction between indigenous and European law" persists (Betts 2007: 740). According to legal anthropologists, virtually every society is legally plural in one way or another, whether or not it had a colonial past. Specifically focused on fragile or conflict-ridden societies, Anna MacDonald and Tim Allen further reiterate that globally the majority of war-affected societies are "regulated in a multifarious domain or assorted and diverse rule systems and institutions" (2015: 283), including multiple justice systems and approaches. Indeed, jurisdictional complexity and multiplicity is hardly unique, neither contemporarily nor historically.

Such is certainly the case in Acholiland, where multiple traditions of justice dating from precolonial, colonial, and postcolonial times coexist. Prior to colonization, what can broadly be referred to as different justice systems operated horizontally in that they were "regulated by a series of relationships, rather than by a state" (McDonald 2014: 71). During this period, wrongdoing and crimes were often dealt with in "open courts," which as described by Erin Baines were "held at different levels of social organization (household, sub-clan, clan, inter-clan and inter-tribal) according to the nature of the conflict (land, domestic conflict, arson, murder)" (2005: 16). There was indeed "not one centre of authority, but many, and their relationships were overlapping" (McDonald 2014: 71).

This plurality of justice systems in Acholiland was further intensified by the British colonial administration, which installed a form of Western legalism alongside, or rather on top of, preexisting forms of social ordering and structuring. To illustrate this imposition of Western justice ideas onto the Acholi context, the first colonial administrator of Gulu district, J. P. Postlewaith, wrote in 1947 that "we meted out justice according to our own ideas without having much real appreciation of natives' own traditions" (37). During the colonial period "the development of law as an institution, and the enforcement of a legal apparatus become a key means of social control" (MacDonald 2014: 75). As noted by Erin Baines, however, this "introduction of the court system by colonialists did not appear to wholly undermine traditional court systems" (2005: 16). Consequently, what marked this period was "the imposition of a new power system conjugated to a new legal culture" (ibid.), and traditional courts and systems of justice were slowly subordinated to a state-administered system.

In the contemporary context, this plurality of systems of authority and administering justice to an extent continues to prevail, although perhaps in a different manifestation. In present-day northern Uganda, the government's local council (LC) system coexists alongside traditional systems organized by clan and village structures. Today people and communities in Acholiland therefore engage with different justice systems, which range from informal and local, often situated within and along village and clan structures, to the official level, such as the LC system or national courts of law. The introduction of the LC system, however, significantly undermined the role and authority of elders and traditional practices, which were subjugated to state-level processes.

Although this plurality of justice systems is often attributed to colonization, in northern Uganda as indeed elsewhere globally, colonialism per se is not always solely responsible for the introduction or manifestation of legal pluralism. In fact, pluralized justice systems existed across a variety of societies and geographies prior to colonialism. While colonialism is thus not exclusively responsible for the introduction of legal pluralism as such, eurocentric and colonial approaches to justice are nevertheless at the very core of a tendency to subjugate indigenous and local justice processes. Theorizing about the plurality of justice systems is thereby characterized by a strong tendency to portray indigenous or traditional and nonstate or informal laws as necessarily subordinate to the official, state-driven, and Western form of justice. This tendency to marginalize the local and informal is particularly pronounced in transitional justice processes, as discussed in more depth below.

Overall this debate about legal pluralism shows that across and within societies, in general and in northern Uganda, plural conceptualizations of justice can coexist. Justice cannot be unanimously understood and applied, and there is sufficient conceptual and empirical ground to challenge the ubiquitous utility of one universally applicable and relativist conception of justice that resonates across and within time and space. This understanding is foundational to my analysis of justice in times of transition.

"The Right Way Forward in the Aftermath of Wrongdoing"—
Understanding Justice in Acholiland

Resonating with these multiple justice conceptions across time and space, in northern Uganda a dominant locally contingent meaning or interpretation of justice appears to prevail. While no commonly agreed-upon translation of the word "justice" exists, the most common conception of justice in Acholi is *ngol matir,* which can broadly be understood as the process of determining "a right way forward in the aftermath of wrongdoing" (Porter 2013: 106). In one of the first examinations of the Acholi language, Catholic missionary Crazzolara translates *ngol* as "to cut," "to pass a sentence," or "to decide a question" (327), while *matir* can be translated as "fair" or "just." In relation to this, Holly Porter explains that "*ngol matir* could be understood literally as to 'cut straight,' though conceptually it is more accurate to say a fair or right judgement" (2013: 98).

Indeed, various research collaborators, for the sake of simplicity, initially translated ngol matir as "fair judgment," or "fair justice." According to this explanation, ngol matir would signify "the decision at the end of a process" (Porter 2013: 98), such as the sentencing or judgment at the end of judicial proceedings. Such an interpretation of justice, however, does not necessarily correspond with the views and priorities of most Acholis, including the lived realities of my informants, as examined below.

Crazzolara's additional interpretation of *ngol* as "to decide a question" in relation to justice, however, much better aligns with Acholi conceptions of justice. According to local understandings of wrongdoing and crime, primarily measured as a disruption of social harmony (Porter 2012), justice, or *ngol matir*—to "decide a question"—can be understood as "to decide a right way forward in the aftermath of wrongdoing" (Porter 2013: 106). In this context, "a right way forward" would ideally be determined in an inclusive and participatory process, involving survivors and offenders, and at times their wider communities, in line with restorative justice theories. In practice this is frequently done through local and traditional justice processes, as described in later parts of this chapter. What this "right way forward" must entail and how it should look, however, is often highly individual and contextual, depending on survivors' lived realities, their social context, the violations committed against them, or the identity of the perpetrator. Based upon this most common conceptualization, I thus follow Porter's approach and utilize the terminology of ngol matir for the purpose of my analysis, understood within the widened frame of "a right way forward in the aftermath of wrongdoing" (Porter 2017).

Such an interpretation of justice as a right way forward is consistent with the widened understanding of justice employed throughout legal anthropology scholarship, and it is much more accommodating of a variety of psychopolitical as well as socioeconomic components, elements, and processes. This approach thereby also stands in contrast to and moves beyond the institutionalized and legalistic construction of transitional justice prevalent throughout much of the literature. Such local understandings of justice vis-à-vis standardized transitional justice approaches illustrate the frictions that arise when global norms grate against local conceptions of justice. Therefore, and as summarized by Millar, "justice is not some platonic ideal, but something experienced within a context, and therefore, variable and reliant on local interpretation" (2011: 517).

TRANSITIONAL JUSTICE

Moving from a general focus on justice to a more specific examination of justice in transition after violent conflict and mass atrocities, in this section I conceptualize an understanding of transitional justice as underpinning the analysis to come. Applied to transitions after armed conflicts, dictatorship, or authoritarian regimes, justice in response to past mass violence and extensive human rights violations is commonly categorized as transitional justice, which according to the United Nations Secretary General (2014: 4) can be defined as "a full range of processes and mechanisms associated with a society's attempt to come to terms with a legacy of large-scale past abuses, in order to ensure accountability, serve justice and achieve reconciliation. These may include both judicial and non-judicial mechanisms, with different levels of international involvement (or none at all) and individual prosecutions, reparations, truth-seeking, institutional reform, vetting, and dismissals, or a combination thereof."

In referring to both judicial and nonjudicial mechanisms, the UNSG's understanding of transitional justice extends the scope of most earlier definitions, which primarily emerged from a legal standpoint and often placed a strong (if not exclusive) emphasis on judicial accountability to facilitate transitions and deliver justice at the expense of non- or quasi-judicial and noninstitutionalized processes.

By broadly working with the UN's definition, I nevertheless emphasize that the suggested catalog of prosecutions, reparations, and various other institutionalized mechanisms should be understood not as an exhaustive list but as an indication of potential measures. Instead, and depending on context, a variety of noninstitutionalized and "unrecognizable" transitional justice measures (Martin 2016) can often likewise be included. The holistic study of justice in transition should thus also entail consideration for, and a critical examination of, "everyday" practices of the way individuals and communities reconstruct their lives and rebuild relationships and societies in the aftermath of armed conflicts. Borrowing from Richmond, the "everyday" in this context refers to "a space in which local individuals and communities live and develop political strategies in their local environment. . . . It is representative of the deeper local-local, engaging with needs, rights, custom, individual, community, agency and mobilization in political terms" (2010: 6).

In light of this evolution, Mallinder observes that "as the field of transitional justice has developed, informal approaches to justice have attracted increasing attention as a way of redressing past crimes" (2014: 4). As emphasized by Erin Baines, "Justice is a social project among many others, and the study of justice should include the various strategies employed by the war-affected populations to deal with the legacies of mass violence" (2010: 7). Instead of exclusively examining what Das and Kleinman (2001: 16) refer to as "grand narratives of forgiveness and redemption," this growing body of "remaking a world" scholarship is increasingly attentive to local and individual experiences of coming to terms with human rights abuses and transitioning out of conflict. In light of this broadened angle, I find Alcalá and Baines's broad conceptualization of transitional justice particularly helpful, as it refers to "the many individual and collective ways in which people pursue mundane activities and practices to restore the basic fabrics of meaningful social relations, negotiations or re-creative protective mechanisms and provide some sense of continuity in their lives and sense of self in relation to others in the aftermath of violence and conflict" (2012: 278).

As indicated by these definitional developments, the concept of transitional justice (TJ) thus experienced its own transition, emerging from its exceptionalist origins toward becoming a normalized, institutionalized, mainstreamed, and globalized practice. For Hansen (2014) this growth and expansion of TJ can be categorized along horizontal and vertical lines. On the one hand, justice processes are increasingly applied to diverse transitional contexts and a wide range of situations. These include not only postconflict settings or postauthoritarian and postdictatorial transitions, but increasingly also still ongoing conflict zones. Not only the points of departure, however, but also the end goals of transitional justice processes are increasingly recognized as being more diverse than initially assumed. Although in recent years TJ has been increasingly emancipated from the bonds of the paradigmatic transition, such processes are often still expected to directly promote democratization, human rights, the rule of law, and peace-building, often within neoliberal frameworks. I concur with Brandon Hamber, however, in arguing that "in reality, these processes are seldom linear, and reconstruction involves many processes that are not always captured by phrases such as peacebuilding or transitional justice" (2016: 8). Instead, the complex, unsettling, and fluid nature of transitional justice processes across time and space evidences that "dealing with the past is a continuing process, rather than confined to a specific 'transitional' period" (Kent 2012: 205).

Such is evidently the case in northern Uganda, where the Juba Peace Agreement of 2008, although not finally signed by the Lord's Resistance Army (LRA), was widely assumed to set in motion a justice and reconstruction process to be characterized by a linear transition from protracted war to liberal peace. As previously discussed, Uganda is a relatively diverse and comprehensive transitional justice landscape. Despite the proposal and involvement of different transitional justice mechanisms—such as the International Crimes Division (ICD), investigations by the ICC, and a draft national transitional justice policy—however, the reality on the ground a decade later looks anything but linear; it rather reflects the messiness and ambiguity of such processes.

As part of this expansion, transitional justice has also become increasingly attentive to the gender dynamics of political transitions, including gendered harms and crimes of sexual and gender-based violence (mostly against women and girls). Even though TJ continues to have a "capture problem with gendered harms" (Ní Aoláin 2012: 20), the past two decades in particular have radically changed and further developed the treatment of gender-based violence. At the same time, however, gendered approaches to TJ are dominated by a strong focus on sexual violence and an emphasis on retributive justice and criminal prosecutions. This arguably resulted in rather limited and exclusionary gender justice developments, marginalizing quasi-judicial or noninstitutionalized justice measures and overshadowing gendered inequalities toward women as well as sexual and gender-based violence against men and boys and against individuals with diverse sexual orientations and gender identities.

The focus of the literature on prosecutorial means reflects, and has arguably been influenced by, a sustained focus on conflict-related sexual violence in the international criminal justice arena—and most notably at the International Criminal Tribunals for the former Yugoslavia (ICTY) and Rwanda (ICTR). These two ad-hoc tribunals in particular are widely credited with the responsibility for the contemporary jurisprudence on sexual violence in the context of armed conflict and are seen as having established landmark and precedence cases concerning sexual violence.

While most of the scholarly literature and most cases at the ad hoc tribunals and at the International Criminal Court (ICC) focus on gendered and sexualized violence against women, very few proceedings have involved cases of sexual violence against men, most notably so at the ICTY. The only two times that male sexual violence and rape were explicitly charged and tried under international criminal law was in the ICTY's *Prosecutor v. Ranko Cesic* case, and in the ICC's case against Jean Pierre Bemba in the Central African Republic, although the initial judgment in the Bemba case was appealed and overturned again in 2018. The ICC's investigation into the Kenya situation similarly included evidence suggesting that even though most crimes of sexual violence were committed against women and girls, men and boys were also affected by different forms of SGBV. Yet, and although the ICC prosecutor initially included these charges under the rubric of "other forms of sexual violence," ICC judges disagreed, arguing that the described crimes do not constitute sexual violence. According to the trial chamber, "not every act of sexual violence which targets part of the body commonly associated with sexuality should be considered as an act of sexual violence" (RLP 2013: 31). This limited body of jurisprudence and case law led international legal scholar Sivakumaran to attest that "the actual prosecutions of male sexual violence have been rather disappointing" (2013: 87).

At the same time, the vertical expansion of transitional justice facilitated an increasing participation and importance of local actors, including communities of victims and survivors, as well as local processes—such as grassroots measures or traditional justice rituals. What throughout the literature is described as "localizing transitional justice" thereby seeks to incorporate local norms, mechanisms, and ceremonies into TJ practice and aims to ensure that the voices, concerns, and needs of local actors and populations are integrated into these processes. The United Nations in 2004 recognized the benefits of customary local practices for larger TJ processes, by emphasizing that "due regard must be given to indigenous and informal traditions for administering justice" so that these processes can "continue their often vital role . . . in conformity with both international standards and local traditions" (18). The UN report, acknowledging the potential of locally embedded and culturally specific mechanisms, therefore emphasizes "the importance of local consultation, ownership and leadership, and recognizes the role of local mechanisms" (Anyeko et al. 2012: 110).

The growing attention to the local can largely be seen as a result of a growing disconnection between international norms and processes and local needs, priorities, and conceptions of justice. Indeed, international or national institutionalized processes are often inaccessible for conflict-affected communities, and/or disconnected from local belief systems, as well as from survivors' needs and priorities. Local customary or traditional justice systems are therefore often portrayed as better accessible and more culturally and socially legitimate for community-based or rural populations.

At the same time, however, and as noted by Shaw and Waldorf, local justice processes are primarily seen as "*complements* to national or international processes" (2010: 4). This implies that local justice is often treated as subordinate to processes at other levels. In the context of peace-building, developmental assistance, and transitional justice, the local is situated at the bottom of a hierarchy. A hierarchical level-based definition of the "local," Shaw and Waldorf (2010) argue, risks depoliticizing locality and "constructing it as a residual category characterized by separation [from the global, national, regional, etc.]" (6). As a result of this depoliticization, locality is often equated with the absence of modernity and is consequently downplayed in value and importance. The infantilization of the local then results in a marginalization of the experiences and perspectives of the people within this residual space, which most often constitute the vast majority of conflict-affected communities.

Traditional and localized justice processes have also taken on a prominent role in discourses and practices around dealing with the legacy of the conflict in northern Uganda. Different informal measures, such as the ritual of *mato oput,* are widely presented as locally appropriate alternatives to formalized and top-down administered means, and especially to the punitive approach of the ICC.[2] Civil society representatives as well as cultural and religious leaders in particular have emerged as prominent advocates of this approach, arguing that these measures are culturally sensitive and best equipped to deal with the complex nature of the conflict and postconflict transition. In ways different from formalized processes, those mechanisms help to bring conflicting parties together with the aim of promoting reconciliation and restoration of relationships and social harmony.

Such rituals and ceremonies have a rich tradition in Acholiland. Often deeply rooted in Acholi cosmology (Gingyera-Pinycwa 1992; p'Bitek 1986), they were employed to deal primarily with interpersonal and interclan disputes. Within the context of the armed conflict and its aftermath, these traditional mechanisms were often modified and applied to deal with conflict-related harms. Nevertheless, critics have questioned the potential applicability of traditional Acholi ceremonies in dealing with mass atrocities, including with crimes of gender-based violence. On a more general level, Tim Allen (2006) raises concerns regarding the politicization of these practices, arguing that they are merely an "invention of tradition," while Branch (2008) claims that especially the practice of *mato oput* is affected by neocolonial interventions, especially by the quite artificially created institution *Ker Kwaro Acholi* (KKA) or by intervening NGOs.

A report from 2005 furthermore found that the majority of Acholi elders interviewed for the study did not think that these processes were feasible in the context of the armed conflict (Baines 2005). This potential inapplicability arises, in part, because traditional cultural beliefs and practices in northern Uganda were heavily impacted by the conflict, and in particular by widespread forced displacement. Furthermore, different rituals, such as *mato oput,* require the active participation of both the victim and perpetrator (and often their families/clans), which in the context of protracted armed conflict, characterized by abduction, high rates of killings, and large-scale displacement, is often difficult to achieve (Baines 2007). And lastly, during the war and in the postconflict period, "many Elders argued that poverty limited their ability to carry out rituals" (Baines 2005: 13), which requires compensational payments and the sacrifice of animals, for instance. Partly in response to these economic barriers, in recent years, different NGOs intervened to support communities in organizing these rituals, which however significantly downplayed the local agency and participation that makes these processes so unique.

A Vacuum of Justice for Male Survivors in Uganda

Despite increasing consideration for accountability for gender-based violence in general, as outlined above, little attention has been paid to justice in response to sexual violence against men. This absence of gender-sensitive and harm-responsive justice with utility across diverse postconflict and transitional settings is particularly evident and pronounced in northern Uganda, where previous, existing, and proposed transitional justice developments fail to account for crimes of sexual violence against men and arguably for gender-based violence more broadly.

Although the current proceedings of the ICC against former LRA commander Dominic Ongwen, and those of the domestic International Crimes Division (ICD) under the High Court of Uganda against former LRA commander Thomas Kwoyelo, include various charges of SGBV against women and girls, they do not include crimes of sexual violence against men. The investigations by the ICC's Office of the Prosecutor (OTP) to date also solely focus on crimes perpetrated by the rebel forces but not by the government army, which has been subjected to sustained criticism for one-sidedness. At the same time, the Rome Statute mandates the court to investigate crimes committed after 1 July 2002, when the statute entered into force. Since almost all crimes of sexual violence against men in Acholiland occurred during the late 1980s and early 1990s, however, the ICC cannot investigate them.

At the same time, the ICD is unlikely to be a viable avenue for male sexual violence survivors to seek justice, as it operates within the government's jurisdiction, and therefore "any prosecution of government-linked war crimes under the current government is highly unlikely" (MacDonald and Porter 2016: 703), let alone any accountability for crimes of male-directed sexual violence. To further complicate things, the Ugandan Penal Code (UPC), which forms the country's primary legal framework, also explicitly defines rape in gender-exclusive terms, solely recognizing women and girls as victims of sexual and gender-based violence and thereby explicitly excluding male survivors (see below).

The Ugandan government's draft national transitional justice policy (JLOS) further reflects these gendered blind spots.[3] For instance, the policy includes only two vague references to gender and only one reference to sexual violence, thus fundamentally lacking any consideration for gendered experiences and harms, let alone any attention to male survivors specifically.[4] Considering that UN women contributed to earlier drafts of the policy, this marginalization and exclusion of gender in the current version of the draft is particularly surprising.

Traditional, customary, and localized justice means, which take on a prominent role in northern Uganda, are often equally ill equipped to remedy gendered harms, including sexual violence against men. Because of their masculine and heteronormative framework, these measures are likely to ignore gendered conflict-related experiences and leave very little room to engage with masculinities outside the hegemonic norms, let alone with male sexual and gendered harms. The majority of Acholi traditional rituals also serve a different purpose, and primarily deal with killings and spiritual cleansing, making them technically inapplicable to cases of male rape. Furthermore, most rituals take place (semi)publicly on the local level, which implies that male survivors' experiences would be publicly revealed to their communities and families. Coupled with various other technical limitations, such as the seeming impossibility (yet technical requirement) of mostly non-Acholi perpetrator participation, these intersecting factors render traditional justice processes inappropriate and highly unlikely to potentially remedy cases of male rape.

Conditioned by these intersecting gaps, the overall transitional justice landscape in Uganda is strikingly insensitive to male survivors' sexual harms. This absence and unresponsiveness of formal processes to male sexual violence survivors and their gendered harms are further compounded by a profound Acholi lived reality of a deep-seated frustration with and mistrust of the Ugandan government to deliver justice. Echoing survivors' sentiments from across various postconflict sites, the majority of research participants in this study expressed frustration, dissatisfaction, and a lack of trust regarding state-administered or top-down elite-driven justice mechanisms. Below I further demonstrate this vacuum of gender-sensitive and harm-responsive justice by systematically evidencing the unresponsiveness of different justice measures to male sexual harms.

MALE SURVIVORS' VIEWS ON JUSTICE

Drawing on this contextual and conceptual overview of (transitional) justice developments, in northern Uganda and beyond, the remainder of this chapter homes in specifically on how Acholi male sexual violence survivors think about and understand justice in response to their sexual and gendered harms. The workshop discussions with survivors essentially foregrounded three central themes as potential avenues of attaining justice. Each characterized by a diversity of at times competing views, these themes form the framework of analysis throughout the remainder of this chapter: (1) recognition and official acknowledgment; (2) criminal prosecutions; and (3) reparations, including (a) material compensation and (b) physical rehabilitation. The analytical structure I impose in accordance with these themes represents the views expressed by the male survivors who participated in this study, how they spoke about what justice means to them, and how to achieve a sense of justice for them. What becomes evident is that these diverse justice measures are frequently linked and interdependent, thereby illustrating that transitional justice processes often need to be externally coherent. It is important to note, however, that survivors' justice-related needs are, of course, never static and potentially evolve and change over time. The analysis offered here therefore provides a snapshot into male survivors' contemporary justice conceptions and priorities.

At the core of this analysis lies the observation that despite a heterogeneity of perspectives, a consensus seems to prevail among survivors that justice processes need to directly respond to their uniquely gendered harms as a result of the sexual violations. In particular, recognition and official government acknowledgment, which can manifest in various ways, were seen to potentially address the marginalization of survivors' silenced violations. Reparations, and especially material compensation and physical rehabilitation, are further expected to reenable male survivors to provide for their families and thus live up to socially constructed gendered expectations and responsibilities. Based on these findings, I argue that most Acholi male sexual violence survivors seem to desire "justice as a better future" (Nickson and Braithwaite 2014: 449), in which they are able to regain a minimally functioning life, fully participate in community activities, and renegotiate their impacted masculine identities. Male survivors' views on and preferences of justice thereby follow anthropologist Veena Das, who has explored how processes of social reconstruction are often enacted through not only "some grand project of recovery," but also through the enactment of "everyday tasks of surviving"—including being able to do the work of the everyday (Das 2000: 222). Drawing on this groundbreaking work by Veena Das, Gray, Stern, and Dolan call for processes of attaining justice and social repair in the aftermath of violence that are "centrally and unavoidably social," not undertaken by "an autonomous subject as imagined by liberal theory, but rather by a socially embedded and relational subject" (2019: 8)—and thus in line with the broader, relational understanding of justice put forward above.

Government Acknowledgment: "To me, justice means recognizing suffering"

To begin with, wider recognition and in particular official government acknowledgment constitute prime justice needs for the majority of male survivors who participated in this study. While in the previous chapter, I discussed how support groups enable survivors to strive for wider societal recognition, and how this links to recognition-theoretical conceptions of justice, here I focus primarily on acknowledgment by the government in line with survivors' viewpoints.

In both theoretical and practical terms, recognition and acknowledgment can be seen as inherently linked. This is locally reflected in linguistic and cultural terms: In the Acholi language, acknowledgment translates as *niyee,* and recognition is translated as *moko niyee,* confirming acknowledgment. Recognition and acknowledgment are thus viewed as distinct yet fundamentally linked, and (full) recognition can depend upon acknowledgment. In the context of this study, and as articulated by survivors, acknowledgment primarily must be official, issued by individual and/or institutional perpetrators, whereas recognition can be offered more widely and on a societal level, not exclusively dependent upon the perpetrators' involvement.

Throughout the transitional justice literature, official and/or perpetrator acknowledgment is often regarded as a key component of delivering justice, linked to a variety of different transitional justice measures, including reparations. Wendy Lambourne, for instance, argues that "having perpetrators acknowledge what they have done and its impact on victims can be crucial for justice," highlighting "the need for acknowledgment as an important part of transitional justice" (2009: 41). Approaching acknowledgment more from a psychological perspective, Shnabel and Ulrich similarly elaborate that for justice, "victims are likely to want perpetrators to acknowledge their responsibility for the injustice they have caused" (2013: 117). And for de Greiff (2008), "acknowledgment is important precisely because it constitutes a form of recognizing the significance and value of persons" (14), and primarily of their victimization.

Mirroring these conceptual reflections, according to male sexual violence survivors in Acholiland, "justice is when the government acknowledges what happened to us." Various service providers working with male survivors in interviews with me similarly emphasized that "in terms of justice, acknowledgment by the government of the violations is crucial." The survivors who participated in this study thus primarily demand official, institutional acknowledgment by the government responsible for commanding and perpetrating these crimes. Interestingly, survivors spoke less prominently about acknowledgment by *individual* perpetrating soldiers, seemingly recognizing the government army's collective command responsibility.

For the majority of survivors, government acknowledgment must ideally be manifested through official statements and/or apologies. The chairperson of one the three subgroups affirmed that "to acknowledge the crimes, the government should give an apology," while another male survivor similarly stated that "there needs to be acknowledgment in the form of an apology." This need for official acknowledgment for harms suffered by the civilian population during the conflict is not exclusive to male sexual violence survivors, as victims across the conflict-affected north demand government acknowledgment for the crimes committed against them. What is unique about male sexual violence survivors' quests for government acknowledgment, however, is that these crimes remain particularly silenced, marginalized, and ignored compared with other violations. One survivor declared that "the government should come out and acknowledge what they did. . . . In most cases, when there are big meetings, we are not recognized, but they go into recognizing other vulnerable groups of people, like the disabled, the widows, the orphans. What about us? We don't have any voice, and that will only change if the government acknowledges what happened to us."

Whereas a whole catalog of conflict-related human rights violations, including government perpetrated abuses, is increasingly brought to the forefront within the contemporary transitional context and is even partially acknowledged by the government, crimes of male-directed sexual violence continue to remain marginalized and silenced.[5] We recall that in Acholiland's hetero-patriarchal society, the rape of men is largely unacknowledged or considered not possible to have occurred. In light of this lack of affirmation, male survivors want their experiences officially acknowledged and thereby validated.

For numerous survivors, acknowledgment is furthermore regarded as a crucial precondition for accessing other remedies, responses, and, importantly, reparations, further demonstrating the interconnections among different justice-related measures. For instance, one survivor emphasized the importance of acknowledgment as a first step to access reparations, by explaining that for me, the government . . . needs to acknowledge what happened. What will the government do if it fails to acknowledge the acts of sexual violations in Acholiland? For the government to do something, and to, for instance, pay us compensation, they first need to acknowledge that they did this to us, and then that would also be justice."

Various survivors indeed articulated that acknowledgment is relevant and valuable only if followed by reparations, and vice versa, reparations can only be meaningful if they are provided as a means of acknowledging the specific sexual violations and survivors' harms: "If there is compensation that means there is full acknowledgment. If it stays with just acknowledging without keeping the promise and paying, that is not real acknowledgment." Such concerns align with conceptual and empirical observations that victims often criticize public apologies of acknowledgment "as being empty words if these apologies are not accompanied by reparations" (Llewellyn and Philpott 2014: 6). Acknowledgment itself would thus not be sufficient but would have to be accompanied by additional measures, such as compensation, thereby supporting Hamber and Wilson's argument that "for most people, more is needed than simple recognition and acknowledgment" (2003: 43).

Obtaining government acknowledgment for crimes committed by state forces, however, is fraught with inherent cultural, social and political challenges, further exacerbated by the gendered dimensions of the violations within a heteropatriarchal context. "The government will not acknowledge this because it happened long ago and they were the ones perpetrating it, so they will not recognize and respond," one male survivor attested. Another survivor similarly stated that "acknowledgment is very important for us, but the biggest challenge . . . is how do we propel the government to acknowledge the wrongs committed against us? We do not have any clear way of convincing the government to do that. That is why everything lies in the hands of the government."

These concerns suggest a deep-seated frustration over the profound lack of measures and provisions by the government for male survivors, including a lack of affirmation of their experiences. On a more general level, when state forces have been involved in perpetrating human rights violations, official acknowledgment may often materialize only after regime changes. Indeed, when the power structures that are responsible for widespread human rights abuses are also in charge of designing and implementing national and top-down justice measures, government-perpetrated crimes almost inevitably fall off the radar. We recall that in northern Uganda the government from which survivors demand acknowledgment is the same regime that was responsible for the perpetration of sexual violence against men more than twenty-five years ago. Among the conflict-affected community in Acholiland at large, a widespread belief prevails that without a regime change, there will be no accountability for NRA atrocities.

In addition to these political barriers, acknowledgment for sexual crimes against men is specifically characterized by a variety of gendered, social, and cultural challenges and therefore seems particularly elusive. In Acholiland's heteronormative and patriarchal setting, male vulnerability is regarded as incompatible with hegemonic masculinities (chapter 4), and male sexual abuse is perceived as de facto nonexistent. Conditioned by the social stigmatization attached to male rape, some survivors themselves previously and currently do not want their experiences of abuse publicly known or recognized. Furthermore, publicized acknowledgment of male sexual victimization can carry wide-reaching psychosocial consequences for survivors and can imply the risk that male survivors face social stigmatization from their families and communities, or that they can be criminalized for same-sex acts, which are punishable by life in prison in Uganda. This unveils a seeming paradox: Male survivors demand acknowledgment for their marginalized and silenced experiences despite the risk that (public) awareness may cause stigmatization, leading to social and psychological harms. Therefore, many survivors want the government to acknowledge the widespread perpetration of these crimes in general but without necessarily publicly revealing survivors' identities.

At the same time informal ways to acknowledge and memorialize the suffering of survivors exist. These include, for instance, communal and local monuments and memorials, which in a broader sense can be classified as symbolic reparations. In northern Uganda community-led monuments and memorials constitute common ways of remembering conflict-related experiences and atrocities across Acholiland. For instance, according to a population-based survey on attitudes about justice, almost all (95 percent) "of the respondents said they wanted memorials to be established to remember what happened in Northern Uganda" (Pham et al. 2007: 34). To some extent, these sentiments for community-based memorialization also resonate with male survivors' conceptions. Indeed, since the government has not acknowledged any responsibility for the perpetration of male rape, some survivors also seek other forms of recognition. According to one male survivor, "If you have everything but no memorial, there will be no justice. If a memorial is not there, . . . there is no acknowledgment and recognition."

Across Acholiland, a variety of community-based memorialization initiatives exist, including at least one memorial that includes acknowledgment of male rape. In 2015 the community of Burcoro in Awach subcounty, where male rape was particularly widespread, received logistical and financial assistance from the Justice and Reconciliation Project (JRP) to erect a monument in memory of a 1991 NRA-executed massacre that included acts of tek-gungu. The memorial structure is in the shape of a tree—since one of the massacre victims was tied to a tree and

FIGURE 3. Monument in Burcoro, Awach subcounty.

executed by a firing squad—and is located at the former execution spot. A variety of human rights abuses and crimes perpetrated during the massacre, such as killings and acts of torture, are marked on the different branches of the tree. One of the branches, clearly visible to everyone who inspects the monument from the front, reminds the viewer of crimes of "sexual abuse," "rape," as well as "sodomy," which is how male rape is often referred to in English across the region.

For many male survivors from Burcoro, this monument and its specific mentioning of sexual violence against men is an important aspect of recognizing their experiences and thus obtaining justice, even though it is not a form of official government acknowledgment. Such a localized memorialization initiative cannot replace government acknowledgment, but it can function in addition and complementary to official state recognition. These informal memorials ultimately serve a purpose different from official government acknowledgment and memorialization efforts: They strive to make visible the communities' recognition of sexual violence against men and demonstrate that male sexual violence survivors should be treated equally to victims of other conflict-related experiences. Therefore, in a context where male sexual violence survivors are marginalized and silenced, community-based memorialization of male-directed sexual violence can carry its own particular value and importance, for the community as well as specifically for survivors.

Criminal Justice and Prosecutions

Criminal prosecutions were another prominent justice-related theme that emerged during the workshop discussions with the survivors. Ultimately survivors' perspectives on criminal justice and prosecutions vary: While some viewed criminal proceedings as potential avenues for attaining justice, most survivors expressed a fundamental mistrust in the criminal justice system and did not view prosecutions to be feasible or necessarily desirable in the current social and political context. Conditioned by the seeming impossibility of prosecutions for redressing male sexual abuse, criminal justice therefore does not seem to be a current priority for the majority of survivors in this study. Male survivors' views thus tend to stand in contrast to the legalistic orientation of the global transitional justice project, which continues to present criminal prosecutions as the benchmark from which other justice processes merely follow. This privileging of legalistic measures specifically characterizes the growing body of scholarship on SGBV accountability in general and the admittedly limited literature on sexual violence against men and transitional justice in particular (see Schulz 2015, 2020a).

Yet despite these dominant sentiments, some survivors do believe that criminal prosecutions are potential avenues for attaining justice. One survivor stated plainly, "I want the issue [the crimes] to be taken to court, because if the discussion is pushed to court, I would see justice," while another said that "to me, justice is fighting impunity." Interestingly, however, survivors seemed not to prefer trials as a means of retribution. During the workshops no male survivor explicitly expressed a desire for criminal accountability and punishment of the perpetrators out of retributive motives. Similarly, other prominent and commonplace objectives of (international) criminal justice, such as deterrence and the investigation of command responsibilities to identify wider patterns of crime and violence, were not raised by survivors as desired outcomes of prosecutorial processes. Apart from one exception of a survivor for whom prosecutions "can block the continuation of the same problem [of male rape]," survivors did not specifically emphasize deterrence, for instance, as a desired outcome of criminal prosecutions.

Instead, several survivors explicitly raised prosecutions as avenues to materialize acknowledgment and to access reparations. One male survivor attested that "if we take this to court, it means our violations are acknowledged at the official level, and we will also be able to get reparations." Another survivor suggested that "we first ask the government to acknowledge and then compensate. If they do not agree, we need to take them to court to get the acknowledgment and compensation through the courts." Further illustrating these perceptions of prosecutions as avenues to obtain acknowledgment and reparations, another male survivor stated that "justice is when the government will be taken to court and acknowledge what happened to us." Although retributive justice theorists have emphasized that criminal proceedings can contribute to acknowledging victims' suffering as a crucial ingredient of delivering justice, recognition is nevertheless seen as only a by-product of criminal prosecutions rather than its primary objective. For many male survivors in northern Uganda, however, it appears that official acknowledgment through the courts constitute a primary desired outcome of judicial proceedings.

At the same time, and despite these rather isolated positive views on criminal justice, the majority of survivors indeed expressed skepticism and negative perceptions regarding prosecutions. These attitudes particularly concern the feasibility of criminal proceedings, conditioned by various legal, social, cultural, and political barriers, many of which are heavily gendered. This lack of faith in the criminal justice system consequently implies that prosecutions do not constitute a contemporary priority for most male survivors. This may likely be the case because prosecutions would not directly address survivors' postconflict needs. Instead of retrospectively criminalizing perpetrators, survivors prioritize processes that help them in their current situation, such as rehabilitative assistance and a return to "normality" through reparations.

Many survivors were well aware of the technical limitations of the legal protection and coverage of male survivors by Ugandan law. During a discussion about prosecutions and the national justice system, one survivor noted that "the law does not prohibit male rape. We may want to take it to court, but we cannot because of the law." In fact, the Ugandan Penal Code defines rape in gender-exclusive and essentializing terms as affecting women only: "Any person who has unlawful carnal knowledge of a *woman or girl,* without her consent, or with her consent, if the consent is obtained by force or by means of threats or intimidation of any kind or by fear of bodily harm, or by means of false representations as to the nature of the act, or in the case of a married *woman,* by personating her husband, commits the felony termed rape (Ugandan Penal Code Act 1998, chapter 14, section 123: 56, emphasis added).

This systematic exclusion of male survivors from legal protection is neither atypical nor exclusive to men in northern Uganda. According to research by Chris Dolan and RLP, "90 per cent of men in conflict-affected countries are in situations where the law provides no [or only inadequate] protection for them if they become victims of sexual violence" (Dolan 2014: 6).

In addition to this lack of legal coverage, Uganda's criminalization of homosexuality further renders the prospects of justice through the court system for Acholi male rape survivors to be very unlikely. When homosexuality is outlawed and criminalized, reporting crimes of male sexual violence, which in northern Uganda are often equated with homosexuality, can lead to incriminations and prosecutions of survivors themselves. Many survivors worried that if they officially reported the crimes to the police, they would be accused of homosexuality, and hence mostly chose not to report the violations. In addition to illuminating these very real disincentives for male survivors to judicially report the sexual violations committed against them, this also shows that the judicial exclusion of male sexual violence victims is not only composed of legal layers, but is also intrinsically linked to and compounded by informal, socially based gendered beliefs.

Besides these technical and gendered barriers of the formal justice system, there are immediate political restrictions when it comes to prosecutions. Many male survivors noted security constraints in relation to attempts to use judicial means against the current regime responsible for the perpetration of these crimes: "Taking the government to court also implies security issues and risks. And it is of course difficult to take the sitting government to court," one male survivor noted.

Similarly, when the state apparatus tasked with delivering justice through the national system is responsible for crimes for which redress and accountability are sought, survivors often do not expect legal justice to be served and eventually give up their hopes for retribution. In such contexts, survivors often decide not to pursue criminal cases through the official system and instead turn to alternative approaches that may be preferred for accessibility and harm-responsiveness. The fact that the identities of most perpetrators, or of those who commanded these crimes, remain unknown to the survivors further complicates the prospects for prosecutions. As summarized by one survivor, "The perpetrators of this violence are majorly non-Acholis. We do not know them, we do not know where they are, and whether they are still alive, and if we want to prosecute, whom do we prosecute? Whom do we put our complaints against? We don't know."

These concerns about the seeming impossibilities of judicial justice through the court system must further be contextualized within a wider Acholi lived reality of "a deep distrust of higher authorities to dispense justice in their interest" (Porter 2012: 81). Many Acholis, including the vast majority of male survivors, have lost faith in these formal systems and ways of dispensing justice. Various survivor statements illustrate this distrust: "For me I know that with this government, if you take this issue [of the sexual violation] to court, there will be no justice," one male survivor proclaimed. Another survivor similarly expressed his general dissatisfaction with the system by stating that in general, "court issues delay a lot in this country." Most likely because of the legal constraints of the ICC's mandate in this context and the distant form of justice it symbolizes, the court in The Hague was not once mentioned by survivors during the discussions.

The combination of these intersecting factors—the lack of coverage and protection from the law, the criminalization of homosexuality, security constraints, and the seeming impossibility of prosecuting the sitting government, coupled with deeply rooted mistrust in the Ugandan justice system as well as gendered societal beliefs and practices—render the prospect for prosecutions in this context highly unlikely. Conditioned by these challenges and limitations, prosecutions thus appear not to constitute a priority for most male sexual violence survivors in northern Uganda.

Gender-Sensitive Reparations

Instead, for the majority of survivors, reparations in response to their sexual and gendered harms constitute a fundamental component of justice. Male survivors' perspectives thereby reflect the centrality of compensation to Acholi conceptions of justice more broadly. Although diverse, survivors' views on reparations primarily

focus on two elements: material compensation and physical rehabilitation. Drawing on these views, it becomes evident that reparations, and in particular material
compensation and rehabilitation, can constitute harm-centric and gender-sensitive
justice mechanisms in response to male sexual violence.

Reparations are often classified as among the most victim-centric transitional
justice mechanisms, and a growing body of scholarship focuses on reparations. In
practice and implementation, reparations can broadly include restitution, compensation, rehabilitation (including access to medical and psychological care), satisfaction, and guarantees of nonrepetition. In postwar northern Uganda and at the
state level, both the Juba Agreement on Accountability and Reconciliation (AAR)
and the draft transitional justice policy include proposals for a holistic reparations
program. Thus far, however, since the policy has not yet been legislated, a reparations program has neither been designed nor implemented, and survivors across
the subregion continuously express frustration and dissatisfaction over the lack
of reparative measures. At the same time the TJ policy, including its reparations
framework, is characterized by a striking absence of any sustained consideration
for gender, let alone any mention of sexual violence survivors, neither male nor
female.

These gendered blind spots in Uganda reflect practical and "conceptual gaps in
the legal and policy framework for reparations addressing conflict-related sexual
violence" globally (Ní Aoláin, O'Rourke, and Swaine 2015: 97). As noted by Ní
Aoláin et al., any remedies for conflict-related sexual violence, including reparations, "must be sensitive, flexible, and encapsulate gender-appropriate approaches"
(2015: 110). However, while increasing attention is paid to women's experiences
and female sexual violence survivors in relation to gendered reparations (Rubio-
Marin 2009; Walker 2016; Duggan et al,. 2008), albeit characterized by various
limitations and restrictions (Rubio-Marin and de Greiff 2007), "tailored intervention to address male-centred sexual harms remains elusive and marginalized" (Ní
Aoláin, O'Rourke, and Swaine 2015: 109). As a result, "a limited understanding
of who can be a victim of sexual harms means that violence against men is often
unseen and unaccounted for when states and other international actors conceive
and implement reparations" (ibid.: 97).

Despite this national and global unresponsiveness of reparations programs to
male sexual harms, the majority of male survivors who participated in this study
expressed strong demands for reparative measures in the form of material compensation, including most prominently the provision of agricultural tools, as well
as physical rehabilitation, rather than monetary compensation. These means were
expected to help survivors in their current socioeconomic situation and thereby
immediately respond to their gendered harms. Such compensation measures
also reflect reparations types commonly included in traditional Acholi justice
processes, which are "largely paid in the form of livestock" (Baines 2005: 15). For
instance, one survivor emphasized that "for justice we can ask the government

to provide reparations to us, if it is in terms of restocking [of livestock], it would be a source of livelihood, and that is what I will wipe my tears with. And if it is monetary, I will also use the money appropriately knowing that it comes from my violent background."

As articulated by another survivor, "Now that I am weak, the government could compensate me with oxen or ox ploughs to dig and to allow me to sell stuff and support the children." Another survivor said that "we should be supported and compensated; for example animals should be given to us, to be kept for us, or oxen for work to access and plough the land."

According to these viewpoints, providing male survivors with agricultural tools and other material provisions is expected to help them move on with their lives by elevating them (back) into a position in which they can (again) provide for their families. As discussed in chapter 4, the sexual violations and the resulting physical and psychological consequences and harms prevented the majority of male survivors from providing for their families, as they are socially expected to as men and according to hegemonic masculinity constructions. In response to these harms, and through the provision of material compensation, various survivors hope to be reenabled to engage in agricultural activities or manual labor, thereby returning to a sense of normality through everyday practices. From the perspectives of male survivors, material compensation would thus allow them to build a better future for themselves. Compensation would therefore be about "justice as a better future."

Male survivors' longing to be restored to their physical and psychological states prior to the harms resonates with Rubio-Marin and de Greiff's (2007) conception of gender-sensitive reparations, which must broadly aim to "rehabilitate victims, to improve their quality of life or, at the least, to optimize their chances of recovering a minimally functional life" (331). In this capacity, the provision of material compensation would be a gender-sensitive and harm-responsive form of reparation.

On a critical note, however, and similar to the dynamics of repairing gender identities discussed in relation to the victims' groups (see chapter 5), this sense of "normality" from the perspectives of men can potentially translate into an unequal *status quo ante*, characterized by male prestige and patriarchal privilege. As introduced in the previous chapter, MacKenzie and Foster theorize these dynamics as "masculinity nostalgia"—referring to "a romanticized 'return to normal' that included men as heads of household, economic breadwinners, primary decision-makers and sovereigns of the family" (2017: 15). In this reading, justice is perceived to be attained if survivors' sense of hegemonic masculinity within a hetero-patriarchal gender ordering is reconstituted. Quests for stability, security, and justice, however, inevitably remain fraught if "dependent on, or intertwined with, a commitment to restoring oppressive gender norms" (MacKenzie and Foster 2017: 15). Therefore, caution is required so that gender-sensitive and harm-responsive reparations do not only repair the previous unequal status quo but rather set in place processes of shaping new and potentially more egalitarian gender identities and relations.

Other demands for compensation included proposals to construct health centers and schools in the areas where the survivors live so that their families and communities could benefit. In line with these sentiments, a variety of male survivors also asked for their families to be helped with the payment of school fees. A 2015 study of survivors' experiences of sexual violence in northern Uganda found that the inability to pay school fees constitutes one of the greatest challenges for female and male survivors of gender-based violence alike (Apiyo and McClain Opiyo 2015). Such demands for education fees and communal schools or health centers express survivors' concerns that the government "must not only compensate us but also our families." Summarizing these considerations, one male survivor asserted that "we have all become very weak, and if justice is to prevail, then they should look at the children that we have and support them, for instance in school, because we don't have the ability and energy anymore to do anything to change the lives of these children."

Because many male survivors are now elderly, their postconflict justice-related needs thus extend to redressing not only their harms but also to assisting and supporting their families' needs, evidencing the horizontal and vertical ripple effects of gendered harms and of postconflict justice processes.

Furthermore, for the vast majority of male survivors, compensation is regarded as a meaningful component of justice only if accompanied by, or delivered as a form of, acknowledgment and recognition. As articulated by one survivor, "Reparations are only a way of justice if they come with acknowledgment by the government," a normative position taken by the majority of survivors who participated in the study. According to male survivors' views, reparations thus also have an important symbolic dimension by demonstrating "signs of recognition of victims as . . . equal citizens" (Rubio-Marin and de Greiff 2007: 331). At the same time, and comparable to survivors' views on prosecutions, various respondents expressed skepticism concerning the prospects of receiving compensation. Given the absence of a comprehensive reparation scheme and the lack of any consideration for gendered experiences and especially male-directed sexual violence in the national TJ policy, the prospect for compensation appears particularly remote.

Physical Rehabilitation

In addition to material compensation, rehabilitation constitutes another justice-related priority for many male survivors. As defined by Pablo de Greiff, rehabilitation broadly "refers to measures that provide social, medical and psychological care" (2008: 3) to victims of violence and armed conflict.

During our workshop discussions, various survivors affirmed that "if there is any kind of physical rehabilitation, that would definitely be a form of redress." According to one male survivor, "My major justice need is rehabilitation. So when

I am physically rehabilitated, I will get healing and strength, and I will get a normal life like any other community member." This emphasis on hoping to obtain a normal life like any other community member is important for understanding this notion of justice through rehabilitation. These concerns are thus closely linked to a return to the ordinary in the aftermath of human rights violations. In male survivors' perspectives, physical rehabilitation—through, for instance, medical treatment and psychological assistance—implies the potential to transform and restore their physical abilities, including to conduct physical labor. Rehabilitation is thus expected to reenable survivors to provide for their families and live up to gendered societal expectations, aligning with their views on reparations more broadly. Summarizing these concerns in relation to justice, one male survivor explained "I have no energy to dig so I am thinking that if we could get treatment and rehabilitation for the health problems, that would be justice."

Similar to material compensation, physical rehabilitation would thus enable survivors to reestablish a sense of normality in a transformative sense. Koloma Beck (2012) explains that "normality refers to the social processes in which the structures of the everyday environment are established, reproduced and negotiated" (53). For Martin (2016), the frame of normality is an "important concept to engage with in postconflict contexts" (401). In Sierra Leone, for instance, many survivors "were able to find peace and justice by regaining a sense of normality and were able to do this through everyday practices" (ibid.). Tapping into this growing debate about the *everydayness* of remaking a world and of attaining justice, the analysis here shows that physical rehabilitation can enable male survivors in northern Uganda to (re)gain this sense of normality, thus fundamentally constituting the "right way forward in the aftermath of violence" in a broadened sense of justice and in a gender-sensitive and harm-reactive manner. At the same time, however, and as critiqued above, these processes risk reestablishing patriarchal gender hierarchies by reinstalling men as primary providers and thus elevating them back into positions of dominance and power.

In northern Uganda's vacuum of state-administered measures, various service providers, including the Refugee Law Project, offer different rehabilitation measures for war victims. Under their now phased-out Beyond Juba Project (BJP), RLP provided psychological services and physical rehabilitation measures for a variety of conflict-affected communities across Acholiland, including male sexual violence survivors. As a result of these efforts, numerous survivors in the groups also received counseling to begin a process of addressing the psychological dimensions of their harms. Various male survivors were also referred for medical treatment to Saint Mary's Hospital in Lacor, just outside Gulu town, to attend to their physical injuries as a result of rape. These steps responded to some of the most severe harms experienced by male survivors.

For some of the survivors who received physical rehabilitation under RLP's project, in the absence of state-driven reparations, these measures constituted a form of redress and a component of justice. Various survivors who received physical rehabilitative support explicitly attested that its outcome helped them to renegotiate their masculine identities. "Through the medical treatment, I was able to work again and provide for my family like a man," one male survivor stated. Other survivors who advocated for rehabilitation, but have not yet received any assistance, likewise confirmed that such measures could constitute an aspect of justice, which would help them to renegotiate their masculine selves.

At the same time, however, for another sizable group of survivors, physical rehabilitation does not suffice as a form of justice if provided by RLP, humanitarian agencies, or nonstate actors because it crucially lacks the government acknowledgment component. According to these perspectives, "rehabilitating us should have been the responsibility of the government who committed these crimes. It is goodwill if RLP helps us with these measures, but not the sign of justice. When the government would come and say that they did something to me and that they help me now with rehabilitation, then that is justice to me."

Therefore, for various survivors physical rehabilitation has to be provided by the government for it to be a form of justice, and it needs to be accompanied by (while in itself symbolizing a form of) official acknowledgment. If provided by nongovernmental actors, these forms of rehabilitation would rather qualify as development work rather than justice. Despite once again illustrating a variety of divergent perceptions, such views accentuate the centrality of government acknowledgment for survivors and its connections to prosecutions, compensation, and rehabilitation.

Yet while the majority of male survivors view reparations positively, a small minority of survivors who participated in this study also represented an opposing viewpoint (see Schulz 2018c for a detailed analysis of this viewpoint). According to this perspective, compensational payments were considered as a form of dowry, locally conceptualized as *luk* (see Porter 2017), to be paid to the survivors by the perpetrating government. In this reading, reparations, if regarded as *luk*, risk further cementing survivors' perceived gendered subordination as previously initiated through the sexual violations. If viewed as dowry, reparations can thus further entrench gendered harms rather than redressing suffering and vulnerabilities, as they are typically theorized to, carrying important implications for the intersections of reparations, victimhood, and gender. This viewpoint also demonstrates that reparations (and perceptions thereof) are value loaded and inevitably depend on local gendered, cultural, and societal contexts, as well as conflict-affected communities' locally specific and subjective interpretations.

IMPLICATIONS FOR SEXUAL VIOLENCE AND JUSTICE

Survivors' views on justice are thus evidently characterized by a diversity of at times competing views. For instance, whereas some survivors regard prosecutions as avenues for delivering justice, others do not see retributive means as a priority. Likewise, some survivors view physical rehabilitation provided by nonstate actors as contributing to justice, while others consider that rehabilitative measures can constitute justice only if linked to official government acknowledgment.

This variety of perspectives among survivors should not be surprising, and it has previously been documented in northern Uganda as well as elsewhere globally. The examples offered here thus contribute to this awareness and illustrate the individuality of postconflict needs among conflict-affected communities, including justice-related concerns. At the same time, and despite increasing awareness, it appears that this realization – that justice needs are often highly individual and differ among survivors – has not yet been fully integrated into transitional justice scholarship and practice, especially in the legalistically and institutionally dominated literature. When it comes to survivors' perceptions and priorities of justice, gross generalizations are frequently made about how to deliver justice for everyone. In the specific context of redressing sexual violence against men, strong and unquestioned assumptions prevail that legalistic and institutionalized measures are needed to deliver justice. The analysis presented here confirms instead that justice-related needs and perspectives are essentially products of culture, cosmology, sociality, and gender within each local context, and are therefore highly local in nature.

Survivors' needs therefore cannot easily be transferred to other conflicts or be generalized across and within cases. In her influential book *Settling Accounts Revisited,* Diane Orentlicher (2007) questions those kinds of generalizations: "Given the extraordinary range of experiences and cultures, how could anyone imagine there to be a universally relevant formula for transitional justice?" (18). The example of the survivors for whom compensation would be a form of dowry illustrates these cultural and cosmological contingencies of justice needs. In addition to these contextual specificities, the findings presented here specifically illuminate that survivors' views on justice processes are not even necessarily unified among survivors of a specific violation within one particular case. Rather, individual survivors' needs within one particular social and geographical locality often vary, shaped by survivors' micro-, mezzo-, and macro-environments. As convincingly argued by Cullinan (2001), "Generalised and conventionally summarised victims' expectations tend to denigrate the complex and inconsistent human identity of such victims and survivors, ignoring the extent to which needs vary from victim to victim and change across time" (19). This individuality of justice needs among conflict-affected communities inevitably raises the complex conceptual and empirical question of how to articulate broad claims in transitional and postconflict settings and thus carries broader implications beyond this case.

Institutionalized, top-down transitional justice processes, which dominate practices of dealing with the past—such as the JLOS-administered draft transitional justice policy in northern Uganda and the ICC's intervention on the African continent more widely—are ill-equipped to take into account this individuality, thereby frequently doing a great disservice to survivors and their individual quests for justice. In light of this, I emphasize that prescriptive, mimetic, and elite-driven top-down approaches to transition must be complemented with processes that foster survivors' agency and are participatory and bottom-up. At the same time, official processes need to be designed in more flexible ways that accommodate survivors' voices and allow preferences to be incorporated into the design and implementation. The recognition of survivors' groups as a potential avenue for delivering justice in transition (chapter 5) is a first step in this direction.

These findings similarly emphasize the importance of consulting survivors about their justice needs and demands before designing and implementing post-conflict justice processes. The centrality of victim participation and consultations for transitional justice processes has previously been recognized in scholarship and practice alike. The United Nations (2014), for instance, emphasizes the importance of effectively consulting victims about their perspectives on postconflict justice. Despite increasing recognition of the importance of victim inclusion and participation, however, sustained engagement with victim constituencies still does not constitute an established practice for most transitional justice processes globally. Across time and space, the vast majority of transitional justice mechanisms continues to be top-down and are rarely driven, mandated, or influenced by victims' perspectives. Male sexual violence survivors have thus far not at all been considered by any such contexts globally.

In northern Uganda the draft transitional justice policy likewise recognizes the importance of victim consultations and in part claims to have done so. But these efforts were limited and insufficient and at most engaged very small and nonrepresentative parts of the population. Victim communities often express frustration over the lack of consultation, attesting that their views have not been sufficiently recorded. Prior to this study, Acholi male survivors of sexual violence in particular were net yet properly consulted about their viewpoints on justice either by relevant (national or international) transitional justice policy-makers or by researchers, thus evidencing the marginalization of male survivors' harms and experiences. At the same time, victim consultations carried out under the auspices of the government responsible for grave human rights violations itself cannot be expected to realistically capture survivors' honest views on justice, in particular relating to redress for state-perpetrated crimes. To ensure that the voices, perspectives, and needs of a broader range of victims are effectively captured, and to work toward meaningful and genuine consultations, such efforts have to be geographically widespread and large scale, ideally carried out by independent (often nonstate) actors.

Scholars, policy-makers, and transitional justice practitioners would surely highlight the difficulties (and seeming impossibilities) of consulting each conflict-affected individual in a particular locality about their justice-related needs and preferences, including the challenges of being able to respond to these individually.

Being aware of and sympathizing with these challenges, however, I nevertheless stress the importance of victim consultations, including studies like this, which are underpinned by the viewpoints of survivors. In concert with others, I emphasize the importance of evidence-based transitional justice and therefore urge transitional justice scholars and practitioners to better engage in dialogues, for programs to be based on consultations, data, and evidence, and for researchers to more openly and transparently communicate their findings beyond pay-walled journals accessible only within the academy. Arguably, and without wanting to give the work at hand too much credit, open access publications like this book may be a first and important step in that direction.

These different paradoxes illustrate one of the tragic realities of transitional justice: The apparent insufficiency of generic postconflict and transitional responses is frequently matched by a seeming impossibility of delivering individualized responses. Based on his personal experiences of several years of imprisonment in concentration camps during the Holocaust, Jean Améry in *At the Mind's Limit* (1980) observed that in the aftermath of mass atrocity "justice could only be hypothetical anyway" (64). In light of these observations, caution is recommended with regard to expectations for transitional justice processes, as resolving these paradoxes and meeting these heightened expectations proves intrinsically difficult. These concerns are certainly applicable to postconflict processes for conflict-affected communities in northern Uganda at large and for male sexual violence survivors in particular, who prior to this book remained largely muted and who continue to be ignored by the country's diverse transitional justice landscape.

CONCLUSION

Taking these challenges into account, this chapter illuminated how Acholi male sexual violence survivors conceptualize justice and how their views fit into and correspond with contemporary transitional justice developments in northern Uganda. The analysis thereby reveals that Acholi male survivors' justice needs and conceptions are strongly centered around demands for acknowledgment and recognition, as well as immediate physical and material assistance to redress their multiple sexual and gendered harms. Survivors articulated demands to have their silenced and neglected experiences officially acknowledged and legitimized by the institutional perpetrators. These viewpoints accentuate the centrality of recognition for male survivors' sexual and gender harms. In addition, material compensation and physical rehabilitation, as integral elements of reparations, can constitute important avenues for male survivors to achieve harm-responsive and gender-sensitive justice. These two forms of reparations are expected to elevate male survivors back into a position where they are able to work and provide for their families, as they are socially conditioned to as men within hegemonic masculinity constructions. Reparations are therefore seen as responding to the violations' impact on survivors' gender identities in reparative and in part even transformative ways.

At the same time, however, the prospects of justice for male survivors in accordance with their needs remain highly elusive and improbable in the contemporary context. The government has not yet acknowledged any responsibility for most of the human rights violations perpetrated by the NRA in the north and certainly not yet for crimes of sexual violence (against women and men). Further, criminal prosecutions on both the national and international level are characterized by numerous legal, judicial, political, and societal barriers, many of which are heavily gendered. Uganda's transitional justice policy proposes a comprehensive reparations framework, but it maintains strikingly gendered blind spots and lacks consideration of sexual violence (against women and men). These gaps, combined with the fact that the policy has yet to be implemented, negatively affect the possibility for male survivors to have their demands for recognition and reparations met.

In light of these gendered barriers and blind spots of official and formalized transitional justice processes in Uganda, unofficial and noninstitutionalized means— such as survivors' groups, localized memorialization initiatives, and nonstate actors' rehabilitative provisions—imply the potential to better address male survivors' gendered harms and thus to achieve a sense of justice. To deliver harm-responsive and gender-sensitive justice for male survivors of sexual violence in northern Uganda as indeed elsewhere, postconflict justice must thus be divorced from the constraints of institutionalism and legalism. To eventually accomplish this, and thus to redress SGBV crimes inclusively and holistically, a survivor-centric approach is needed—as put forward in the concluding chapter.

7

Toward a Survivor-Centric Approach

By way of centralizing the voices and experiences of male sexual violence survivors, this book has sought to paint a holistic and detailed picture of the dynamics surrounding wartime sexual violence against men in northern Uganda. Owing to the prevailing marginalization of conflict-related sexual violence against men across time and space, empirical insights into male survivors' lived realities thus far have remained remarkably underexplored and mostly absent from existing scholarship. It was my intention, therefore, to integrate male survivors' perspectives and experiences into heretofore largely normatively infused and conceptually dominated debates, to move forward the frontiers of knowledge on the gender dynamics of armed conflicts and on the civil war in northern Uganda

The analysis pursued in this book reveals that in northern Uganda, wartime sexual violence against men was geographically widespread and perpetrated as part of wider systematic and strategic warfare operations against the civilian Acholi population. Yet, whereas the LRA rebels' atrocities have been subjected to extensive scholarly and media debate, human rights violations committed by the Ugandan government's armed forces, on the other hand, are insufficiently explored. In this context crimes of sexual violence against men perpetrated by the government's National Resistance Army in the early stages of the war are particularly poorly documented. Throughout existing scholarship on the conflict in northern Uganda as well as on the local level, among the war-affected population, crimes of sexual violence against men are heavily silenced and often only circulate as rumors, if talked about at all. This neglect of crimes of sexual violence against men in northern Uganda is thereby symptomatic for the persistent global silencing and marginalizing of male-directed sexual violence throughout scholarship and policy making alike. By way of situating these crimes within their wider sociopolitical history and overlapping conflict dynamics, I have sought to shed some light on the context, extent, and dynamics surrounding these crimes in the northern Ugandan context.

Throughout this book I have been particularly interested in how male survivors have experienced these crimes, including their impact in gendered manifestations. Toward this end, I have sought to show how situated within hetero-patriarchal gender relations and evaluated against a normative hegemonic model of masculinity, crimes of sexual violence against men significantly impact male survivors' masculinities in different ways and strike at multiple levels of what it means to be a man in this sociocultural context (chapter 4). I have shown that the impact of sexual violence on Acholi male survivors' gender identities is a longitudinal process, rather than a one-time event, that unfolds via numerous physical, psychological, and physiological harms. In this context physical acts of sexual violence, and in particular penetrative anal rape, subordinate male survivors along gendered hierarchies, thereby communicating gendered victimhood. These processes are further exacerbated through different layered and gendered harms that demonstrate male survivors' inabilities to protect (themselves and their families), provide, and procreate, as is expected of them according to local constructions of hegemonic masculinity.

In order to make sense of these harms, I have put forward the analytical and conceptual framework of "displacement from gendered personhood," to adequately reflect the context-specific, multilayered, dynamic, and fluid character of these processes of perceived gender subordination. I have positioned this framework as an alternative to the dominant notion of "emasculation" by way of "feminization" or "homosexualiztion" as commonly employed in the literature, which tends to freeze dynamic experiences in time and space and to mask over the complexities of these deeply embedded processes. The framework of "displacement from gendered personhood" instead acknowledges the fluidity and contextual contingencies of survivors' experiences, recognizing it as a "layered and compounded process," in which the effects of violence itself are "further compounded over time through myriad gendered and sexual harms," challenging survivors' "masculine selves and roles on various levels" (Schulz 2018b: 1118).

At the same time, however, the analysis pursued in this book shows—and the conceptual framework reflects—that this "unmaking" of survivors' gendered personhood commonly occurs in tandem with multifaceted processes of "remaking" the self and gendered subjectivities. To this end, survivors also exercise agency and thrive to access services and assistance in order to (re)constitute their personhood in myriad exogenous and endogenous ways, including by advocating for justice and by engaging with their experiences in the context of survivors' groups. In northern Uganda, however, conditioned by heteronormative assumptions about masculinities and vulnerabilities, there is a striking lack of services and assistance for male sexual violence survivors, with only very few exceptions. As a result, most survivors have not yet been able to share their experiences, and the majority have not received any physical or psychological treatment, let alone any form of justice or redress. Within this vacuum of assistance and services, male survivors in northern

Uganda began creating their own forums to advocate for their needs in the form of survivors' groups. These groups enable male survivors to exercise agency in different ways while at the same time facilitating a sense of justice on the microlevel. Through peer-to-peer counseling, joint agricultural and income-generating activities, and by offering safe spaces for storytelling and disclosure, the groups facilitate a process that responds to survivors' most prevalent gendered harms, enabling them to renegotiate their gender identities, repair relationships, and mitigate isolation, as well as to obtain a sense of recognition of their marginalized and silenced experiences. As a result, numerous survivors attest that "the group is also a sense of justice."

Despite this engagement in the groups, Acholi male survivors nevertheless also demand different forms of justice and redress at other residual levels. While thus far only a handful of studies conceptually and descriptively engaged with the nexus between postconflict justice and sexual violence against men, the analysis in this book sheds important light on male survivors' perspectives on justice. Despite a heterogeneity of justice needs, survivors' priorities broadly center around recognition, acknowledgment, and reparations. This focus stands in contrast to the often unitary focus on international criminal accountability in redressing SGBV, including against men, throughout most of the literature and policy-making efforts. Instead, survivors view official acknowledgment, which can take various forms, as implying the potential to address the marginalization of their largely silenced violations. At the same time, reparations, and especially material compensation and physical rehabilitation, are expected to reenable male survivors to provide for their families and thus live up to socially constructed gendered expectations and responsibilities. Based on these findings, most Acholi male sexual violence survivors seem to desire "justice as a better future" (Nickson and Braithwaite 2014: 449), in which they are able to fully participate in community life and renegotiate their previously impacted masculine identities.

At the core of this book therefore lies the argumentation that although crimes of sexual violence significantly impact male survivors' gender identities in myriad and intertwined ways, compounded over time, these experiences do not necessarily define survivors as ever-vulnerable victims without a voice and agency. Instead, and as illustrated through the case study narrative of Okwera that opened this book, more than twenty-five years after the violations, survivors actively engage with and respond to their experiences, for instance in the context of survivors' groups and by advocating for justice. Survivors' experiences are diverse, variable, and potentially fluid and can thus best be understood as a form of displacement from gendered personhood. In fact, whereas the vast majority of survivors who participated in this study reported harmful effects on their gender identities as a result of the sexual violations, various survivors over time were also able to engage with and respond to these experiences, and partly reverse or undo them, in different ways.

By paying attention to these aspects and facets of survivors' lived realities, including their contemporary postconflict concerns and priorities, this book has sought to paint a detailed and nuanced account of the implications of wartime sexual violence and of male survivors' experiences. It is important to acknowledge, however, that there is significant variation in the experiences of the survivors whose stories are included in this book, as well as beyond other survivors in Acholiland, let alone elsewhere globally. I therefore emphasize that the arguments pursued here apply to a particularly concentrated sample of survivors, all of whom are members in organized support groups, and that survivors who are not engaged in such associations may very well be expected to have partially different experiences.

REVISITING ASSUMPTIONS ABOUT GENDER, CONFLICT, VIOLENCE, AND JUSTICE

The different viewpoints presented here and the arguments pursued throughout this book nonetheless carry important implications for research on gender and armed conflict more widely, as well as for scholarship on conflict-related sexual violence and postconflict processes in particular.

As identified in the introduction, dominant research on gender and armed conflict only slowly and marginally examines the roles and positioning of masculinities in theaters of war. Throughout this growing body of literature, only scant attention is paid to men's conflict-related experiences as explicitly gendered. If and when masculinities perspectives are employed, which is increasingly becoming the case, the focus of these examinations predominantly rests on hyper- and militarized masculinities and their conceptual linkages with violence, at the expense of other, alternative, nonheteronormative, and subordinated conceptions of manhood. Such portrayals, however, frequently omit attention to male vulnerabilities and men and boys as victims in armed conflicts. By examining male sexual violence survivors' gendered and sexual harms and vulnerabilities, I have therefore sought to situate this book as part of an ongoing process of diversifying and complexifying masculinities perspectives in, and gendered analyses of, wars and armed conflict.

Another dominant position in the literature views male-directed sexual violence, if attended to at all, as a peripheral phenomenon and an exception to the norm. As a result, male survivors frequently remain of marginal concern for scholars and policy makers alike. By demonstrating that sexual violence against men is perpetrated more frequently than commonly assumed, in northern Uganda and various other contexts, the research underpinning this book thus carries implications for scholarship on gender and armed conflict, particularly for the growing research field on wartime sexual violence. The empirical deconstruction of male survivors' harms and the development of the conceptual frame of "displacement from gendered personhood," likewise force us to revisit domination assumptions about conflict-related sexual violence against men.

The findings and arguments put forward in this book also speak to the growing postconflict and transitional justice literature. In particular, the findings underpinning this analysis complement a growing list of critical inquiries that challenge the legal and institutional preoccupation of justice in transition processes and that instead advocate for a deeper, broader, and thicker understanding of justice that takes into account survivors' everyday needs and priorities (see Robins 2011; Kent 2012; Gready and Robins 2014; McEvoy 2007), in line with a survivor-centric approach, as explained below. Indeed, throughout this book I show that in the absence of avenues at the macrolevel, justice often takes places at the microlevel and for the male survivors who participated in this study specifically in the context of survivors' groups. The examination offered here thereby adds a masculinities lens and specific attention to male sexual harms to this growing body of everyday postconflict and social reconstruction scholarship, something that has largely been underdeveloped.

Closely linked to these observations, the findings and insights in this book accentuate the need to think more creatively outside the prevailing template about what justice can look like for conflict-affected communities. For instance, recognizing survivors' groups as an important vehicle for exercising agency and thereby conveying a sense of justice is part of a larger strategy of creating "spaces for people to determine, shape and develop solutions for themselves" (Lundy and McGovern 2008: 292). Echoing Sharp, this can facilitate a "more holistic approach to the scope of justice issues addressed in transition" (2013: 152), interrogating the margins and peripheries of standardized and often technocratic and prescribed transitional justice approaches.

A SURVIVOR-CENTRIC APPROACH

Inevitably any focused research project bound by scope and time constraints can constitute only an initial investigation of a particular question or topic. Clearly more research and careful inquiries across different case sites are needed to further uncover the manifold ways in which conflict-related sexual and gender-based violence is targeted against men, how such violations impact male victims, and how survivors seek to engage with and respond to their harms and vulnerabilities. What remains strikingly absent from existing analyses, including admittedly from this book, are queer perspectives to uncover how individuals with diverse sexual orientation and gender identities experience conflict and are affected by and targeted through sexual and gender-based violence.

By and large—and although over the last decade a growing body of scholarship has been generated on sexual violence against men—most studies on the topic remain largely descriptive, undertheorized, and characterized by a dearth of empirically grounded survivors' perspectives. Having privileged and analyzed Acholi male survivors' experiences, voices, and viewpoints throughout this book, I have sought to depart from this dominant trend of ignoring or silencing survivors' perspectives. I therefore position this book as an empirically driven counter to the largely descriptive and at times normatively infused bodies of literature on conflict-related sexual violence as well as on postconflict justice and reconstructions, offering numerous inroads into underexplored intersections and themes.

Explicitly foregrounding male survivors' experiences and views thereby leads me to revisit and reshape dominant assumptions inherent in research on the gendered aspects of armed conflict, sexual violence, and postconflict justice. For instance, my analysis of survivors' groups as spaces to exercise agency and as pathways through which justice on the microlevel can be conveyed is an immediate outcome of male survivors' views articulated during the workshop discussions and would most likely not have surfaced if interviews had been solely conducted with external service providers and so-called (often self-proclaimed) experts. To pick up again the proverb offered in the introduction, which guided my research, that "a long stick cannot kill a snake," by getting close to and centralizing male survivors' views and their experiences, I have been able to paint a more holistic picture of their lived realities.

However, one persistent problem that I, as well as others, have repeatedly observed is that a significant number of studies on conflict-related sexual violence (against all genders) seem to negate the ethical imperatives and the implications of research for survivors. Various researchers and studies frequently do not (and perhaps often cannot) involve research participants in the research process as equal and active protagonists. As a result of this, ethical sensitivity and integrity often seem to fall by the wayside, and interventionist and exploitative methodologies prevail. The implications of such approaches to the survivors who are subjected to research, and to the organization(s) that work tirelessly to establish safe spaces, are severe and stand in contrast to the self-centric and egoistic gains for intervening researchers. Having situated my research project as part of RLP's continuous and sustainable process of engagement with male survivors, I have actively and deliberately sought to address and engage with these very real and profound challenges.

If done properly and in an ethically sensitive manner, research processes can also constitute an emancipatory and empowering exercise for survivors themselves. Various survivors who participated in this study repeatedly emphasized that "it is good that we are now speaking" and that "talking has really helped, and it was important to get this out." Nonetheless, despite my tireless efforts to try to facilitate an ethically sensitive and empowering environment, I likely cannot entirely free myself from any blame for externally intervening. However, I raise an important aspect of imperative significance: that ethical considerations must be centralized and prioritized during research with (potentially) vulnerable populations in (post)conflict and transitional settings—as I have sought to do within the context of this study.

To conclude, then, what are the implications and lessons to be drawn from this inquiry? Quite generally, of course, more scholarly and political attention needs to be directed to wartime sexual violence against men and to male survivors' experience—as clearly this type of violence is committed more frequently and occurs on a much larger scale than is commonly understood and acknowledged. Specifically applied to the context of northern Uganda, where crimes of tek-gungu circulate as rumors but remain insufficiently explored and only marginally recognized, it is my intention and hope that the documentation provided in this book contributes toward creating awareness for this notoriously underexplored aspect of the conflict. This newly gained recognition, in turn, is important for understanding how to address these gendered crimes and harms, as well as for survivors' continuous quests for acknowledgment, recognition, and justice. In the eyes of several survivors, documenting an understanding of the crimes perpetrated against them also constitutes a form of recognition and is thus fundamentally important for survivors on numerous levels.

Directly related to this, the vacuum of postconflict assistance for male sexual violence survivors, in Uganda and globally, signifies the importance of paying more sustained attention to informal, "everyday," and survivor-driven approaches of remaking a world in the aftermath of violence, suffering, and harm. While state-driven, official, and top-down approaches frequently are fraught with and bound by sociopolitical, cultural, and gendered constraints and barriers, processes that are more autonomously (co)driven or influenced by survivors themselves, such as survivors' groups, imply the potential for survivors to engage with their harms and experiences on their own terms. Instead of focusing on and exclusively investing in formal and institutionalized process, therefore, more consideration should be given and more sustainable resources need to be allocated to such measures and to the actors and agencies supporting these processes. While still confronted with certain constraints, such a microlevel and survivor-centric approach can get us closer to restoring minimally functioning lives for survivors, to gaining redress or justice, and ultimately to remaking a world.

In policy terms, such procedures align with the survivors-centric approach as stipulated in the most recent UN Security Council Resolution 2467, adopted in April 2019, which constitutes the latest piece of the puzzle that makes up the UN Women Peace and Security agenda. In addition to, for the first time ever, *repeatedly* mentioning and recognizing male survivors of sexual violence, this resolution emphasizes a survivor-centered approach that ultimately must serve survivors on their own terms. The preamble of the resolution specifically recognizes the need to adopt "a survivor-centred approach in preventing and responding to sexual violence in conflict and postconflict situations, ensuring that prevention and response are non-discriminatory and specific, and respect the rights and prioritise needs of survivors, including groups that are particularly vulnerable or may be specifically targeted" (3).

According to the propositions stipulated in the resolution, victims in conflict-affected settings should no longer be seen as only passive and helpless victims in need of external help and assistance but should instead be treated as actors with agency and choices. The resolution thereby emphasizes the urgency of providing access to justice for survivors and of addressing their socioeconomic needs. How precisely that can materialize and what it would look like in practice, however, remains arguably absent from the UNSC resolution. Indeed, while a survivor-centric approach has gained traction and prominence not only in the policy sphere but also in the postconflict literature in recent years, the term has not yet necessarily been filled with meaning and has only rarely been implemented, if ever. How a survivor-centric approach specifically applies to the gender-conditioned needs, vulnerabilities, and experiences of male sexual violence survivors has thus far not yet been explored at all, but has been put into some shape and form throughout the pages of this book.

In methodological terms, such a survivor-centric approach immediately builds upon, centralizes, and privileges survivors' experiences, viewpoints, and concerns. As emphasized in the preceding chapters, this entails an investigation of survivors' needs and priorities in response to their harms and experiences by way of getting close to their lived realities, utilizing the proverbial "short stick," as explained in the introduction. Employing this methodological focus has enabled me to show that for male survivors of sexual violence in northern Uganda, a survivor-centric approach encapsulates different measures that immediately address the diverse physical, psychological, and physiological impacts that the sexual violations have had, often over the course of years if not decades. Similarly a survivor-centric approach also enables the men who have participated in this study to engage with their experiences in a diversity of ways, at different levels, in order to come to terms with their sexual and gendered harms. In the context of this book, such an approach is most strongly put into practice through the Men of Courage support group that the survivors' have formed and operate, which enables them to engage with their experiences on their own terms, based on their needs and priorities. In light of the potential that these groups offer as avenues for postconflict recovery, and how they can link to and form part of the UN's envisaged survivor-centric approach in responding to SGBV, more attention needs to be paid and more resources need to be allocated to such measures and to the agencies supporting and facilitating these processes, such as the Men of Courage group and the Refugee Law Project in northern Uganda.

NOTES

1. INTRODUCTION: MALE SURVIVORS' EXPERIENCES IN CONTEXT

1. See, for instance, Enloe 2004; Moser and Clark 2001; Zalewski 1995; Zarkov 2001.

2. See Cohen 2016; Eriksson Baaz and Stern 2013; Wood 2014.

3. See Connell 1995; Zalewski 1995; Duncanson 2015; Duriesmith 2016.

4. Angela Harris defines hypermasculinity as a form of "masculinity in which the structures against femininity and homosexuality are especially intense and in which physical strength and aggressiveness are paramount" (2000: 793).

5. See Zalewski et al. 2018; Féron 2018; Touquet and Gorris 2016.

6. Parts of this section on the concept of "displacement from gendered personhood" were previously published as Schulz, Philipp (2018), Displacement from gendered personhood: Sexual violence and masculinities in northern Uganda. *International Affairs* 94(5): 1101–1119.

7. Although the focus on one case study implies compromises with regard to the findings' representation and generalizability across other case sites, certain key implications of my data and arguments from northern Uganda can nevertheless be expected to transfer across other conflict contexts as well, in that they imply broader empirical and conceptual applicability.

8. Such direct psychological or psychosocial support, however, was not needed during (or after) any of the interviews or workshop discussions.

9. Having two colleagues present at the workshops to translate allowed for rigorously double-checking exact translation and interpretations of the viewpoint of survivors as articulated during the sessions.

2. CONFLICT-RELATED SEXUAL VIOLENCE AGAINST MEN: A GLOBAL PERSPECTIVE

1. Féron 2018; Zalweski, Drumond et al. 2018; Touquet and Gorris 2016.

2. Different strands of feminist theory include, among others, liberal and mainstream feminism, radical feminism, Marxist feminism, and postcolonial feminism or cultural feminism (see Ahmed 2016).

3. Moser and Clark 2001; Enloe 2000; Tickner 2001.

4. Ní Aoláin et al. 2011; O'Rourke 2013; Duncanson 2015; Zarkov 2001.

5. See Duriesmith 2016; Myrttinen et al. 2016; Duncanson 2015.

6. See Eriksson Baaz and Stern 2009; Higate and Hopton 2005; Higate 2003.

7. That being said, however, there is evidence of female perpetrators of sexual violence across different conflict (and nonconflict) sites (see Sjoberg 2016).

8. See chapter 4 for a more detailed discussion of the concept of hegemonic masculinity and its applicability in the northern Ugandan context.

9. See Amony 2015; Baines 2015; McKenzie 2012.

10. See Carpenter 2003; Dolan 2015; Stemple 2009.

11. Okello and Hovil (2007) note that this definition incorporates various legal, physical, and psychological dimensions of GBV and is broader than previous definitions, which assumed that GBV affects only women. The *conflict-related* prefix as employed here, and as adopted from the United Nations' usage of the term, refers to acts of sexual violence "occurring in a conflict or post-conflict setting that have direct . . . links with the conflict itself" (UN 2014: 2). This includes situations of active armed combat and hostilities as well as internal or external displacement caused by political violence or armed conflict.

12. See Stiglmayer 1994; Seifert 1996; Thornhill and Palmer 2000.

13. Such as UNSCR 1820 (2008), 1888 (2009), 1960 (2010).

14. See Cockburn 2004; Otto 2009; Eriksson Baaz and Stern 2013.

15. A case in point would be US Senator John McCain. As a prisoner of war during the Vietnam War, McCain was subjected to different forms of torture. In his self-representation and the external representation of him and his experience, the fact that McCain survived torture can be seen as awarding him a boost to his masculinity, portraying him as hypermasculine for his ability to survive extraordinary violence.

16. Crimes of sexual humiliation may specifically include forced nudity, forced masturbation, or men and boys being forced or subjected to violent and degrading sexual acts, such as being forced to commit sexual acts with animals or objects (in private and in public) or being dragged with a cord connected to the penis or the testicles (Sivakumaran 2010).

17. Bastick et al. 2007; Touquet and Gorris 2016.

18. In cases of connected sexual harms where men are forced to watch (female) members of their communities being raped (Coulter 2009), the symbolic and perceived emasculation of male victims may occur through demonstrating their inability to protect their families and communities, and thereby their incapacity to fulfill socially constructed gender roles and expectations closely tied to masculinities.

19. In light of these critiques, in the introduction I have alternatively proposed the terminology and framework of "displacement from gendered personhood" (see Edström, Dolan, et al. 2016) to conceptualize these dynamics.

3. TEK-GUNGU: WARTIME SEXUAL VIOLENCE IN NORTHERN UGANDA

1. Although hostilities ceased in 2006, thus representing the perhaps more relevant event ending the armed conflict, the Juba peace negotiations that brought the conflict to a halt ended in 2008.

2. Up until 1995, Uganda's national army was called the National Resistance Army (NRA). Thereafter, it was renamed as the Uganda's People's Defense Force (UPDF). For a more detailed discussion of this transition and transformation, see Katumba-Wamala (2000).

3. A whole ethnographic overview of the Acholi people would go beyond the scope of this chapter. For more detailed information, see p'Bitek 1985, 1986; Finnström 2008. The Acholi as a tribe did not exist as such in precolonial times. Finnström (2003) argues that the Acholi ethnic identity "was reified or codified because of colonialism" (52). The Acholi people are part of the Western Nilotic language group, and part of a larger group of Luo peoples. In one of the first anthropological accounts from Acholiland, Girling (1960) proposes that the designation *Acholi* could originate from *An-coo-li*—"I am a man."

4. See Blattman and Annan 2012 for a thorough discussion about the nature and causes of LRA abduction.

5. Of the five indictees, Joseph Kony and Dominic Ongwen are the only ones still alive.

6. Since the ICC's investigation commenced in 2005, when the conflict was still ongoing, it has been argued that the court's intervention implied the danger of constituting an obstacle to peace at the time. On the other hand, advocates of the court have argued that justice is a precondition for meaningful peace and thus to be prioritized in this context. Although far more complex, these dynamics illustrate the peace-versus-justice question and debate.

7. The earliest occurrence documented by my research took place in 1987, and the latest in 1994.

8. The locations documented on the map have been identified in collaboration with male survivors during the workshops, with RLP colleagues, and with my research assistant Kenneth. The listed towns, trading centers, and villages indicate locations where sexual violence against men has been documented.

9. The illustration is published in an article by Sverker Finnström (2009: 64) and has kindly been made available to me by the author.

10. The gendered implications of these localities and the impact on male survivors' masculinities and identities as men will be examined more carefully in the following chapter.

11. In the early years of the conflict, the LRA did not yet engage in frequent battle with the Ugandan army, nor did the rebels attack the civilian population. Only in the early- and mid-1990s, after having gained considerable strength, did the LRA engage in more frequent military combat with the NRA and turn against the civilian population (see Allen and Vlassenroot 2012).

12. Such a practice would lend further empirical support to my assessment that sexual violence by the NRA against Acholi civilians, including against men, constituted part of a wider and systematic tactic or strategy.

13. See Dolan 2014; Johnson et al. 2008; Zalewski, Drumond, et al. 2018.

14. This was approximately four years after the initial violation.

15. As described more fully in the following chapter, homosexuality is legally and politically outlawed and criminalized in Uganda (Alava 2016) punishable by life in prison.

16. The gendered implications of this inability to work and thus to provide for their families as expected of them in accordance with the normative hegemonic model of masculinity in Acholiland (Dolan 2011, 2002) are thoroughly unpacked in the following chapter.

17. In chapter 5, I examine more carefully how within this vacuum of available psychosocial services for male survivors of sexual violence, support groups constitute an avenue

for them to engage with their experiences, including through peer counseling, as a way of exercising agency.

18. See Dolan 2014; Edström, Dolan, et al. 2016.

4. "I USED TO BE A STRONG MAN, BUT NOW I AM NOT": GENDERED VULNERABILITIES AND HARMS

1. The three-piece method, or *kandooya* in Acholi, "is a form of torture in which the arms are tied tightly behind the back at the wrists and elbows. *Kandooya* strains the chest and impedes breathing, and sometimes severely damages the nerves of the arms" (Behrend 1999: 34). To the extent of my knowledge, predominantly men have been targeted by this method.

2. It is also important to acknowledge that gender must be seen as fluid and comprising a spectrum, rather than two dichotomous and easily discernible categories (Sjoberg 2016). However, because of the heteronormative categorization into femininities and masculinities within the Acholi cultural context, I focus on dichotomous portrayals of masculinities and femininities respectively.

3. This contrast, however, presents gender identities as binaries, thereby ignoring a whole variety of potential nonbinary identities.

4. Myrttinen et al 2016; Demetriou 2001; Hamber 2016; Beasley 2008.

5. This conflation often falsely posits that hegemonic masculinity is the same as violent masculinity.

6. A *cuna* process is the "traditional Acholi courtship culminating in the payment of bridewealth" (Baines and Rosenoff Gauvin 2014: 288). *Cuna* means that a young man marries a woman following both families' complete knowledge, support, and approval (ibid.).

7. Lwambo 2013; Ratele 2008; Gilmore 1990.

8. An earlier, shortened version of this section was published as Philipp Schulz, (2018), Displacement from gendered personhood: Sexual violence and masculinities in northern Uganda. *International Affairs* 94(5): 1101–1119.

9. These socially constructed incompatibilities appear somehow ironic in light of Fineman's conception of vulnerability as universal and inherent in the human condition (2008).

10. All survivors who participated in this study live in rural settings, where the most common form of work available is agricultural work or other physical labor, such as brick making.

5. EXERCISING AGENCY: SURVIVORS' SUPPORT GROUPS

1. For a previous attempt to theorize political agency, see: Heleen Touquet and Philipp Schulz (2020), Navigating vulnerabilities and masculinities: How gendered contexts shape the agency of male sexual violence survivors, *Security Dialogue*. Online First: 1–19.

2. In April 2013 Refugee Law Project (Uganda), in partnership with First Step (Cambodia), Male Survivors of Sexual Abuse Trust (New Zealand), Men of Hope (Uganda), Men of Peace (Uganda), Men of Courage (Uganda), and with input from International Human Rights Law Clinic, the University of California at Berkeley (United States) initiated the South-South Institute on Sexual Violence against Men and Boys in Conflict and

Forced Displacement. The institute aims to create a new and different space within which victims, survivors, activists, practitioners, and academics can come together to discuss the largely ignored dimension of conflict-related sexual violence against men.

3. More information about the Beyond Juba Project, especially in relation to wider peace-building and transitional justice processes, see www.beyondjuba.org.

4. Some of the findings presented here were previously published as Philipp Schulz (2019), "To me, justice means to be in a group": Survivors' Groups as a Pathway to Justice in Northern Uganda, *Journal of Human Rights Practice*. Online First: 1–22. The discussion here, however, is much more in depth and supported by additional material.

5. In this context, where the government was responsible for the perpetration of these crimes, demands for government acknowledgment imply perpetrator acknowledgment. Official government acknowledgment and recognition as fundamental justice needs for male survivors will be discussed separately in the next chapter.

6. For a more detailed discussion of this, see Schulz 2019b.

6. JUSTICE, RECOGNITION, AND REPARATIONS

1. Some of the findings presented in the analysis below were previously published as Schulz, Philipp (2020a), Examining Male Wartime Rape Survivors' Perspectives on Justice in Northern Uganda. *Social & Legal Studies.* 29(1): 19–40.

2. *Mato Oput* broadly translates as "drinking (*mato*) of the bitter root (*oput*)." As summarized by Anyeko et al. (2012), *mato oput* is a voluntary process that begins with negotiations and mediation between the families involved to develop trust and establish the truth. Thereafter negotiations are held about the amount of compensation to be paid. "The practice . . . concludes with a ceremony and feast during which clan representatives share a drink made of sheep's blood and roots from the bitter *oput* plant, symbolizing the washing away of bitterness between the clans" (111).

3. The policy is yet to be passed by the parliament and yet to be legislated and implemented. See McDonald (2014) for a detailed analysis and critique of the policy and the process by which it came into existence.

4. These vague references are with regard to gender equality and the policy's objective of mainstreaming gender concerns in transitional justice. The reference to sexual violence is in the policy's background section, outlining relevant international legal frameworks but not discussing concrete justice measures in direct response to sexual violence.

5. Official government acknowledgement of NRA-perpetrated atrocities during the early years of the conflict, however, is severely limited and only constitutes an exception to the norm. If and where the government has acknowledged the occurrence of NRA-perpetrated violence, President Museveni has also been quick to deny any responsibility, instead blaming the loose composition of NRA cadre at that time.

Acan, G. 2015. *Not Yet Sunset: A Story of Survival and Perseverance in LRA Captivity.* Kampala: Fountain Publishers.

Acharya, A. 2014. Global International Relations (IR) and Regional Worlds: A New Agenda for International Studies. *International Studies Quarterly* 58(4): 647–659.

Achebe, C. 1958. *Things Fall Apart.* London: Penguin Books.

Ackerly, B., and True, J. 2008. Reflexivity in Practice: Power and Ethics in Feminist Research on International Relations. *International Studies Quarterly* 10(4): 693–707.

Aijazi, O., and Baines, E. 2017. Relationality, Culpability and Consent in Wartime: Men's Experiences of Forced Marriage. *International Journal of Transitional Justice* 11(3): 1–21.

Akullo Otwili, E., and Schulz, P. 2012. *Paying Back What Belongs to Us. Victims' Groups in Northern Uganda and Their Quest for Reparations.* JRP Field Note 16. Gulu: Justice and Reconciliation Project (JRP).

Alava, H. 2016. Homosexuality, the Holy Family and a Failed Mass Wedding in Catholic Northern Uganda. *Critical African Studies* 9(1): 1–20.

Alcalá, P. R., and Baines, E. 2012 Editorial Note. *International Journal of Transitional Justice* 6(3): 385–393.

Alcoff, L. 1991. The Problem of Speaking for Others. *Cultural Critique* (20): 5–32.

Alison, M. 2007. Wartime Sexual Violence: Women's Human Rights and Questions of Masculinity. *Review of International Studies* 33(1): 75–90.

Allen, T. 2015. Vigilantes, Witches and Vampires: How Moral Populism Shapes Social Accountability in Northern Uganda. *International Journal on Minority and Group Rights* 22(3): 360–386.

Allen, T. 2006. *Trial Justice: The International Criminal Court and the Lord's Resistance Army.* London: Zed Books.

Allen, T. 1991. Understanding Alice: Uganda's Holy Spirit Movement in Context. *Africa* 61(3): 370–399.

Allen, T. 1987. *Kwete and Kweri: Acholi Farm Work Groups in Southern Sudan.* Department of Administrative Studies, University of Manchester.

Allen, T., and Vlassenroot, K. 2010. *The Lord's Resistance Army: Myth and Reality.* London: Zed Books.

Améry, J. 1980. *At the Mind's Limits.* Bloomington: Indiana University Press.

Amony, E. 2015. *I Am Evelyn Amony. Reclaiming My Life from the Lord's Resistance Army (LRA).* Madison: University of Wisconsin Press.

Annan, J., and Blattman, C. 2010. On the Nature and Causes of LRA Abduction: What the Abductees Say. In Allen, T., and Vlassneroot, K. (eds.). *The Lord's Resistance Army. Myth and Reality.* London: Zed Books.

Anyeko, K., Baines, E., Komakech, E., Ojok, B., Ogora, L. O., and Victor, L. 2012. "The Cooling of Hearts": Community Truth-Telling in Northern Uganda. *Human Rights Review* 13(1): 107–124.

Apiyo, N., and McClain Opiyo, L. 2015: *My Body, A Battlefield Survivors' Experiences of Conflict Sexual Violence in Koch Ongako.* JRP Field Note 22. November 2015. Gulu: Justice and Reconciliation Project.

Apoko, A. 1967. At Home in the Village: Growing Up in Acholi. *East African Childhood: Three Versions*: 45–75.

Arendt, H. 1958. *The Human Condition.* Chicago: University of Chicago Press.

Auchter, J. 2017. Forced Male Circumcision: Gender-Based Violence in Kenya. *International Affairs* 93(6): 1339–1356.

Baines, E. 2016. *Buried in the Heart: Women, Complex Victimhood and the War in Northern Uganda.* Cambridge: Cambridge University Press.

Baines, E. 2015. "Today, I Want to Speak Out the Truth": Victim Agency, Responsibility, and Transitional Justice. *International Political Sociology* 9(4): 316–332.

Baines, E. 2014. Forced Marriage as a Political Project: Sexual Rules and Relations in the Lord's Resistance Army. *Journal of Peace Research* 51(3): 405–417.

Baines, E. 2010. Spirits and Social Reconstruction after Mass Violence: Rethinking Transitional Justice. *African Affairs* 109(436): 409–430.

Baines, E. 2007. The Haunting of Alice: Local Approaches to Justice and Reconciliation in Northern Uganda. *International Journal of Transitional Justice* 1(1): 91–114.

Baines, E. 2005. *Roco Wat I Acholi: Restoring Relationships in Acholiland: Traditional Approaches to Justice and Reintegration.* Liu Institute for Global Issues and Gulu District NGO Forum. Vancouver: University of British Columbia, Liu Institute for Global Issues.

Baines, E., and Rosenoff-Gauvin, L. 2014. Motherhood and Social Repair after War and Displacement in Northern Uganda. *Journal of Refugee Studies* 27(1): 282–300.

Baines, E., and Stewart, B. 2011. "I cannot accept what I have not done": Storytelling, Gender and Transitional Justice. *Journal of Human Rights Practice* 3(3): 1–19.

Baker, G., and Ricardo, C. 2005. Young Males and Masculinity in Sub-Saharan Africa: HIV/AIDS, Conflict, and Violence. *The World Bank Social Papers* 26: 9–14.

Barnett, C. 2012. Situating the Geographies of Injustice in Democratic Theory. *Geoforum* 43: 677–686.

Beasley, C. 2008. Rethinking Hegemonic Masculinity in a Globalizing World. *Men and Masculinities* 11(1): 86–103.

Behrend, H. 1999. *Alice Lakwena and the Holy Spirits: War in Northern Uganda, 1985–97.* Athens: Ohio University Press.

Bell, C., and O'Rourke, C. 2007. Does Feminism Need a Theory of Transitional Justice? An Introductory Essay. *International Journal of Transitional Justice* 1(1): 23–44.

Björkdahl, A., and Selimovic, J. M. 2015. Gendering Agency in Transitional Justice. *Security Dialogue* 46(2): 165–182.

Branch, A. 2011. *Displacing Human Rights: War and Intervention in Northern Uganda.* Oxford: Oxford University Press.

Branch, A. 2010. The Roots of LRA Violence: Political Crisis and Politicized Ethnicity in Acholiland. IIn Allen, T., and Vlassenroot, K. (eds.), *The Lord's Resistance Army: Myth and Reality.* London: Zed Press.

Branch, A. 2005. Neither Peace nor Justice: Political Violence and the Peasantry in Northern Uganda, 1986–1998. *African Studies Quarterly* 8(2): 1–31.

Bolten, C. 2014. *I did it to save my life. Love and Survival in Sierra Leone.* Berkeley: University of California Press.

Brownmiller, S. 1975. *Against Our Will. Men, Women and Rape.* New York: Simon and Schuster.

Butler, J. 1990. *Gender Trouble: Feminism and the Subversion of Identity.* New York: Routledge.

Cahn, N., and Ni Aoláin, F. D. 2010. Gender, Masculinities and Transition in Conflicted Societies. *New England Law Review* 44: 101–122.

Carpenter, R. C. 2006. Recognizing Gender-Based Violence against Civilian Men and Boys in Conflict Situations. *Security Dialogue* 37(1) 83–103.

Carpenter, R. C. 2003. "Women and Children First": Gender, Norms, and Humanitarian Evacuation in the Balkans 1991–95. *International Organization* 57(4): 661–694.

Centre for the Study of Violence and Reconciliation (CSVR) and Khulumani Support Group. 1998. *Submission to the Truth and Reconciliation Commission: Survivors' Perceptions of the Truth and Reconciliation Commission and Suggestions for the Final Report.* Report based on eleven reconciliation and rehabilitation workshops undertaken by the Centre for the Study of Violence and Reconciliation between 7 August 1997 and 1 February 1998. Johannesburg: Centre for the Study of Violence and Reconciliation.

Charlesworth, H., Chinkin C., and Wright, S. 1991, Feminist Approaches to International Law, *American Journal of International* Law 85(4): 613–45.

Charman, T. 2018. Sexual Violence or Torture? The Framing of Sexual Violence against Men in Armed Conflict in Amnesty International and Human Rights Watch Reports. In Zalewski, M., et al. (eds.), *Sexual Violence against Men in Global Politics.* London: Routledge.

Cleaver, F. 2002. *Masculinities Matter!: Men, Gender and Development.* London: Zed Books.

Cockburn, C. 2010. Gender Relations as Causal in Militarization and War. *International Feminist Journal of Politics* 12(2): 139–157.

Cockburn, C. 2001. The Gendered Dynamics of Armed Conflict and Political Violence. In Moser, C., and Clark, F. (eds.), *Victims, Perpetrators or Actors. Gender, Armed Conflict and Political Violence.* Chicago: University of Chicago Press: 13–35.

Cohen, D. K. 2016. *Rape during Civil War.* Ithaca: Cornell University Press.

Cohen, D. K. 2013. Explaining Rape During Civil War: Cross-National Evidence (1980–2009). *American Political Science Review* 107(3): 461–477.

Cohn, C., and Enloe, C. 2003. A Conversation with Cynthia Enloe: Feminists Look at Masculinity and the Men Who Wage War. *Signs: Journal of Women in Culture and Society* 28(4): 1187–1107.

Connell, R. W. 2002. Masculinities, the Reduction of Violence and the Pursuit of Peace. In Cockburn, C., and Zarkov, Z. (eds.), *The Postwar Moment: Militaries, Masculinities and International Peacekeeping, Bosnia and the Netherlands*. London: Lawrence and Wishart.

Connell, R. W. 1995. *Masculinities*. 2nd edition. Berkeley: University of California Press.

Connell, R. W., and Messerschmidt, J. W. 2005. Hegemonic Masculinity: Rethinking the Concept. *Gender and Society* 19(6): 829–859.

Corntassel, J., Chaw-win-is, and T'lakwadzi. 2009. Indigenous Storytelling, Truth-Telling, and Community Approaches to Reconciliation. *ESC: English Studies in Canada* 35(1): 137–159.

Coulter, C. 2009. *Bush Wives and Girl Soldiers. Women's Lives through War and Peace in Sierra Leone*. Ithaca: Cornell University Press.

Crazzolara, J. P. 1938. *A Study of the Acooli Language: Grammar and Vocabulary*. London: Oxford University Press.

Cullinan, S. 2001. *Torture Survivors' Perceptions of Reparation: Preliminary Survey*. London: Redress Trust.

Daniel, V. 1996. *Charred Lullabies: Chapters in an Anthropology of Violence*. Princeton: Princeton University Press.

Das, V. 2007. *Life and Words: Violence and the Descent into the Ordinary*. Berkeley: University of California Press.

Das, V., Kleinman, A., Ramphele, M., and Reynolds, P. 2000. *Violence and Subjectivity*. Berkeley: University of California Press.

Das, V., Kleinman, A., Lock, M., Ramphele, M., and Reynolds, P. 2001. *Remaking a World: Violence, Social Suffering and Recovery*. Berkeley: University of California Press.

de Greiff, P. 2012. Theorizing Transitional Justice. *Nomos* 51: 31–77.

de Waardt, M. 2016. Naming and Shaming Victims: The Semantics of Victimhood. *International Journal of Transitional Justice* 10(3): 432–450.

Demetriou, D. Z. 2001. Connell's Concept of Hegemonic Masculinity: A Critique. *Theory and Society* 30(3): 337–361.

Denov, M. 2007. *Girls in Fighting Forces. Moving beyond Victimhood*. A Summary of the Research Findings on Girls and Armed Conflict from CIDA's Child Protection Research Fund. McGill University.

Dery, I. 2019. "To be a man is not easy": Everyday Economic Marginality and Configurations of Masculinity among Rural Ghanaian Youth. *Masculinities and Social Change* 8(2): 171–194

Dolan, C. 2015. Letting Go of the Gender Binary: Charting New Pathways for Humanitarian Interventions on Gender-Based Violence. *International Review of the Red Cross* 96(894): 485–501.

Dolan, C. 2014. Into the Mainstream: Addressing Sexual Violence against Men and Boys in Conflict: A briefing paper prepared for the workshop held at the Overseas Development Institute.

Dolan, C. 2011. Militarized, Religious and Neo-Colonial: The Triple-Bind Confronting Men in Contemporary Uganda. In Cornwall, A., Edström, J., and Greig, A. (eds.), *Men and Development: Politicising Masculinities*. London: Zed Books: 126–138.

Dolan, C. 2009. *Social Torture: The Case of Northern Uganda, 1986–2006*. Oxford and New York: Berghahn Books.

Dolan, C. 2002. Collapsing Masculinities and Weak States: A Case Study of Northern Uganda. In Cleaver, F. (ed.), *Masculinity Matters: Men, Masculinities and Gender Relations in Development*. London: Zed Books: 57–83.

Dolan, C., Shahrokh, T., Edström, J., and Kabafunzaki, D. K. 2017. Engaged Excellence or Excellent Engagement? Collaborating Critically to Amplify the Voices of Male Survivors of Conflict-Related Sexual Violence. *IDS Bulletin* 47(6).

Duncanson, C. 2015. Hegemonic Masculinity and the Possibility of Change in Gender Relations. *Men and Masculinities* 18(2): 231–248.

Duriesmith, D. 2016. *Masculinity and New War. The Gendered Dynamics of Contemporary Armed Conflict*. New York: Routledge.

Drumond, P. 2018. Sex, Violence and Heteronormativity: Revisiting Performances of Sexual Violence against Men in former Yugoslavia. In Zalewski, M., Drumond, P., Prügl, E., and Stern, M. (eds.), *Sexual Violence against Men in Global Politics*. London: Routledge: 152–166.

Edström, J., Dolan, C., Shahrokh, T., and David, O. 2016. Therapeutic Activism: Men of Hope Refugee Association Uganda Breaking the Silence over Male Rape in Conflict-Related Sexual Violence. *IDS Evidence Report 182*. Brighton: Institute for Development Studies.

Enloe, C. 2017. *The Big Push. Exposing and Challenging the Persistence of Patriarchy*. Berkeley: University of California Press.

Enloe, C. 2004. *The Curious Feminist: Searching for Women in a New Age of Empire*. Berkeley: University of California Press.

Enloe, C. 2000. *Maneuvers: The International Politics of Militarizing Women's Lives*. Berkeley: University of California Press.

Enloe, C. 1989. *Bananas, Beaches and Bases: Making Feminist Sense of International Politics*. Berkeley: University of California Press.

Eriksson Baaz, M., and Stern, M. 2013. *Sexual Violence as a Weapon of War? Perceptions, Prescriptions, Problems in the Congo and Beyond*. London: Zed Books.

Eriksson Baaz, M., and Stern, M. 2009. Why Do Soldiers Rape? Masculinity, Violence, and Sexuality in the Armed Forces in the Congo (DRC). *International Studies Quarterly* 53(2): 495–518.

Esuruku, R. S. 2011. Beyond Masculinity: Gender, Conflict and Post-Conflict Reconstruction in Northern Uganda. *Journal of Science and Sustainable Development* 4(25): 25–40.

Fanon, F. 1963. *Wretched of the Earth*. New York: Grove Press.

Féron, E. 2018. *Wartime Sexual Violence against Men: Masculinities and Power in Conflict Zones*. New York and London: Rowman and Littlefield.

Fineman, M. A. 2008. The Vulnerable Subject: Anchoring Equality in the Human Condition. *Yale Journal of Law and Feminism* 20(1): 8–40.

Finnström, S. 2015. War Stories and Troubled Peace: Revisiting Some Secrets of Northern Uganda. *Current Anthropology* 56(12): 222–230

Finnström, S. 2009. Gendered War and Rumors of Saddam Hussein in Uganda. *Anthropology and Humanism* 34(1): 61–70.

Finnström, S. 2008. *Living with Bad Surroundings: War, History, and Everyday Moments in Northern Uganda*. Duke University Press.

Foucault, M. 1978. *The History of Sexuality.* New York, London: Penguin Books.

Fujii, L. 2018. *Interviewing in Social Science Research: A Relational Approach.* New York: Routledge.

Gilmore, D. D. 1990. *Manhood in the Making: Cultural Concepts of Masculinity.* New Haven: Yale University Press.

Gilson, E. G. 2016. Vulnerability and Victimization: Rethinking Key Concepts in Feminist Discourses on Sexual Violence. *Signs: Journal of Women in Culture and Society* 42(1): 71–98.

Gingyera-Pinycwa, A. 1992. *Northern Uganda in National Politics.* Kampala: Fountain Publishers.

Girling, F. K. 1960. *The Acholi of Uganda.* London: Her Majesty's Stationery Office.

Government of the Republic of Uganda. 1998. *The Uganda Penal Code Act.* Kampala: Government of Uganda.

Gray, H., and Stern, M. 2019. Risky Dis/entanglements: Torture and Sexual Violence in Conflict. *European Journal of International Relations.* 25(4): 1035–1058.

Gray, H., Stern, M., and Dolan, C. 2019. Torture and Sexual Violence in War and Conflict: The Unmaking and Remaking of Subjects of Violence. *Review of International Studies:* 1–20.

Gready, P., and Robins, S. 2014. From Transitional to Transformative Justice: A New Agenda for Practice. *International Journal of Transitional Justice* 8(3): 339–361.

Hagen, J. 2016. Queering Women, Peace and Security. *International Affairs* 92(2): 313–332.

Haldemann, F. 2009. Another Kind of Justice: Transitional Justice as Recognition. *Cornell International Law Journal* 41: 675–737.

Hamber, B. 2016. There Is a Crack in Everything: Problematising Masculinities, Peacebuilding and Transitional Justice. *Human Rights Review* 17(1): 1–25.

Hamber, B., and Wilson, R. A. 2003. Symbolic Closure through Memory, Reparation and Revenge in Post-Conflict Societies. *Journal of Human Rights* 1(1): 35–53.

Hansen, T. O. 2014. The Vertical and Horizontal Expansion of Transitional Justice: Explanations and Implications for a Contested Field. In Buckley-Zistel, S., et al. (eds.), *Transitional Justice Theories.* New York: Routledge.

Harris, A. P. 2000. Gender, Violence, Race, and Criminal Justice. *Stanford Law Review* 52: 777–807.

Häkli, J., and Kallio, K. P. 2013. Subject, Action and Polis: Theorizing Political Agency. *Progress in Human Geography* 38(2): 181–200.

Hearn, J. 1998. *The Violences of Men: How Men Talk about and How Agencies Respond to Men's Violence to Women.* Thousand Oaks: Sage Publishing.

Henry, N. 2009. Witness to Rape: The Limits and Potential of International War Crimes Trials for Victims of Wartime Sexual Violence. *International Journal of Transitional Justice,* 3(1): 114–134.

Hollander, T. 2014. Men, Masculinities, and the Demise of a State: Examining Masculinities in the Context of Economic, Political, and Social Crisis in a Small Town in the Democratic Republic of the Congo. *Men and Masculinities* 17(4): 417–439.

Honneth, A. 1995. *The Struggle for Recognition: The Moral Grammar of Social Conflicts.* Cambridge, MA: MIT Press.

Humphrey, M., and Valverde, E. 2008. Human Rights Politics and Injustice: Transitional Justice in Argentina and South Africa. *International Journal of Transitional Justice* 2(1): 83–105.

Hutchings, K. 2008. Making Sense of Masculinity and War. *Men and Masculinities* 10(4): 389–404.

Jackson, M. 2002. *The Politics of Storytelling: Violence, Transgression, and Intersubjectivity.* Copenhagen: Museum Tusculanum Press.

Johnson, K., Asher, J., Rosborough, S., Raja, A., Panjabi, R., Beadling, C., and Lawry, L. 2008. Association of Combatant Status and Sexual Violence with Health and Mental Health Outcomes in Post-Conflict Liberia. *Journal of the American Medical Association (JAMA)* 300(6): 676–690.

Johnson, K., Scott, J., Rughita, B., Kisielewski, M., Asher, J., Ong, R., and Lawry, L. 2010. Association of Sexual Violence and Human Rights Violations with Physical and Mental Health in Territories of the Eastern Democratic Republic of the Congo. *Journal of the American Medical Association (JAMA)* 304(5): 553–562.

Justice and Reconciliation Project (JRP). 2013. *The Beasts at Burcoro: Recounting Atrocities by the NRA's 22nd Battalion in Burcoro Village in April 1991.* JRP Field Note 17. Gulu, Uganda: Justice and Reconciliation Project.

Justice Law and Order Sector (JLOS). 2017. *National Transitional Justice Policy.* Prepared by the National Transitional Justice Working Group. 8th draft. Kampala: Justice Law and Order Sector/Ministry of Justice of the Republic of Uganda.

Katumba-Wamala, E. 2000. The National Resistance Army (NRA) as a Guerilla Force. *Small Wars and Insurgencies* 11(3): 160–171.

Keating, C. 2013. Resistant Silences. In Malhotra, S., and Rowe, A. C. (eds.), *Silence, Feminism, Power: Reflections at the Edges of Sound.* London: Palgrave MacMillan: 25–33.

Kent, L. 2014. Narratives of Suffering and Endurance: Coercive Sexual Relationships, Truth Commissions and Possibilities of Gender Justice in Timor-Leste. *International Journal of Transitional Justice* 8(2): 289–313.

Kent, L. 2012. *The Dynamics of Transitional Justice: International Models and Local Realities in East Timor.* London: Routledge.

Kimmel, M. 2010. *Misframing Men. Essays on the Politics of Contemporary Masculinities.* New Brunswick: Rutgers University Press.

Kimmel, M. 1996. *Manhood in America: A Cultural History.* Oxford: Oxford University Press.

Kirby, P. 2013. How Is Rape a Weapon of War? Feminist International Relations, Modes of Critical Explanation and the Study of Wartime Sexual Violence. *European Journal of International Relations* 19(4): 797–821.

Koloma Beck, T. 2012. *The Normality of Civil War: Armed Groups and Everyday Life in Angola.* Frankfurt, New York: Campus.

Kreft, A. 2019. *Sexual Violence in Armed Conflict. Threat, Mobilization and Gender Norms.* PhD dissertation. University of Gothenburg.

Kronsell, A. 2005. Gendered Practices in Institutions of Hegemonic Masculinity: Reflections from Feminist Standpoint Theory. *International Feminist Journal of Politics* 7(2): 280–298.

Lambourne, W. 2013. Transformative Justice, Reconciliation, and Peace-Building. In Buckley-Zistel, S. (ed.), *Transitional Justice Theories.* London: Routledge: 19–39.

Lake, D. A. 2016. White Man's IR: An Intellectual Confession. *Perspectives on Politics* 14(4): 1112–1122.

Latigo, J. O. 2008. Northern Uganda: Tradition-Based Practices in the Acholi region. In Huyse, L., et al. (eds.), *Traditional Justice and Reconciliation after Violent Conflict: Learning from African Experiences.* Stockholm: International IDEA: 85–121.

Leiby, M. 2009a. Digging in the Archives: The Promise and Perils of Primary Documents. *Politics and Society* 37(1): 75–99.

Leiby, M. 2009b. Wartime Sexual Violence in Guatemala and Peru. *International Studies Quarterly* 53(2): 445–468.

Lewis, C. 2014. Systemic Silencing: Addressing Sexual Violence against Men and Boys in Armed Conflict and Its Aftermath. In Heathcote, G., and Otto, D. (eds.), *Rethinking Peacekeeping, Gender Equality and Collective Security.* London: Palgrave Macmillan: 203–223.

Llewellyn, J. J., and Philpott, D. 2014. *Restorative Justice, Reconciliation, and Peacebuilding.* Oxford: Oxford University Press.

Lorde, A. 1983. There Is No Hierarchy of Oppressions. *Bulletin Homophobia and Education*: Council on Interracial Books for Children 14(3/4): 9.

Loveluck, L. 2019. Syrian Forces Use Widespread Sexual Violence to Humiliate and Silence Male Prisoners, New Report Says. *Washington Post*, 11 March 2019, https://www .washingtonpost.com/world/syrian-forces-use-widespread-sexual-violence-to-humiliate -and-silence-male-prisoners-new-report-says/2019/03/11/2e1f5b12–43e4–11e9–9726 –50f151ab44b9_story.html.

Lwambo, D. 2013. "Before the war, I was a man": Men and Masculinities in the Eastern Democratic Republic of Congo. *Gender and Development* 21(1): 47–66.

MacDonald, A. (2014) *Justice in Transition? Transitional Justice and Its Discontents in Uganda.* PhD dissertation. Department of War Studies, King's College London.

MacDonald, A., and Allen, T. 2015. Social Accountability in War Zones—Confronting Local Realities of Law and Justice. *International Journal on Minority and Group Rights* 22(3): 279–308.

MacDonald, A., and Porter, H. 2016. The Trial of Thomas Kwoyelo: Opportunity or Spectre? Reflections from the Ground on the First LRA Prosecution. *Africa* 86(4): 698–722.

MacGinty, R., and Richmond, O. 2013. The Local Turn in Peace Building: A Critical Agenda for Peace. *Third World Quarterly* 34(5): 763–783.

MacKenzie, M. H. 2012. *Female Soldiers in Sierra Leone: Sex, Security, and Post-Conflict Development.* New York: New York University Press.

MacKenzie, M. H., and Foster, A. 2017. Masculinity Nostalgia: How War and Occupation Inspire a Yearning for Gender Order. *Security Dialogue* 48(3): 206–223.

Madlingozi, T. 2010. On Transitional Justice Entrepreneurs and the Production of Victims. *Journal of Human Rights Practice* 2(2): 208–228.

Mahmood, S. 2001. Feminist Theory, Embodiment, and the Docile Agent: Some Reflections on the Egyptian Islamic Revival. *Cultural Anthropology* 16(2): 202–236.

Mallinder, L. 2014. Amnesties in the Pursuit of Reconciliation, Peacebuilding and Restorative Justice. In Llewellyn, J., and Philpott, D. (eds.), *Restorative Justice, Reconciliation, and Peacebuilding.* Oxford: Oxford University Press.

Mamdani, M. 1988. Uganda in Transition: Two Years of the NRA/NRM. *Third World Quarterly* 10(3): 1155–1181.

Martin, L. 2016. Practicing Normality: An Examination of Unrecognizable Transitional Justice Mechanisms in Post-Conflict Sierra Leone. *Journal of Intervention and Statebuilding* 10(3): 400–418.

McEvoy, K. 2007. Beyond Legalism: Towards a Thicker Understanding of Transitional Justice. *Journal of Law and Society* 34(4): 411–440.

McEvoy, K., and McConnachie, K. 2013. Victims and Transitional Justice: Voice, Agency and Blame. *Social and Legal Studies* 22(4): 489–513.

Meger, S. 2016. *Rape, Loot, Pillage: The Political Economy of Sexual Violence in Armed Conflict.* Oxford: Oxford University Press.

Men of Hope. 2015. *Annual Report.* Kampala: Men of Hope Refugee Association Uganda.

Men of Peace. 2014. *Together We Can: 2014 Activity Report.* Nakivale, Uganda: Men of Peace Association.

Menzel, A. 2018. The Perils of Recognising Local Agency: A Situational Concept of Agency and the Case of Victims of Sexual Violence and the Sierra Leone Truth and Reconciliation Commission (TRC). *Journal of International Relations and Development.* 1–23.

Merry, S. E. 1988. Legal Pluralism. *Law and Society Review* 22(5): 869–896.

Mertus, J. 2004. Shouting from the Bottom of the Well: The Impact of International Trials for Wartime Rape on Women's Agency. *International Feminist Journal of Politics* 6(1): 110–128.

Millar, G. 2011. Local Evaluations of Justice through Truth Telling in Sierra Leone: Postwar Needs and Transitional Justice. *Human Rights Review* 12(4): 515–535.

Millett, K. 1970. *Sexual Politics.* New York: Doubleday.

Minow, M. 1998. *Between Vengeance and Forgiveness: Facing History after Genocide and Mass Violence.* Boston: Beacon Press.

Morrel, R., Jewkes, R., and Lindegger, G. 2012. Hegemonic Masculinity/Masculinities in South Africa: Culture, Power, and Gender Politics. *Men and Masculinities* 15(1): 11–30.

Moser, C., and Clark, F. 2001. *Victims, Perpetrators or Actors: Gender, Armed Conflict and Political Violence.* London and New York: Zed Books.

Mutibwa, P. M. 1992. *Uganda since Independence: A Story of Unfulfilled Hopes.* Trenton: Africa World Press.

Myrttinen, H., Khattab, L., and Naujoks, J. 2016. Re-thinking Hegemonic Masculinities in Conflict-Affected Contexts. *Critical Military Studies* 3(2): 103–119.

Nader, L. 1965. The Anthropological Study of Law. *American Anthropologist* 67(6): 3–32.

Ní Aoláin, F. 2012. Advancing Feminist Positioning in the Field of Transitional Justice. *International Journal of Transitional Justice* 6(2): 205–228.

Ni Aoláin, F. D., O'Rourke, C., and Swaine, A. 2015. Transforming Reparations for Conflict-Related Sexual Violence: Principles and Practice. *Harvard Law Review* 28: 97–146.

Ni Aoláin, F., Haynes, D. F., and Cahn, N. 2011. *On the Frontlines: Gender, War, and the Post-Conflict Process.* Oxford: Oxford University Press.

Nordstrom, C. 1997. *A Different Kind of War Story.* Philadelphia: University of Pennsylvania Press.

Odoch Pido, J. 2000. Personhood and Art: Social Change and Commentary among the Acoli. *African Philosophy as Cultural Inquiry*: 105–135.

Okello, M. C., Dolan, C., et al. 2012. *Where Law Meets Reality: Forging African Transitional Justice.* Cape Town: Pambazuka Press.

Okello, M. C., and Hovil, L. 2007. Confronting the Reality of Gender-Based Violence in Northern Uganda. *International Journal of Transitional Justice* 1(3): 433–443.

Okuku, J. 2002. *Ethnicity, State Power and the Democratisation Process in Uganda*. Uppsala: Nordic Africa Institute.

Oloka-Onyango, J. 2000. New Wine or New Bottles? Movement Politics and One-Partyism in Uganda. In Mugaju, J., and Oloka-Onyango, J. (eds.), *No-Party Democracy in Uganda: Myths and Realities*. Kampala: Fountain Publishers.

Omara-Otunnu, A. 1995. The Dynamics of Conflict in Uganda. In Furley, O. (ed.), *Conflict in Africa*. London and New York: I.B. Tauris Publishers.

Onyango, E. O. 2012. *Manhood on the Margins: Failing to Be a Man in Post-Conflict Northern Uganda*. Brighton: MICROCON Research Working Paper 68.

Onyango, M. A., and Hampanda, K. 2011. Social Constructions of Masculinity and Male Survivors of Wartime Sexual Violence: An Analytical Review. *International Journal of Sexual Health* 23(4): 237–247.

Onyango-Odongo, J. M. 1976. The Early History of the Central Lwo. In Onyango-Odongo, J. M., Webster, J. B. (eds.), *The Central Lwo during the Aconya*. Nairobi: East African Literature Bureau.

Orentlicher, D. F. 2007. "Settling Accounts" Revisited: Reconciling Global Norms with Local Agency. *International Journal of Transitional Justice* 1(1): 10–22.

O'Rourke, C. 2013. *Gender Politics in Transitional Justice*. London: Routledge

Otunnu, O. 2002. Causes and Consequences of the War in Acholiland. In Okello, L. (ed.), *Protracted Conflict, Elusive Peace. Initiatives to End the Violence in Northern Uganda*. London: Conciliation Resources, Kacoke Madit and ACCORD.

Ouzgane, L., and Morrell, R. (eds.). 2005. *African Masculinities. Men in Africa from the Late Nineteenth Century to the Present*. New York: Palgrave.

Patterson, M., and Renwick Monroe, K. 1998. Narrative in Political Science. *Review of Political Science* 1(1): 315–331.

p'Bitek, O. 1986. *Artist, the Ruler: Essays on Art, Culture and Values*. Nairobi: Heinemann Kenya.

p'Bitek, O. 1985. *Acholi Proverbs*. Nairobi: Heinemann Kenya.

p'Bitek, O. 1984. *Song of Lawino and Song of Ocol*. Nairobi: Heinemann Kenya.

p'Bitek, O. 1964. Acholi Love. *Transition* 17: 28–33.

p'Chong, C. L. 2000. Okot p'Bitek: The Cultural Matrix of the Acholi in His Writings. In Breitinger, E. (ed.), *Uganda: The Cultural Landscape*. Kampala: Fountain Publishers: 83–96.

Peterson, V. S. 2010. Gendered Identities, Ideologies, and Practices in the Context of War and Militarism. In Sjoberg, L., and Via, S. (eds.), *Gender, War, and Militarism: Feminist Perspectives*. Santa Barbara: ABC-CLIO: 17–29.

Pham, P., Vinck, P., Stover, E., Moss, A., Wierda, M., and Bailey, R. 2007. *When the War Ends. A Population-Based Survey on Attitudes about Peace, Justice, and Social Reconstruction in Northern Uganda*. Berkeley and New York: Human Rights Center, University of California Berkeley and International Center for Transitional Justice.

Pittaway, E., Bartolomei, L., and Hugman, R. 2010. "Stop stealing our stories": The Ethics of Research with Vulnerable Groups. *Journal of Human Rights Practice* 2(2): 229–251.

Porter, A. 2013. "What Is Constructed Can Be Transformed": Masculinities in Post-Conflict Societies in Africa. *International Peacekeeping* 20(4): 486–506.

Porter, H. 2016. *After Rape: Violence, Justice, and Social Harmony in Uganda*. Cambridge: Cambridge University Press.

Porter, H. 2013. *After Rape: Justice and Social Harmony in Northern Uganda*. PhD dissertation. London School of Economics and Political Science.

Porter, H. 2012. Justice and Rape on the Periphery: The Supremacy of Social Harmony in the Space between Local Solutions and Formal Judicial Systems in Northern Uganda. *Journal of Eastern African Studies* 6(1): 81–97.

Postlethwaite, J.R.P. 1947. *I Look Back*. London: TV Boardman.

Ratele, K. 2014. Currents against Gender Transformation of South African Men: Relocating Marginality to the Centre of Research and Theory of Masculinities. *NORMA: International Journal for Masculinity Studies* 9(1): 30–44.

Ratele, K. 2007. *From Boys to Men: Social Constructions of Masculinity in Contemporary Society*. Cape Town: University of Cape Town Press.

Refugee Law Project (RLP). 2014a. *Julius Okwera: A Survivor's Journey through Pain, Despair and Hope!* Kampala: Refugee Law Project, School of Law, Makerere University.

Refugee Law Project (RLP). 2014b. *Compendium of Conflicts in Uganda. Findings of the National Reconciliation and Transitional Justice Audit*. Kampala: Refugee Law Project, School of Law, Makerere University.

Refugee Law Project (RLP), 2013. Promoting Accountability for Conflict-Related Sexual Violence against Men: A Comparative Legal Analysis of International and Domestic Laws Relating to IDP and Refugee Men in Uganda. *Refugee Law Project Working Paper* (24).

Refugee Law Project (RLP). 2011. *They Slept with Me*. Video documentary. Kampala: Refugee Law Project, School of Law, Makerere University.

Reinharz, S. and Davidman, L. 1992. *Feminist Methods in Social Research*. Oxford: Oxford University Press.

Richmond, O. P. 2011. De-romanticising the Local, De-Mystifying the International: Hybridity in Timor Leste and the Solomon Islands. *Pacific Review* 24(1): 115–136.

Robins, S. 2011. *Addressing the Needs of Families of the Missing: A Test of Contemporary Approaches to Transitional Justice*. PhD dissertation. York: University of York, Post-War Reconstruction and Development Unit.

Robins, S. 2009. Whose Voices? Understanding Victims' Needs in Transition. Nepali Voices: Perceptions of Truth, Justice, Reconciliation, Reparations and the Transition in Nepal. *Journal of Human Rights Practice* 1(2): 320–331.

Robins, S., and Wilson, E. 2015. Participatory Methodologies with Victims: An Emancipatory Approach to Transitional Justice Research. *Canadian Journal of Law and Society* 30(2): 219–236.

Rombouts, H. 2004. *Victim Organisations and the Politics of Reparation: A Case-Study on Rwanda*. Mortsel: Intersentia.

Rosenoff-Gauvin, L. 2013. In and out of Culture: Okot p'Bitek's Work and Social Repair in Post-Conflict Acoliland. *Oral Tradition* 28(1).

Ross, F. C. 2003. On Having Voice and Being Heard: Some After-Effects of Testifying before the South African Truth and Reconciliation Commission. *Anthropological Theory* 3(3): 325–341.

Rubio-Marín, R. 2009. *The Gender of Reparations: Unsettling Sexual Hierarchies while Redressing Human Rights Violations*. Cambridge: Cambridge University Press.

Rubio-Marín, R., and de Greiff, P. 2007. Women and Reparations. *International Journal of Transitional Justice* 1(3): 318–337.

Rubio-Marin, R., and Sandoval, C. 2011. Engendering the Reparations Jurisprudence of the Inter-American Court of Human Rights: The Promise of the Cotton Field Judgment. *Human Rights Quarterly* 33(4): 1062–1091.

Ryan, C. (2017). Oporto! Oporto! Reflections on the Motorcycle as Methodological Tool, and on Having Lunch with "the Men." *International Feminist Journal of Politics* 19(3): 376–378.

Scarry, E. 1985. *The Body in Pain: The Making and Unmaking of the World*. Oxford: Oxford University Press.

Schulz, P. 2020a. Examining Male Wartime Rape Survivors' Perspectives on Justice in Northern Uganda. *Social & Legal Studies*. 29(1): 19–40.

Schulz, P. 2020b. Recognizing Research Participants' Fluid Positionalities in (Post-)Conflict Zones. *Qualitative Research* 00(0): 1–18.

Schulz, P. 2019a. "To me, justice means to be in a group": Survivors' Groups as a Pathway to Justice in Northern Uganda. *Journal of Human Rights Practice*. 11(1): 171–189.

Schulz, P. 2019b. Gendered Postconflict Justice: Male Survivors of Sexual Violence in Northern Uganda. In Kurze, A., and Lamont, C. (eds.), *New Critical Spaces in Transitional Justice. Gender, Art and Memory*. Bloomington: Indiana University Press: 89–112.

Schulz, P. 2018a. Displacement from Gendered Personhood: Sexual Violence and masculinities in northern Uganda. *International Affairs* 94(5): 1101–1119.

Schulz, P. 2018b. The "Ethical Loneliness" of Male Sexual Violence Survivors in Northern Uganda: Gendered Reflections on Silencing. *International Feminist Journal of Politics* 20(4): 583–601.

Schulz, P. 2016. Evelyn Amony. I Am Evelyn Amony: Reclaiming My Life from the Lord's Resistance Army. *International Feminist Journal of Politics* 18(2): 312–314.

Schulz, P., and Touquet, H. 2020. Queering Explanatory Frameworks for Wartime Sexual Violence against Men. *International Affairs* 96(6): 1–18.

Scott, J. C. 1990. *Domination and the Arts of Resistance. Hidden Transcripts*. New Haven, CT: Yale University Press.

Select Committee on Sexual Violence in Conflict. 2016. *Sexual Violence in Conflict: A War Crime. Report of Session 2015–16*. London: House of Lords.

Sen, A. 2017. Ethics and the Foundation of Global Justice. *Ethics and International Affairs* 31(3): 261–270.

Sharlach, L. B. 2001. *Sexual Violence as Political Terror*. PhD dissertation. University of California, Davis.

Sharp, D. N. 2014. Emancipating Transitional Justice from the Bonds of the Paradigmatic Transition. *International Journal of Transitional Justice* 9(1): 150–169.

Shaw, R., and Waldorf, L. 2010. *Localizing Transitional Justice: Interventions and Priorities after Mass Violence*. Redwood City: Stanford University Press.

Sivakumaran, S. 2013. Prosecuting Sexual Violence against Men and Boys. In de Brouwer, A. M., Ku., C. et al. (eds.), *Sexual Violence as an International Crime: Interdisciplinary Approaches*. Cambridge: Intersentia: 79–97.

Sivakumaran, S. 2007. Sexual Violence against Men in Armed Conflict. *European Journal of International Law* 18(2): 253–276.

Sivakumaran, S. 2005. Male/Male Rape and the "Taint" of Homosexuality. *Human Rights Quarterly* 27(4): 1274–1306.

Sjoberg, L. 2016. *Women as Wartime Rapists: Beyond Sensation and Stereotyping*. New York: New York University Press.

Sjoberg, L. 2013. *Gendering Global Conflict: Toward a Feminist Theory of War*. New York: Columbia University Press.

Sjoberg, L., and Via, S. 2010. *Gender, War, and Militarism: Feminist Perspectives*. Santa Barbara: ABC-CLIO.

Skjelsbaek, I. 2001. Sexual Violence and War: Mapping out a Complex Relationship. *European Journal of International Relations* 7(2): 211–237.

Solangon, S., and Patel, P. 2012. Sexual Violence against Men in Countries Affected by Armed Conflict. *Conflict, Security and Development* 12(4): 417–442.

Stauffer, J. 2015. *Ethical Loneliness: The Injustice of Not Being Heard*. New York: Columbia University Press.

Stemple, L. 2009. Male Rape and Human Rights. *Hastings Law Journal* 60: 605–646.

Tapscott, R. 2018. Policing Men: Militarized Masculinity, Youth Livelihoods, and Security in Conflict-Affected Northern Uganda. *Disasters* 42(1): 119–139.

Tapscott, R. 2017. Local Security and the (Un)making of Public Authority in Gulu, Northern Uganda. *African Affairs* 116(462): 39–59.

Teitel, R. G. 2015. *Globalizing Transitional Justice*. Oxford: Oxford University Press.

Theidon, K. 2012. *Intimate Enemies: Violence and Reconciliation in Peru*. Philadelphia: University of Pennsylvania Press.

Thomson, S. 2019. Engaged Silences as Political Agency in Postgenocide Rwanda: Jeanne's Story. In Parpart, J., and Parashar, S. (eds.), *Rethinking Silence, Voice and Agency in Contested Gendered Terrains: Beyond the Binary*. London: Routledge.

Tickner, J. A., and Sjoberg, L. 2013. *Feminism and International Relations: Conversations about the Past, Present and Future*. New York: Routledge.

Touquet, H. 2018. *Unsilenced: Male Survivors Speak of Conflict-Related Sexual Violence in Sri Lanka*. London: International Truth and Justice Project.

Touquet, H., and Gorris, E. 2016. Out of the Shadows? Male Victims in Conceptualizations of Wartime Sexual Violence. *Reproductive Health Matters* 24(47): 1–11.

Touquet, H., and Schulz, P. 2020. Navigating Vulnerabilities and Masculinities: How Gendered Contexts Shape the Agency of Male Sexual Violence Survivors. Security Dialogue: 1–18.

United Nations (UN). 2014. *Analytical Study Focusing on Gender-Based and Sexual Violence in Relation to Transitional Justice*. New York: Office of the United Nations High Commissioner for Human Rights.

United Nations (UN). 2013. *Report of Workshop on Sexual Violence against Men and Boys in Conflict Situations*. New York: Office of the Special Representative of the Secretary-General on Sexual Violence in Conflict.

UNHCR. 2018. *"We keep it in our heart": Sexual Violence against Men and Boys in the Syria Crisis*. New York and Geneva: United Nations High Commissioner for Refugees.

UNOCHA 2008. *Discussion Paper 2: The Nature, Scope and Motivation for Sexual Violence against Men and Boys in Conflict*. New York: United Nations Office for the Coordination of Humanitarian Affairs.

UNSG. 2004. *The Rule of Law and Transitional Justice in Conflict and Post-Conflict Societies*. Report of the Secretary General. 23 August 2004. S/2004/616. New York: United Nations Secretary General.

Utas, M. 2005. Victimcy, Girlfriending, Soldiering: Tactic Agency in a Young Woman's Social Navigation of the Liberian War Zone. *Anthropological Quarterly* 78(2): 403–430.

Walker, R. 2010. Violence, the Everyday and the Question of the Ordinary. *Contemporary South Asia* 18(1): 9–24

Whyte, D. 2018. *Consolations: The Solace, Nourishment and Underlying Meaning of Everyday Words.* Langley, WA: Many Rivers Press.

Women's Refugee Commission (WRC). 2018. *It's Happening to Our Men as Well. Sexual Violence against Rohingya Men and Boys.* New York: WRC.

Wood, E. J. 2018. Rape as a Practice of War: Toward a Typology of Political Violence. *Politics and Society* 46(4): 513–537.

Wood, E. J. 2014. Conflict-Related Sexual Violence and the Policy Implications of Recent Research. *International Review of the Red Cross* 96(894): 1–22.

Wood, E. J. 2006. Variation in Sexual Violence during War. *Politics and Society* 34(3): 307–342.

Wright, H. 2014. *Masculinities, Conflict and Peacebuilding: Perspectives on Men through a Gender Lens.* London: Saferworld.

Zalewski, M. 2018. Provocations in Debates about Sexual Violence against Men. In Zalewski, M., Drumond, P. Prügl, E., and Stern, M. (eds.), *Sexual Violence against Men in Global Politics.* London: Routledge: 25–43.

Zalewski, M. 1995. "Well, What Is the Feminist Perspective on Bosnia?" *International Affairs* 71(2): 339–356.

Zalewski, M., Drumond, P. Prügl, E., and Stern, M. 2018. *Sexual Violence against Men in Global Politics.* London: Routledge.

Zarkov, D. 2001. The Body of the Other Man. In Moser, C., and Clark, F. (eds.), *Victims, Perpetrators or Actors: Gender, Armed Conflict and Political Violence.* London and New York: Zed Books: 69–82.

INDEX

Note: Numbers in italics followed by "fig." indicate figures; numbers in italics followed by "map" indicate maps.

Acholi cosmology, 88, 97, 140

Acholiland, 9, 12, 14, 17, 34, 50, *58map*, *59map*, 63, 66, 75, 77, 81, 93, 99, 115, 117, 132; British colonial administration in, 49–50, 134; conflict-related male rape in, 23–24; explanations for sexual violence against men in, 62–66; forms of male-directed sexual violence in, 61–66; gender dynamics and, 45; gender identities in, 82–92; gender relations in, 83–85; hegemonic masculinities in, 82–92, 171n16; legal pluralism in, 133–35; rituals and ceremonies in, 140; storytelling and, 123

Acholi language, 14, 16, 61, 85

Acholi population, 48, 52, 56, 65

Acholi soldiers, 50, 51, 60

Acholi Times, 111

Acholi War Debt Claimants Associations, 114

acknowledgment, 166; justice and, 132, 142, 143–47, 159, 162; from Ugandan government, 25, 143–47, 159, 173n2, 173n5. *See also* recognition

advocacy work, 48, 56, 103, 115, 117, 126

agency, 5, 14, 101; definition of, 108–9; example of, 110–11; exercise of, 24–25, 102–30, 161, 165; political, 103, 105–6, 108–12, 125; relational, 125; storytelling and, 122–25; theorizing, 108–12; victimhood and, 104–8; voice and, 122–25; of women, 31, 106–8

Agreement on Accountability and Reconciliation (AAR), 54

Allen, Tim, 51, 57, 133, 140

Amony, Evelyn, 107–8

Anti-Homosexuality Bill, 39

armed conflict: feminist approaches to theorizing, 6; feminist scholarship on, 27–28; gender and, 6, 24; gender dynamics and, 4; masculinities and, 6, 24, 28–30, 81, 90, 91, 163, 163–64; masculinity and, 7; patriarchy and, 6; revisiting assumptions about, 163–64; violence and, 24–25. *See also* sexual violence, conflict-related

assistance, 4, 12, 114, 115, 119, 122, 162, 166; economic. *See also* compensation; reparations

Baines, Erin, 71, 83, 85, 104–6, 108, 110, 123–24, 128, 133–34, 137

bedo adana, 83, 109

Behrend, Heike, 49, 56

Beyond Juba Project (BJP), 116, 154, 173n3

binaries, 6–7

British colonialism, 49–50, 134

"bush wives," 71, 106, 107

butu tek-tek, 61

189

physical rehabilitation, 142, 143, 151–55, 158, 162; nonstate actors and, 159
political agency, 103, 105–6, 108–11, 125; theorizing, 108–12
Porter, Holly, 13–14, 61, 71, 83–84, 89–90, 135
positionality, 15–17
postconflict literature, 164
postconflict reconstruction, 113, 122–23
power: gendered power relations, 70, 78, 79, 93, 94–95; sex and, 94–96
Preventing Sexual Violence Initiative (PSVI), 42
private sphere, vs. public sphere, 61–62, 97
prosecutions, 142, 147–50, 155–56

rape, 1–2, 32, 34, 63, 170n18; consequences of, 66–70, 97–100; gang rape, 62; male rape, 1–2, 3, 32, 48–73, 58map, 97–100; map of Acholiland documenting cases of, 58map, 64; penetrative anal rape, 24, 33, 61, 92–96, 100; perpetration of along major and military-strategic roads (Map 3), 58; physical consequences of, 67–68, 97–100; physiological consequences of, 69–70; psychological consequences of, 68–69; in US military, 94; "weapon of war" narrative and, 42–43, 63, 104. See also sexual and gender-based violence (SGBV); sexual violence, conflict-related; tek-gungu (male rape)
recognition, 129, 131–59, 162, 166; justice and, 132, 142, 143–47, 162; struggle for, 118, 125–28; by Ugandan government, 113, 143–47
Refugee Law Project (RLP), 1, 3, 14–15, 17–19, 21–23, 38–39, 48, 56, 60, 102, 111, 115–19, 122, 126, 139, 154–55, 165, 167, 172–73n2
relational agency, 125
relationships: reestablishing, 118, 120–22; repairing, 128–29, 162
reparations, 113, 131–59; gender-sensitive, 150–53; justice and, 132, 142, 143, 145, 158–59, 162
research: ethical imperatives and, 165; implications for survivors, 165–66
retaliation, 61
Rome Statute of the International Criminal Court, 35–36
Rwanda, genocide in, 33–34, 113

Saint Mary's Hospital, Lacor, 116, 154
services, 12; restricted access to, 114–15, 161–62, 166; vacuum for male survivors in Uganda, 161–62, 171–72n17
sex: erectile dysfunction and, 69–70, 98–99; heterosexuality and, 89–90; power and, 94–96
"sex slaves," 106, 107

sexual and gender-based violence (SGBV), 6–7, 31–32, 34, 44, 61, 62, 126, 132, 138, 159, 167, 170n11; classifications and definitions of, 32–35, 41; definitions of, 33; forms of, 61; strategic, 41, 63; transitional justice and, 138; against women and girls, 53, 56, 70–71, 106, 170n18. See also sexual violence, conflict-related; sexual violence against men
sexual harassment, 37
sexual harms, 12, 13, 170n18
sexual humiliation: crimes of, 170n16. See also humiliation
sexual identities, 15–16
sexual violation, 1–2. See also rape; sexual and gender-based violence (SGBV)
sexual violence, conflict-related, 4, 26–47, 32, 33, 36–37, 46–47, 163–64, 170n11; explanations for, 44–47; forms of, 33; gender and, 42, 74–101; gendered effects on masculinity, 74–101; as gender subordination, 46–47; justice and, 155–58; misrepresented as torture, 34–35; as opportunistic, 41, 42, 44, 46, 63–66; in public vs. private sphere, 61–62, 97; sexual needs and, 41–42; sexual violence and, 27–31; state armed forces and, 63; as tactic or strategy, 44, 46, 63, 63–66, 104, 171n12; victimhood and, 104–5; in wartime, 5–9, 44–47. See also sexual violence against men
sexual violence against men, 1–2, 3, 4, 8–9, 9, 26–47, 37, 39, 48–73, 56, 57, 61–62, 64, 71–72, 97–100, 141; challenges of quantifying, 39–40; as communicative and performative act, 45; conceptualizing, 31–36; conflict-related, 26–47; consequences of, 66–70, 97–100; crimes of, 28; emasculation and, 44–46; existing evidence, 36–39; explanations for, 40–47, 62–66; feminist approaches to, 6; feminization and, 44–46; forms of, 61–66; frequency of, 163; by government soldiers, 14; justice and, 140–42; physical consequences of, 67–68, 97–100; physiological consequences of, 69–70; presence and dynamics of, 57–61; as a process, 92–100; psychological consequences of, 68, 68–69; in the public sphere, 62; recognition of, 125–26; scope and prevalence of, 36–40; silencing of, 159. See also tek-gungu (male rape)
shame, 2, 3, 4, 68–69
"short stick," 13, 118, 130, 167
silence, 111, 122; agentive, 111; breaking, 124–29; forms and functions of, 111; navigating, 104, 105, 110–11, 112; protective, 112; spatial-geographic dimensions of, 111–12
Sivakumaran, S., 10, 28, 34, 43, 95, 139

violence, 129; armed conflict and, 24–25; cycles of, 50, 70; hegemonic masculinities and, 90, 172n5; masculinities and, 6–7, 24, 81–82, 90, 172n5; opportunisitic, 41, 42, 44, 46, 63–66; revisiting assumptions about, 163–64; strategic, 41, 42, 44, 46, 63–66, 104; "violences of men," 7, 29. *See also* sexual and gender-based violence (SGBV); *specific forms of violence*

voice, agency and, 122–25

vulnerabilities, 12; as a feminized concept, 93–94; gendered, 24; masculinities and, 8–9, 45, 93–94, 104–5, 146

war. *See* armed conflict

war in Northern Uganda, historical roots of, 48–56

"weapon of war" narrative, 42–43, 63, 104

womanhood, 84–85. *See also* femininities

women: agency of, 31, 106–8; armed conflict and, 24–25; sexual and gender-based violence (SGBV) against, 70–71, 106; subordination of, 84–85; violence and, 24–25

Women Peace and Security (WPS) agenda, 32, 33

Women's Advocacy Network (WAN), 115

Wood, Elisabeth, 37, 41, 63, 65

Founded in 1893,
UNIVERSITY OF CALIFORNIA PRESS
publishes bold, progressive books and journals
on topics in the arts, humanities, social sciences,
and natural sciences—with a focus on social
justice issues—that inspire thought and action
among readers worldwide.

The UC PRESS FOUNDATION
raises funds to uphold the press's vital role
as an independent, nonprofit publisher, and
receives philanthropic support from a wide
range of individuals and institutions—and from
committed readers like you. To learn more, visit
ucpress.edu/supportus.